CORPORATIONS
ARE NOT
PEOPLE

WHY THEY HAVE MORE
RIGHTS THAN YOU DO AND
WHAT YOU CAN DO ABOUT IT

JEFFREY D. CLEMENTS

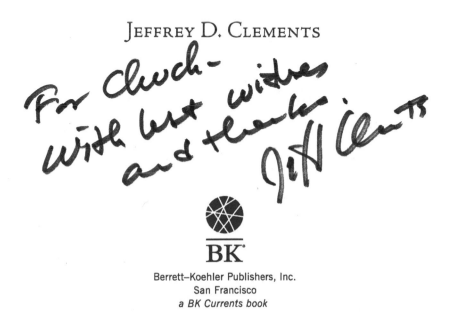

*For Chuck —
With best wishes
and thanks*

Jeff Clements

BK

Berrett–Koehler Publishers, Inc.
San Francisco
a BK Currents book

Berrett-Koehler Publishers, Inc.
235 Montgomery Street, Suite 650
San Francisco, CA 94104-2916
Tel: (415) 288-0260   Fax: (415) 362-2512   www.bkconnection.com

Ordering Information

Quantity sales. Special discounts are available on quantity purchases by corporations, associations, and others. For details, contact the "Special Sales Department" at the Berrett-Koehler address above.

Individual sales. Berrett-Koehler publications are available through most bookstores. They can also be ordered directly from Berrett-Koehler:
Tel: (800) 929-2929; Fax: (802) 864-7626; www.bkconnection.com

Orders for college textbook/course adoption use. Please contact Berrett-Koehler:
Tel: (800) 929-2929; Fax: (802) 864-7626.

Orders by U.S. trade bookstores and wholesalers. Please contact Ingram Publisher Services:
Tel: (800) 509-4887; Fax: (800) 838-1149; E-mail: customer.service@ingrampublisherservices.com; or visit www.ingrampublisherservices.com/Ordering for details about electronic ordering.

Berrett-Koehler and the BK logo are registered trademarks of Berrett-Koehler Publishers, Inc.

Printed in the United States of America

Berrett-Koehler books are printed on long-lasting acid-free paper. When it is available, we choose paper that has been manufactured by environmentally responsible processes. These may include using trees grown in sustainable forests, incorporating recycled paper, minimizing chlorine in bleaching, or recycling the energy produced at the paper mill.

Library of Congress Cataloging-in-Publication Data

Clements, Jeffrey D.
    Corporations are not people : why they have more rights than you do and what you
        can do about it / Jeffrey D. Clements. -- 1st ed.
        p. cm.
    Includes bibliographical references and index.
    ISBN 978-1-60994-105-5 (pbk.)
    1. Business and politics--United States. 2. Corporations--Political aspects--United States.
    3. Corporations--Political activity--United States. I. Title.
    JK467.C55 2011
    322'.30973--dc23
                                                                                2011043953

First Edition

17 16 15 14 13 12   10 9 8 7 6 5 4 3 2 1

Interior design and project management: Dovetail Publishing Services
Cover design: Mark van Bronkhorst, MvB Design

For Bob Clements

CONTENTS

PREFACE

Of course corporations are not people. Do we really need a book about that obvious truth? Unfortunately, we do.

After the United States Supreme Court's decision in *Citizens United* v. *Federal Election Commission* in 2010, the identity of corporations and their place in our government of the people is not so obvious anymore, at least not to the Supreme Court and to the armies of corporate lawyers pushing for more corporate constitutional rights. And the fact that corporations are not people does not seem to be obvious to too many cowed and trembling lawmakers at all levels of government. There are exceptions, to be sure, but in the face of wildly unbalanced corporate money and influence, too few of our elected officials stand with conviction and firmness to state the obvious about corporations in defense of the public interest.

Citizens United is the biggest and most radical (to use a word from the dissent of Justice Stevens) decision in a regular series of recent Supreme Court decisions in favor of corporations. In *Citizens United*, the Supreme Court overturned decades of precedent, reversed a century of legislative effort to keep corporate money from corrupting democracy, and upended the American ideal that we are a government of people rather than a government of corporate wealth. The decision, in many ways, symbolizes how far off track we have fallen from our ideal of the American Republic, governed by the people.

In the pages that follow, I hope to show what *Citizens United* is all about, where it came from, and what I think this triumph of corporate power means for you and for all Americans. Much of the book is about what I see as the devastating effect of unbalanced corporate power, sustained and strengthened by a deliberate, organized, and extremely well funded campaign to transform—I would say, pervert—our Bill of Rights into a charter for corporations as much and even more than for people.

I also hope to show, however, why we do not have to leave it at that depressing juncture. As I describe in Chapter Seven, thanks to the mechanism of constitutional amendment that has come through before when our democracy is on the line, we can fight back to restore government of the people and to save our country. Thousands of people have started that work already, working for the People's Rights Amendment as the Twenty-Eighth Amendment to the Constitution. I hope that you will join us; the Resources section that follows Chapter Seven offers some ways you can do that.

Many people across the country have taken up the effort to preserve our nation and world against unbalanced corporate power and have shared their ideas, time, spirit, and hard work with me. I hope that all of them will know how much they have influenced this book and how grateful I am, even if I could not list everyone here.

Bill Moyers is at the top of the list of a few who deserve special mention. Bill has been a hero and a teacher for me and for so many Americans. He tells the truth. Calmly and clearly, to be sure, but make no mistake, he tells the truth, out loud for all to hear. He never gives up on the journey of America and of humanity, and his curiosity, determination, and grace make that journey live for all of us. I cannot say how grateful and honored I am to have him write the Foreword to this book.

I am blessed to be part of the Clements family. Thank you to Marilyn Clements and this wonderful extended clan of opinionated, smart, loving, patriotic people, who work hard for the good, stand for principle, and believe in writing and in books. They put in hours helping me to make this one better.

I am deeply appreciative of so many who early on understood the danger of *Citizens United* and corporate power, who have worked so hard, and who are bringing such hope and purpose to the cause of liberty and democracy. They have picked up the constitutional amendment banner used so well by our forefathers and foremothers. These modern-day heroes do not accept that our generation is less determined or less true to the American cause of freedom and democracy than those who came before. They reject defeatism. They are standing for people's rights and against corporate rights, and they have inspired much of this book.

One of these heroes is John Bonifaz, a determined visionary and leader. On top of launching Free Speech for People, a nationwide campaign to overturn *Citizens United*, he took the time to read drafts and helped make this book better than it would have been. I thank John and all of the friends and supporters who are helping move Free Speech for People and the People's Rights Amendment forward.

Many others generously shared their time, ideas, comments, and criticisms. My colleague Gwen Stowe, associate at Free Speech for People and manager at Clements Law Office, LLC, made far more contributions to all aspects of this project than I can list. Pam Kogut, my old friend and colleague, first at the Massachusetts attorney general's office and now at Clements Law Office, LLC, provided smart edits and wise suggestions. I am lucky to work with Pam and Gwen.

I also am grateful for the terrific work of Neal Maillet and the Berrett-Kohler team and for many people who provided comments, suggestions, and correction of errors, including David Korten,

Daniel Greenwood, Rob Ellman, Shauna Shames, Kristen Mousalli, Ariel Jolicoeur, Ted Nace, Steve Cobble, and David Swanson. I know that the final product is not everything they might have thought possible, but I also know that it is better thanks to them. Thanks, too, to Thom Hartmann.

Finally, as always, my loving gratitude to Nancy, Will, Sophie, and Ben.

Jeff Clements
Concord, Massachusetts
October 2011

FOREWORD
FIGHTING BACK
Bill Moyers

Rarely have so few imposed such damage on so many. When five conservative members of the Supreme Court handed for-profit corporations the right to secretly flood political campaigns with tidal waves of cash on the eve of an election, they moved America closer to outright plutocracy, where political power derived from wealth is devoted to the protection of wealth. It is now official: Just as they have adorned our athletic stadiums and multiple places of public assembly with their logos, corporations can officially put their brand on the government of the United States as well as the executive, legislative, and judicial branches of the fifty states.

The decision in *Citizens United* v. *Federal Election Commission* giving "artificial entities" the same rights of "free speech" as living, breathing human beings will likely prove as infamous as the *Dred Scott* ruling of 1857 that opened the unsettled territories of the United States to slavery whether future inhabitants wanted it or not. It took a civil war and another hundred years of enforced segregation and deprivation before the effects of that ruling were finally exorcised from our laws. God spare us civil strife over the pernicious consequences of *Citizens United*, but unless citizens stand their ground, America will divide even more swiftly into winners and losers with little pity for the latter. *Citizens United* is but the latest battle in the class war waged for thirty years from the top down by the corporate and political right. Instead of creating a fair and level playing field for all, government would become the agent of the powerful and privileged. Public institutions, laws, and regulations, as well as the ideas, norms, and beliefs that aimed to protect the common good and helped create America's iconic middle class, would become increasingly vulnerable. The Nobel Laureate economist Robert Solow succinctly summed up results: "The redistribution of wealth in favor of the wealthy and of power in favor of the powerful." In the wake of *Citizens United*, popular resistance is all that can prevent the richest economic interests in the country from buying the democratic process lock, stock, and barrel.

America has a long record of conflict with corporations. Wealth acquired under capitalism is in and of itself no enemy to democracy, but wealth armed with political power—power to choke off opportunities for others to rise, power to subvert public purposes and deny public needs—is a proven danger to the "general welfare" proclaimed in the Preamble to the Constitution as one of the justifications for America's existence.

In its founding era, Alexander Hamilton created a financial system for our infant republic that mixed subsidies, tariffs, and a central bank to establish a viable economy and sound public credit. James Madison and Thomas Jefferson warned Americans to beware of the political ambitions of that system's managerial class. Madison feared that the "spirit of speculation" would lead to "a government operating by corrupt influence, substituting the motive of private interest in place of public duty." Jefferson hoped that "we shall crush in its birth the aristocracy of our monied corporations which dare already to challenge our government to a trial of strength and [to] bid defiance to the laws of our country." Radical ideas? Class warfare? The voters didn't think so. In 1800, they made Jefferson the third president and then reelected him, and in 1808 they put Madison in the White House for the next eight years.

Andrew Jackson, the overwhelming people's choice of 1828, vetoed the rechartering of the Second Bank of the United States in the summer of 1832. Twenty percent of its stock was government-owned; the rest was held by private investors, some of them foreigners and all of them wealthy. Jackson argued that the bank's official connections and size gave it unfair advantages over local competition. In his veto message, he said: "[This act] seems to be predicated on the erroneous idea that the present stockholders have a prescriptive right not only to the favor but to the bounty of Government. . . . It is to be regretted that the rich and powerful too often bend the acts of government to their selfish purposes." Four months later, Jackson was easily reelected in a decisive victory over plutocracy.

The predators roared back in the Gilded Age that followed the Civil War. Corruption born of the lust for money produced what one historian described as "the morals of a gashouse gang." Judges, state legislators, the parties that selected them and the editors who supported them were purchased as easily as ale at the local pub. Lobbyists roamed the halls of Congress proffering gifts of cash, railroad passes, and fancy entertainments. The U.S. Senate became a "millionaires' club." With government on the auction block, the notion of the "general welfare" wound up on the trash heap; grotesque inequality and poverty festered under the gilding. Sound familiar?

Then came a judicial earthquake. In 1886, a conservative Supreme Court conferred the divine gift of life on the Southern Pacific Railroad and by extension to all other corporations. The railroad was declared to be a "person," protected by the recently enacted Fourteenth Amendment, which said that no person should be deprived of "life, liberty or property without due process of law." Never mind that the amendment was enacted to protect the rights of freed slaves who were now U.S. citizens. Never mind that a corporation possessed neither a body to be kicked nor a soul to be damned (or saved!). The Court decided that it had the same rights of "personhood" as a walking, talking citizen and was entitled to enjoy every liberty protected by the Constitution that flesh-and-blood individuals could claim, even though it did not share their disadvantage of being mortal. It could move where it chose, buy any kind of property it chose, and select its directors and stockholders from anywhere it chose. Welcome to unregulated multinational conglomerates, although unforeseen at the time. Welcome to tax shelters, at home and offshore, and to subsidies galore, paid for by the taxes of unsuspecting working people. Corporations were endowed with the rights of "personhood" but exempted from the responsibilities of citizenship.

That's the doctrine picked up and dusted off by the John Roberts Court in its ruling on *Citizens United*. Ignoring a century of modifying precedent, the court gave our corporate sovereigns a "sky's the limit" right to pour money into political campaigns for the purpose of influencing the outcome. And to do so without public disclosure. We might as well say farewell to the very idea of fair play. Farewell, too, to representative government "of, by, and for the people."

Unless.

Unless "We, the People"—flesh-and-blood humans, outraged at the selling off of our government—fight back.

It's been done before. As my friend and longtime colleague, the historian Bernard Weisberger, wrote recently, the Supreme Court remained a procorporate conservative fortress for the next fifty years after the Southern Pacific decision. Decade after decade it struck down laws aimed to share power with the citizenry and to promote "the general welfare." In 1895, it declared unconstitutional a measure providing for an income tax and gutted the Sherman Antitrust Act by finding a loophole for a sugar trust. In 1905, it killed a New York state law limiting working hours. In 1917, it did likewise to a prohibition against child labor. In 1923, it wiped out another law that set minimum wages for women. In 1935 and 1936, it struck down early New Deal recovery acts.

But in the face of such discouragement, embattled citizens refused to give up. Into their hearts, wrote the progressive Kansas journalist William Allen White, "had come a sense that their civilization needed recasting, that the government had fallen into the hands of self-seekers, that a new relationship should be established between the haves and the have-nots." Not content merely to wring their hands and cry "Woe is us," everyday citizens researched the issues, organized public events to educate their neighbors, held rallies, made speeches, petitioned and canvassed, marched and exhorted. They would elect the twentieth-century governments that restored "the general welfare" as a pillar of American democracy, setting in place legally ordained minimum wages, maximum working hours, child labor laws, workmen's safety and compensation laws, pure foods and safe drugs, Social Security and Medicare, and rules to promote competitive rather than monopolistic financial and business markets.

The social contract that emerged from these victories is part and parcel of the "general welfare" to which the Founders had dedicated our Constitution. The corporate and political right seeks now to weaken and ultimately destroy it. Thanks to their ideological kin on the Supreme Court, they can attack the social contract using their abundant resources of wealth funneled—clandestinely—into political campaigns. During the fall elections of 2010, the first after the *Citizens United* decision, corporate front groups spent $126 million while hiding the identities of the donors, according to the Sunlight Foundation. The United States Chamber of Commerce, which touts itself as a "main street" grass-roots organization, draws most of its funds from about a hundred businesses, including such "main street" sources as BP, Exxon-Mobil, JPMorgan Chase, Massey Coal, Pfizer, Shell, Aetna, and Alcoa. The ink was hardly dry on the *Citizens United* decision when the Chamber organized a covertly funded front and fired volley after volley of missiles, in the form of political ads, into the 2010 campaigns, eventually spending approximately $75 million. Another corporate cover group—the Americans Action Network—spent over $26 million of undisclosed corporate money in six Senate races and 28 House of Representative elections. And "Crossroads GPS" seized on *Citizens United* to raise and spend at least $17 million that NBC News said came from "a small circle of extremely wealthy Wall Street hedge fund and private equity moguls," all determined to water down the financial reforms designed to avoid a collapse of the financial system that their own greed and reckless speculation had helped bring on. As I write in the summer of 2011, the *New York Times* reports that efforts to thwart serious reforms are succeeding. The populist editor Jim Hightower concludes that today's proponents of corporate plutocracy "have simply elevated money itself above votes, establishing cold, hard cash as the real coin of political power. The more you spend on politics, the bigger your voice is in government, making the vast vaults of billionaires and corporations far superior to the voices of mere voters."

Against such odds, discouragement comes easily. But if the generations before us had given up, slaves would be waiting on our tables and picking our crops, women would be turned back at the voting booths, and it would be a crime for workers to organize. Like our forebears, we will not fix the broken promise of America—the promise of "life, liberty, and the pursuit of happiness" for all our citizens, not just the powerful and privileged—if we throw in the proverbial towel. Surrendering to plutocracy is not an option. Confronting a moment in our history that is much like the one Lincoln faced—when "we can nobly save or meanly lose the last best hope on earth"—we must fight back against the forces that are pouring dirty money into the political system, turning it into a sewer.

How to fight back is the message of this book. Jeffrey Clements saw corporate behavior up close during two stints as assistant attorney general in Massachusetts, litigating against the tobacco industry, enforcing fair trade practices, and leading more than one hundred attorneys and staff responsible for consumer and environmental protection, antitrust practices, and the oversight of health care, insurance, and financial services. He came away from the experience repeating to himself this indelible truth: "Corporations are not people." Try it yourself: "Corporations are not people." Again: "Corporations are not people." You are now ready to join what Clements believes is the most promising way to counter *Citizens United*: a campaign for a constitutional amendment affirming that free speech and democracy are for people and that corporations are not people. Impossible? Not at all, says Clements. We have already amended the Constitution twenty-seven times. Amendment campaigns are how we have always made the promise of equality and liberty more real. Difficult? Of course; as Frederick Douglass taught us, power concedes nothing without a struggle. To contend with power, Clements and his colleague John Bonifaz founded Free Speech for People, a nationwide nonpartisan effort to overturn *Citizens United* and corporate rights doctrines that unduly leverage corporate economic power into political power. What Clements calls the People's Rights

Amendment could be our best hope to save the "great American experiment."

To find out why, read on, and as you read, keep in mind the words of Theodore Roosevelt, a Republican, who a century ago stood up to the mighty combines of wealth and power that were buying up our government and called on Americans of all persuasions to join him in opposing the "naked robbery" of the public's trust:

> *It is not a partisan issue; it is more than a political issue; it is a great moral issue. If we condone political theft, if we do not resent the kinds of wrong and injustice that injuriously affect the whole nation, not merely our democratic form of government but our civilization itself cannot endure.*

Introduction
What's at Stake

America's story is one of defiant struggle against the odds for an improbable vision: that all people, created and born free and equal, can live and govern together "in the pursuit of happiness." This dream of a society of free people with equal rights, where people govern themselves, was unlikely indeed in the eighteenth century. In a world of empires, governed by royalty and divided by class, and in our own country, with millions enslaved, where women were considered the property of their husbands, and where land ownership was considered a prerequisite to participation in government, the pursuit—let alone the fulfillment—of this vision was far-fetched indeed.

Yet we Americans never let that vision go, despite dark days. In generation after generation, for more than two centuries, the power of this dream drove us and inspired the world. Despite all of the contradictions, shortcomings, missteps, and failures along the way, this basic American story remains true, and it is an undeniable triumph of the human spirit. Cynics and critics will have their say, but Americans really did come together to defeat the British Empire; to overthrow the evil of slavery and work for justice; to secure

1

equal voting rights for women; to insist that everyone, not only the wealthy, has an equal vote and voice; to suffer, work, and fight year after year to defeat fascist, communist, fundamentalist, and totalitarian challenges to our vision of democracy, equality, and freedom.

People are free. People are equal. People govern. We have lived by that and died for that, and whenever we fell short, we worked and sacrificed for that, to ensure, as Abraham Lincoln said in one of our darkest moments, "that government of the people, by the people, for the people shall not perish from the Earth."

To triumph again over powerful enemies of human equality, dignity, and freedom in our generation, we must properly identify the challenge and bring clarity of thinking and action to making our republic work again. As so often before, success and struggle begin with the simplest of propositions: Corporations are not people.

On January 20, 2010, the Supreme Court of the United States concluded, in effect, that corporations are people and have the people's First Amendment free speech rights. According to the Supreme Court in *Citizens United* v. *Federal Election Commission*, we Americans cannot prevent corporations from using billions of dollars to control who wins and who loses elections or to control what our representatives in Congress and in state and local government do or do not do. In one stroke, the Court erased a century or more of bipartisan law and two previous Supreme Court rulings that affirmed the right, if not the duty, of the people to regulate corporate political spending to preserve the integrity of American democracy. Eight months after *Citizens United*, we had the most expensive election in American history, with nearly $4 billion, much of it secret corporate money channeled and laundered through front groups, spent to define who was good, who was bad, and what issues mattered. Nearly six out of ten eligible American voters did not even bother to vote.

Citizens United is not merely a mistake easily corrected, nor is the case simply about campaign finance or money in politics. *Citi-*

zens United is a corporate power case masquerading as a free speech case. In many ways, the decision was less a break from the recent past than a proclamation about the sad reality of corporate power in America. The Court's declaration in Citizens United that corporations have the same rights as people must strike most Americans as bizarre. To the five justices in the majority and to the corporate legal movement out of which they have come, however, it was more like a victory lap or an end zone dance for the three-decade-long campaign for corporate power and corporate rights.

This campaign, begun in the 1970s, had already succeeded in creating a corporate trump card to strike down federal, state, and local laws enacted for the public's benefit. Even before Citizens United, the fabrication of corporate rights and the reality of corporate power controlled economic, energy, environmental, health, budget, debt, food, agriculture, and foreign policy in America.

The results? Massive job outsourcing abroad; destruction of our manufacturing capacity; wage stagnation for the vast majority of Americans and unprecedented enrichment of the very few; uncontrolled military spending and endless wars to secure energy supplies from a region from which we should have cut our dependence long ago; out-of-control health care spending at the same time that millions of people cannot get health care at all; bloated and unsustainable budgets and debt at every level of government; national and global environmental crisis; loss of wilderness and open land, and the takeover of public hunting and fishing grounds; chain store sprawl and gutting of local economies and communities; obesity, asthma, and public health epidemics; and a growing sense that the connection between Americans and our government has been lost.

Bill Moyers, the acclaimed journalist, has been an optimist for much of his legendary career as he explored faith and reason, war and peace, and the progress of American democracy. Here is what he said in Washington in late 2010:

> *Democracy in America has been a series of narrow escapes, and we may be running out of luck. The most widely shared assumption of our journey as Americans has been the idea of progress, the belief that the present is "better" than the past and things will keep getting better in the future. No matter what befalls us—we keep telling ourselves—"the system works."*
>
> *All bets are now off. The great American experiment in creating a different future together has come down to the worship of individual cunning in the pursuit of wealth and power, with both political parties cravenly subservient to Big Money. The result is an economy that no longer serves ordinary men and women and their families. This, I believe, accounts for so much of the profound sense of betrayal in the country, for the despair about the future. . . .*
>
> *America as a shared project is shattered, leaving us increasingly isolated in our separate realities.*[1]

We do not have to live with this. We can put the American project back together again.

First, though, we need to see where *Citizens United* came from and how much we have lost to the triumph of corporate power. Most of the first six chapters of this book examine these themes from different perspectives. In Chapter Three, I digress to examine what a corporation actually is as a matter of law and fact. This may be a digression, but it lies at the heart of why corporations can have no constitutional rights superior to the rights of the American people to make laws governing corporations. Corporations are not merely private entities, owing no duties to the public. Corporations are legal creations of government.

I close with three essential steps to roll back corporate dominance of government: (1) a twenty-eighth amendment to the Constitution that will overturn *Citizens United* and corporate rights and restore people's rights; (2) corporate accountability and charter reform to ensure that corporations better reflect the public policy reasons for which we allow the legal benefits of incorporation, such as limited liability, in the first place; and (3) election law reform, including increased public funding, greater transparency, and an end to legal political bribery.

❖　❖　❖

Citizens United confronts us again with the basic question of American democracy—what do we mean when we say, as we do in the opening words of the Constitution, "We, the People"? That question drives the central narrative of the American story, and it is why a constitutional amendment campaign to reverse *Citizens United* is so important now.

Amendment campaigns are how we make the American vision of equality and liberty a reality. Amendment campaigns are how we accomplished much that we now take for granted:

- All people are equal.
- Every citizen of every gender, race, and creed gets to vote and participate in our society.
- Women are equal and may vote just as men vote.
- The poor can vote, even if they don't have money for a poll tax.
- Millions of men and women who have lived eighteen, nineteen, and twenty years, old enough to die for their country in war, may not be barred from voting.
- We can, if we, the people, choose to do so, enact progressive income taxes and not place the tax burden only on middle-class and working families.
- We elect the individuals who serve in the U.S. Senate, rather than watch from the sidelines while corporate-dominated political bosses appoint them.

Not one of these principles was established without Americans working for and winning constitutional amendments.

Now we need to work together again, to campaign for a fundamental proposition, encourage a national conversation, and force votes in towns and cities, state legislatures, and Congress, so that people and our representatives state where they stand on this question of our time: Must the American people cede our rights and our government to global corporations? I hope this book will show why this question is so important and how Americans can succeed in restoring our free republic, with equality for all.

Finally, a word about nomenclature. I am not "anticorporate," and this book is not "anticorporate," whatever that means. When I refer to "corporations" and "corporate power" and the like, I am talking about large, global or transnational corporations. Size matters. Complexity and power matter. Whether corporations operate in the economic sphere without dominating the political sphere matters.

Thousands and thousands of corporations in America are just like the corporation I set up for my law firm and just like the kinds of corporations that you may have set up or worked in. They are convenient legal structures for businesses to make economic activity more efficient, productive, flexible, and, we hope, profitable (to be sure, I am not "antiprofit" either).

If I am "anti" anything, I am opposed to any force that takes God-given rights away from people and threatens one of the most remarkable runs of democracy and republican government in the history of humanity. Today that force is the combination of massive and insufficiently controlled global corporations. To succeed in making government of the people real in our generation, we will need to restore our right and duty to check, balance, and restrain that power.

Chapter One
American Democracy Works, and Corporations Fight Back

In 1838, a quarter-century before he became the nation's sixteenth president, a twenty-nine-year-old Abraham Lincoln stepped up to speak at the Young Men's Lyceum in Springfield, Illinois. He spoke about what was to become the cause of his life: the preservation of that great American contribution to the human story, government of, for, and by the people. He insisted that the success or failure of the American experiment was up to us. "If destruction be our lot, we must ourselves be its author and finisher. As a nation of freemen, we must live through all time, or die by suicide."[1]

Lincoln's generation of Americans, and every generation since, has faced daunting questions of whether "destruction be our lot," and we certainly have our share today. Most people can point to a host of complex and related reasons for rising anxiety about our future. Global and national environmental crises seem relentless and increasingly related to energy, economic, military, and food crises. Our unsustainable debt and budgets—national, state, local, family, personal—seem beyond control, reflecting an economy that has not generated significant wage growth in a generation. We have been locked in faraway wars for more than a decade, at war in one form or another for a half-century. Despite our victory over totalitarian communism, we spend more on our military than all other countries combined. We, the descendants of republicans with great suspicion about standing armies, now maintain a costly military empire across more than one hundred countries. On top of all of this and more, too many people now doubt that we are, in fact, a government of the people, and they no longer believe in their hearts that democracy works or that our government responds to what the people want.

We can point to an array of causes, and we can point fingers at each other, but the root of many of these related problems is our collective failure to do what generations of Americans before us did: choose to take responsibility as citizens to manage and control corporate power in our nation. We have lost sight of the implications of the astonishing global wealth and power of transnational corporations. The goals of these corporations do not concern what is best for people, the nation, and the globe.[2] The agenda of the largest corporations will never be the agenda of the American family and the American community. Yet the corporate agenda is now the dominant policy agenda at home and across the world.

Citizens United v. Federal Election Commission

In 2010, in *Citizens United v. Federal Election Commission*, the U.S. Supreme Court proclaimed that the American people are not permitted to determine how much control corporations may have over elections and lawmakers. The Court, in a 5–4 decision, struck down as unconstitutional a federal election law designed to prevent corporations from dominating the outcome of elections. This law was the Bipartisan Campaign Reform Act (also known as McCain-Feingold, after its Republican and Democratic sponsors). The Bipartisan Campaign Reform Act banned "electioneering" spending by corporations—and only corporations—for or against specific candidates within sixty days of a federal election. The law was intended to prevent corporations from bypassing a longstanding prohibition on corporate political contributions to candidates, passed in 1907.

The case is called *Citizens United* because a Virginia nonprofit corporation by that name sued the Federal Election Commission to challenge the corporate spending restriction in the Bipartisan Campaign Reform Act. Citizens United, the corporation, wished to use its corporate money and donations from for-profit corporations to make and distribute what the Court described as a "feature-length advertisement" against Hillary Clinton, who was running for president when the case began. Further, Citizens United sought to do this within the sixty-day period before an election when the law restricted corporate spending on electioneering activity. According to Citizens United, the law violated the First Amendment right of free speech because it prevented Citizens United, a not-for-profit corporation, from engaging in "electioneering activity" and for-profit corporations from contributing to Citizens United's electioneering activity.

Of course, people are free to make a feature-length advertisement attacking a powerful senator running for president, if that's what people wish to do. Nor is anything wrong with people pooling their money to do the same thing. That's essential for political participation. People contribute all the time to organizations, associations, political parties, political action committees and other political committees. At first blush, the background to the case seemed to warrant concern about government restrictions on the free ability of people to pool resources to advocate views.

The Court majority in *Citizens United* was not content to leave the case at first blush. Instead, they saw an opportunity to make new law and to throw out a century of law they thought too restrictive of corporations. In the end, they effectively proclaimed that *all* corporations have a right to spend unlimited money in any American election—federal, state, local, judicial.

The Supreme Court had rejected this argument only a few years earlier, when Justices William Rehnquist and Sandra Day O'Connor were still on the Court. In 2003, in the case of *McConnell* v. *Federal Election Commission*, the Court ruled that the very same corporate spending provision in the McCain-Feingold law did *not* violate the First Amendment. In *McConnell*, the Court agreed that Congress may make different election spending rules for corporations than for people. The Court in *McConnell* followed the 1990 case of *Michigan Chamber of Commerce* v. *Austin*, in which another majority of the Court had ruled that corporate money, aggregated with advantages that come from the government, is not the same as people's money pooled together. Corporate spending in elections can be restricted because government creates the advantages for corporations to make them effective in the economic sphere, and the same advantages pose dangers in the political sphere.

Now in *Citizens United*, the Court, with the additions of a new chief justice, John Roberts, and a new justice, Samuel Alito, threw out *McConnell* and *Austin*. The *Citizens United* Court said its earlier decisions were wrong. The Court struck down the McCain-Feingold law as a violation of free speech rights and invited billions of corporate dollars into American elections.

Justice Anthony Kennedy wrote the opinion in *Citizens United* for the Court. At first, Justice Kennedy's opinion sounds like a ringing defense of free speech and American democracy. He writes that the government may not "ban speech." *Yes!* All "speakers" must be allowed and no "voices" may be silenced. *Yes!* The government cannot restrict a "disadvantaged person or class" from speech. *Yes!* All "citizens, or associations of citizens," must have an unfettered right to get their views about candidates or anything else out to the people. *Of course!*

But wait. Who are these "voices," "speakers" and "disadvantaged persons"? They are corporations, particularly global corporations with *trillions* of dollars in revenue and profits. And what was this onerous "ban on speech"? A rather weak law that said corporations may not, within sixty days of an election, spend corporate "general treasury" money to support or attack candidates for federal office. That's it.

The Court announced its decision on a cold January day in 2010 when most Americans were anxious about millions of job losses, angered by national debt and massive deficits deepened by corporate bailouts, and worried about our military and global strength overstretched by repeated distant wars while China, Germany, and other economic powerhouses at peace charged ahead. Now the Supreme Court says corporations are "disadvantaged persons" with "rights" that trump and invalidate our laws?

Since the decision, *Citizens United* has been widely recognized as a notorious and dangerous mistake by the Court. First, the four dissenting justices on the Court, led by eighty-nine-year-old Justice John Paul Stevens, sounded an alarm. Justice Stevens's ninety-page dissent, among his last work before retiring, may be his greatest legacy.

Stevens, born and raised in Chicago, had enlisted in the U.S. Navy on December 6, 1941, the day before the Japanese attack on Pearl Harbor, and received the Bronze Star for his service in World War II. He then began a twenty-five-year career as a lawyer and represented numerous corporations in antitrust cases. In 1969, Stevens led the investigation and prosecution of corrupt judges in Illinois and was hailed for his fair, honest, and determined approach. A Republican, he was appointed to the Court by President Gerald Ford in 1975. It would be difficult to find a more honest, moderate, and balanced judge.

When the justices assembled to announce the *Citizens United* decision, Stevens took the unusual step of reading his dissent aloud from his seat in the Supreme Court's public chamber. While the reading of the elderly judge at times faltered, his words were unmistakable. Stevens called the Court's action in *Citizens United* a "radical departure from what has been settled First Amendment law." He blasted the Court's conclusion that corporations, "like individuals, contribute to the discussion, debate, and the dissemination of information and ideas that the First Amendment seeks to foster." Justice Stevens said that "glittering generality" obscured the truth about what *Citizens United* really meant for America, already suffering from undue influence of corporate power. Then Justice Stevens said this:

> *The Framers [of our Constitution] thus took it as a given that corporations could be comprehensively regulated in the service of the public welfare. Unlike our colleagues [on the Supreme Court], they had little trouble distinguishing corporations from human beings, and when they constitutionalized the right to free speech in the First Amendment, it was the free speech of individual Americans that they had in mind. . . .*
>
> *At bottom, the Court's opinion is thus a rejection of the common sense of the American people, who have recognized a need to prevent corporations from undermining self-government since the founding, and who have fought against the distinctive corrupting potential of corporate electioneering since the days of Theodore Roosevelt. It is a strange time to repudiate that common sense. While American democracy is imperfect, few*

*outside the majority of this Court would have thought its flaws
included a dearth of corporate money in politics.*

Justice Stevens and his fellow dissenters on the Court were not
alone. President Obama called the decision a "strike at the heart
of democracy." Others, such as Maryland Congresswoman Donna
Edwards, called *Citizens United* the worst case since the Supreme
Court ruled in the 1856 case of *Dred Scott* v. *Sanford* that African Americans could not be citizens. Republican Senator John
McCain said he was "disappointed," and conservative Tea Party
activists went further. A founder of the Tea Party said, "I have a
problem with that. It just allows them to feed the machine. Corporations are not like people. Corporations exist forever; people
don't. Our founding fathers never wanted them; these behemoth
organizations that never die. . . . It puts the people at a tremendous disadvantage."[3]

Polls showed that more than 75 percent of Independents,
Republicans, and Democrats alike rejected the decision. People
formed groups such as Free Speech for People and Move to
Amend to launch a constitutional amendment campaign to overturn the decision and corporate rights, and more than a million
Americans quickly signed petitions calling on Congress to send an
amendment to the States for ratification. Several amendment bills
were introduced in the House and Senate, and resolutions con-
demning the decision and calling for a constitutional amendment
were introduced in towns, cities, and state across the country.

Why this reaction? Most Americans understand the fundamental truth that corporations are not people and that large
corporations already have far too much power in America. The
real people are not buying the metaphors sprinkled throughout
Citizens United and know that corporations are not "speakers" or
"disadvantaged persons." Corporate money is not a "voice."

Roots of *Citizens United*: Earth Day 1970

If so many understood at once the crisis that *Citizens United* poses for America, how did it happen? To answer that question, we need to go back to the 1970s and the formation of the organized corporate campaign to put American democracy on a leash. First came a wave of engaged citizens and responsive government; then came the corporate reaction. *Citizens United* could not have happened without the deliberate drive for corporate power and rights that began more than three decades ago.[4]

After a century of industrialization, Americans had by 1970 had enough of corporations using our rivers, air, oceans, and land as sewers and dumps, leaving most people and communities with the costs and giving the profits to shareholders. One day in April 1970, twenty million Americans of every age and political party came out into the streets and the parks to celebrate the first Earth Day. They demanded a better balance between corporations and people and better stewardship of our land, water, and air. Look at the photos from this first Earth Day and you will see families with children, men in suits and ties and neatly dressed women, working- and middle-class Americans, people of all ages and races.

These millions continued a longstanding American principle of guarding against concentrated corporate power that might overwhelm the larger interests of the nation. This nonpartisan tradition goes back not only to Franklin Roosevelt's New Deal, not only to Theodore Roosevelt's Square Deal, but to the founding of America. James Madison, a chief architect of the Constitution, wrote in the early 1800s that "incorporated Companies with proper limitations and guards, may in particular cases, be useful; but they are at best a necessary evil only."[5] Always willing to be more colorful, Thomas Jefferson said that he hoped to "crush in its birth the aristocracy of our monied corporations, which dare already to challenge our government to a trial of strength and bid defiance to the laws of our country."[6]

In the 1830s, President Andrew Jackson and his allies battled against the partisan activity of the Second Bank of the United States, a corporation. Jackson pressed the urgent question of "whether the people of the United States are to govern through representatives chosen by their unbiased suffrages or whether the money and power of a great corporation are to be secretly exerted to influence their judgment and control their decisions."[7] Even President Martin Van Buren, hardly a radical, warned of "the already overgrown influence of corporate authorities."[8]

That first Earth Day in 1970 again awakened our government to the necessity of restoring the balance of corporate power and public interest, of those who control powerful corporations and the rest of Americans. With a Republican president in the White House and bipartisan support in Congress, the extent of reform that quickly followed in the months and a few short years after the first Earth Day remains astonishing:

- First Environmental Protection Agency
- Clean Water Act
- Federal Water Pollution Control Amendments
- Clean Air Act Extension
- Toxic Substances Control Act
- Safe Drinking Water Act
- Wilderness Act
- Surface Mining Control and Reclamation Act
- Endangered Species Act
- Marine Mammal Protection Act
- Resource Recovery Act
- First fuel economy standards for motor vehicles

These 1970s reforms were long overdue. For a time, they worked extraordinarily well and made a profound difference in the quality of life of the vast majority of Americans. No longer could dumping untreated sewage and toxic waste in our waters be considered a standard business practice; no longer could corporations walk away from hazardous waste and chemical sites; more wilderness areas preserved more of our birthright and that of future Americans; new laws rejected the industry view that we just had to live with the discharge of brain- and organ-damaging lead from millions of cars and the spread of lead paint in every building in the land; access to clean, safe water was assured for far more Americans; and so much more.

The market did not do this. We did this by acting as citizens in a republic.

As with every time in American history, of course, the 1970s were racked with crisis and challenge. Yet the American people worked the levers of democracy, and the government responded. It actually seemed as if some connection existed between those levers—voting, organizing, debating, petitioning, marching—and our government's conduct.

Environmental protection was not all. We often remember the strife and problems of the late 1960s and early 1970s but think of the progress in race and gender equality; ending the Vietnam War; real wage growth for average Americans; global leadership in trade and commerce and manufacturing; steady, comprehensive, creative, and effective resistance across the globe to dictatorial communism; public accountability when the president broke the law; more open government and better congressional oversight; manageable debt and budgets in Washington and the states; employee rights and safety; and a constitutional amendment to enfranchise millions of Americans from eighteen to twenty years old. The people demanded change; our government delivered change.

The biggest corporations on the planet, however, did not celebrate the responsive democracy that followed Earth Day. Instead, they organized to fund a sustained program to take political power and rights for themselves and away from average Americans. With *Citizens United*, we may see the end game of this project, but it has been years in the making.

1971: Lewis Powell and the "Activist-Minded Supreme Court"

In 1971, Lewis Powell, a mild-mannered, courtly, and shrewd corporate lawyer in Richmond, Virginia, soon to be appointed to the United States Supreme Court, wrote a memorandum to his client, the United States Chamber of Commerce. He outlined a critique and a plan that changed America.[9]

Lewis Powell, like the *Citizens United* dissenter Justice John Paul Stevens, was a decorated World War II veteran who returned to his hometown to build a most respected corporate law practice. By all accounts, Powell was a gentleman—reserved, polite, and gracious—and a distinguished lawyer and public servant. Commentators and law professors cite Powell's "qualities of temperament and character" and his "modest" and "restrained" approach to judging.[10] At his funeral in 1998, Sandra Day O'Connor, who had joined the Supreme Court in 1987, said, "For those who seek a model of human kindness, decency, exemplary behavior, and integrity, there will never be a better man."[11] Even the rare critic will cite Lewis Powell's decency and kindness.[12]

Much about these accounts must be true, but none tells the whole story of Lewis Powell. All of them, and even the principal Powell biography, omit the details of how he used his gifts to advance a radical corporate agenda.[13] It is impossible to square this corporatist part of Powell's life and legacy with any conclusion of "modest" or "restrained" judging.

Powell titled his 1971 memo to the Chamber of Commerce "Attack on American Free Enterprise System." He explained, "No thoughtful person can question that the American economic system is under broad attack." In response, corporations must organize and fund a drive to achieve political power through "united action." Powell emphasized the need for a sustained, multiyear corporate campaign to use an "activist-minded Supreme Court" to shape "social, economic and political change" to the advantage of corporations.

Powell continued:

> But independent and uncoordinated activity by individual corporations, as important as this is, will not be sufficient. Strength lies in organization, in careful long-range planning and implementation, in consistency of action over an indefinite period of years, in the scale of financing available only through joint effort, and in the political power available only through united action and national organizations.

The roots of *Citizens United* lie in Powell's 1971 strategy to use "activist" Supreme Court judges to create corporate rights. "Under our constitutional system," Powell told the U.S. Chamber of Commerce, "especially with an activist-minded Supreme Court, the judiciary may be the most important instrument for social, economic and political change."

Powell's call for a corporate rights campaign should not be misunderstood as a "conservative" or "moderate" reaction to the excesses of "liberals" or "big government." Rather, to understand the perspective of Powell and his allies is to understand the difference between a conservative and a corporatist.

Powell and the Tobacco
Corporations Show the Way

By the time of his 1971 memorandum, Lewis Powell was a director of more than a dozen international corporations, including Philip Morris Inc., a global manufacturer and seller of cigarettes. Powell joined Philip Morris as a director in 1964, when the United States surgeon general released the most devastating and comprehensive report to date about the grave dangers of smoking. He remained a director of the cigarette company until his appointment to the Supreme Court in 1971. Powell also advised the Tobacco Institute, the cigarette lobby that finally was exposed and stripped of its corporate charter in the 1990s after decades of using phony science and false statements to create a fraudulent "debate" about smoking and health.[14]

The story of the cigarette corporations and their response to public efforts to address addiction, smoking, and health is a big piece of the larger story of how corporate rights took such significant pieces of the Constitution and American democracy. The ideas expressed by Powell in his 1971 memorandum to the Chamber of Commerce came out of his personal involvement in the aggressive resistance of the cigarette corporations to efforts to address the devastating social and public costs of its lethal products. As a director and an executive committee member of Philip Morris, Powell shared responsibility for the fraudulent attack on the conclusions of scientists and the surgeon general by the cigarette industry and for its false insistence for years that "no proof" showed cigarettes to be unhealthy.

Hints of this work can be seen in the Philip Morris annual reports issued during Powell's tenure as a director, which reflected the broader campaign of the company and the cigarette industry to discredit the science about smoking and health and to misrepresent the facts to keep people smoking and get young people to start. We now know, thanks to the 2007 findings of a federal judge, that many of the assertions in these annual reports were knowingly false. According to the reports themselves, these statements and others were made "on behalf of the Board of Directors," including Powell:

> 1964: "The industry continues to support major research efforts directed towards resolving the many unanswered questions on smoking and health."
>
> 1967: "The year 1967 was marked by an intensification of exaggerated claims made relative to the possible adverse health effects of smoking on health. . . . We deplore the lack of objectivity in so important a controversy. . . . Unfortunately the positive benefits of smoking which are so widely acknowledged are largely ignored by many reports linking cigarettes and health, and little attention is paid to the scientific reports which are favorable to smoking."
>
> 1967: "We would again like to state that there is no biological proof that smoking is causally related to the diseases and conditions claimed to be statistically associated with smoking . . . no proof that the tar and nicotine levels in smoke are significant in relation to health."
>
> 1969: "No biological or clinical proof that smoking is causally related to human disease . . . serious doubt that smoking is a causative factor in heart disease."
>
> 1970: "Often the scientific information which is relied on to indict cigarette smoking is of dubious validity."

Absent convincing evidence, it might be reckless to say that Philip Morris and the other tobacco corporations engaged in a willful, aggressive, wide-ranging conspiracy and racketeering enterprise so that the corporations could sell more products that kill people. But now that the evidence is in, we know that that is exactly what happened. We know this thanks to scientists, victims of the conspiracy, state attorneys general (both Democrats and Republicans), the United States Department of Justice (under both Presidents Bill Clinton and George W. Bush), and Judge Gladys Kessler and a panel of U.S. Court of Appeals judges appointed by Presidents Ronald Reagan, Bill Clinton, and George H. W. Bush.

In 2006, the U.S. Department of Justice took the cigarette corporations to trial, alleging that they had engaged in a racketeering conspiracy. Eighty-four witnesses testified in the nine-month trial, and hundreds of internal corporate secrets were finally exposed. When the verdict came in, Judge Kessler concluded that "overwhelming evidence" proved that the cigarette corporations "conspired together" to fraudulently deny that cigarettes caused cancer, emphysema, and a long list of other fatal diseases; to manipulate levels of highly addictive nicotine to keep people smoking; to market addictive cigarettes to children so that the corporations would have "replacement smokers" for those who quit or died; and that they "concealed evidence, destroyed documents, and abused the attorney-client privilege to prevent the public from knowing about the dangers of smoking and to protect the industry" from justice.[15]

As counsel to the cigarette industry and as a Philip Morris director, Powell already had begun testing the use of activist-minded courts to create corporate rights. In one case in the late 1960s, Powell argued that any suggestion that cigarettes caused cancer and death was "not proved" and was "controversial." Therefore, according to Powell, the Federal Communications Commission wrongly violated the First Amendment rights of cigarette corporations by refusing to require "equal time" for the corporations to respond to any announcement that discouraged cigarette smoking as a health hazard.[16]

Even the U.S. Court of Appeals for the Fourth Circuit, based in the tobacco-friendly South, rejected this claim. Although Powell lost that time, he went on to win far more than he could have imagined after he got on the Supreme Court and helped change the Constitution.

Powell's 1971 memo to the Chamber of Commerce laid out a corporate rights and a corporate power campaign. The Chamber and the largest corporations then implemented these recommendations with zeal, piles of money, patience, and an activist Supreme Court. In equating corporations with "We, the People" in our Constitution, no justice would be more of an activist than Lewis Powell after he joined the Supreme Court in 1972.

1972: Powell Gets His Chance

In January 1972, President Nixon filled two Supreme Court vacancies, appointing Powell to one seat and William Rehnquist, a conservative Republican lawyer from Phoenix, Arizona, to the other. Rehnquist never hid his conservative views, which were well known and, to some, controversial. At the same time, neither Congress nor most Americans knew of Powell's radical corporatist views. In his Senate confirmation hearing, no one asked about his recent proposal to the Chamber of Commerce recommending the use of an "activist-minded Supreme Court" to impose those views on the nation. No one asked because neither Powell nor the Chamber of Commerce disclosed the memo during his confirmation proceedings.[17]

Once on the Court, these two Nixon appointees followed very different paths. Justice Powell would go on to write the Court's unprecedented decisions creating a new concept of "corporate speech" in the First Amendment. Using this new theory, the Court struck down law after law in which the states and Congress sought to balance corporate power with the public interest. With increasing assertiveness by the Supreme Court even after Powell retired in 1987, the new corporate rights theory has invalidated laws addressing the environment, tobacco and public health, food and drugs, financial regulation, and more.[18]

Powell helped shape a new majority to serve the interest of corporations, but for years, several vigorous dissents resisted the concept of corporate rights. The most vigorous came from the conservative Justice William Rehnquist. He grounded his dissents in the fundamental proposition that our Bill of Rights sets out the rights of human beings, and corporations are not people. For years, Rehnquist maintained this principled conservative argument, warning over and over again that corporate rights have no place in our republican form of government.[19]

Here Come the Foundations

Despite the Rehnquist dissents, Powell's vision of an unregulated corporate political "marketplace," where corporations are freed by activist courts from the policy judgment of the majority of people, won out. Powell, of course, could not have acted alone. He could not have moved a majority of the Court to create corporate rights if no one had listened to his advice to organize corporate political power to demand corporate rights. Listen they did—with the help of just the sort of massive corporate funding that Powell proposed.

Corporations and corporate executives funded a wave of new "legal foundations" in the 1970s. These legal foundations were intended to drive into every court and public body in the land the same radical message, repeated over and over again, until the bizarre began to sound normal: corporations are persons with constitutional rights against which the laws of the people must fall.

Huge corporations, including Powell's Philip Morris, invested millions of dollars in the Chamber of Commerce's National Chamber Litigation Center and other legal foundations to bring litigation demanding new corporate rights. In rapid succession, corporations and supporters funded the Pacific Legal Foundation, the Mid-Atlantic Legal Foundation, the Mid-America Legal Foundation, the Great Plains Legal Foundation (Landmark Legal Foundation), the Washington Legal Foundation, the Northeastern Legal Foundation, the New England Legal Foundation, the Southeastern Legal Foundation, the Capital Legal Center, the National Legal Center for the Public Interest, and many others.[20]

These foundations began filing brief after brief challenging state and federal laws across the country, pounding away at the themes of corporations as "persons," "speakers" and holders of constitutional rights. Reading their briefs, one might think that the most powerful, richest corporations in the history of the world were some beleaguered minority fighting to overcome oppression. The foundations and the corporate lawyers argued that "corporations are persons" with the "liberty secured to all persons." They used new phrases like "corporate speech," the "rights of corporate speakers," and "the corporate character of the speaker." They demanded, as if to end an unjust silence, "the right of corporations to be heard" and "the rights of corporations to speak out."

This corporate campaign sought to redefine the very role of corporations in American society. The message was insistent: We should no longer think of corporations as useful but potentially insidious industrial economic tools. We should no longer be concerned that corporations might leverage massive economic power into massive political power or trample the public interest for the profit of the few. Instead, we should think of corporations as pillars of liberty, institutions that Americans can trust. They would protect our freedom for us. They would stand up to "bad" government for us.

A 1977 brief of the Chamber of Commerce, for example, argued that the Court should strike down a state law that limited corporate political spending in citizens' referendum elections because corporations help maintain our freedoms: "Business's social role is to provide the people a valuable service which helps maintain their freedoms. . . . The statute at issue prevents the modern corporation from fulfilling a major social obligation. . . ."[21]

By 1978, the millions of dollars invested in the radical corporate rights campaign began to pay off. The first major victory for the corporate rights advocates came in 1978, with a corporate attack on a Massachusetts law in *First National Bank of Boston* v. *Bellotti*. Several international corporations—including Gillette, the Bank of Boston, and Digital Equipment Corporation—filed a lawsuit after the people of Massachusetts banned corporate political spending intended to influence a citizen referendum. Justice Lewis Powell cast the deciding vote and wrote the 5–4 decision wiping off the books the people's law intended to keep corporate money out of citizen ballot questions.[22] For the first time in American history, corporations had successfully claimed "speech" rights to attack laws regulating corporate money in our elections.

With that success, an emboldened corporate rights campaign next attacked energy and environmental laws. In the 1982 case of *Central Hudson Gas & Electric Corporation* v. *Public Service Corporation of New York*, utility corporations and the array of corporate legal foundations all argued that a New York law prohibiting utility corporations from promoting energy consumption violated the corporations' rights of free speech. The corporations won again, and again Justice Powell wrote the decision for the activist Supreme Court that he had imagined in his 1971 Chamber of Commerce memo. The corporate interest in promoting energy *consumption* for corporate profit trumped the people's interest in energy *conservation*.[23] Over a period of six years, Justice Powell wrote four key corporate rights decisions for the Supreme Court. These unprecedented cases transformed the people's First

Amendment speech freedom into a corporate right to challenge public oversight and corporate regulation.

Powell led a majority of the Court to accept the repeated mantra that "corporations are persons" and corporate "voices" must be free, and the sustained attacks on the people's laws continued for the next two decades. Oil, coal, and utility corporations, tobacco corporations, chemical and pharmaceutical corporations, alcohol corporations, banking and other Wall Street corporations, and many others all successfully claimed corporate speech rights to invalidate federal, state, and local laws. As you will see in Chapter Two, corporations even succeeded in attacking the right of parents to know whether the milk they fed their children came from cows treated with Monsanto's genetically engineered recombinant DNA bovine drug.

In 2007, the U.S. Chamber of Commerce's National Chamber Litigation Center celebrated thirty years of using judicial activism on behalf of corporations and admitted that it was "the brainchild of former U.S. Supreme Court Justice Lewis Powell." The brainchild, with its motto of "Business Is Our ONLY Client," bragged about such "victories" as convincing the Supreme Court to throw out a decision by a jury of people to impose punitive damages for the unlawful conduct of Philip Morris, Inc.[24]

The Consequences

The success of the Powell–Chamber of Commerce plan transformed American law, government, and society, with two devastating consequences for the country. First, corporations gained new political power at the expense of average citizens and voters. Corporations poured out money to lobbying and election campaigns and to help friendly politicians and hurt unfriendly politicians. With even modest reform crushed by corporate rights decisions such as *Bellotti* v. *First National Bank of Boston*—and now much more so, *Citizens United*—corporations could threaten "independent expenditure" campaigns against politicians who did not bend their way. Corporate money to influence legislative votes and politician behavior lost its scandalous, shameful nature. Bags of corporate cash were no longer bags of cash; they were "speech." How could "speech" be corrupt or scandalous?

Washington and many state capitals became playgrounds for corporate lobbyists, and our elected representatives became increasingly disconnected from the will of the people. With the new, organized corporate radicalism, staggering amounts of corporate money flooded Washington and our political system. Between 1998 and 2010, for example, the Chamber of Commerce spent $739 million on lobbying. Pharmaceutical and health care corporations spent more than $2 *billion* on lobbying in the past twelve years. Three corporations seeking military contracts, Northrop Grumman Corporation, Lockheed, and Boeing, spent more than $400 million on lobbying. GE Corporation ($237 million), AT&T ($162 million), the pharmaceutical corporate lobby PI IRMA ($195 million), ExxonMobil ($151 million), Verizon ($149 million), and many more corporations all joined the lobbyfest.[25] Financial, labor, energy, environmental, health, trade, and other legislation and policy tilted in favor of corporate interests; the hurdles for advancing the public interest became much higher.

Second, the successful corporate rights campaign created a corporate trump card over public interest laws. If laws that were inconvenient to corporate business models somehow made it through the corporate lobbyist machine, corporations now had constitutional "rights" to attack the laws in the courts. It no longer mattered if the majority of people and our representatives chose laws to curb pollution, require disclosure, protect the public health, or nurture small businesses and local economies. The democratic process was no longer enough to decide the issue.

After the creation of "corporate speech" rights, it was now up to federal judges to decide whether the law served an "important" state interest and was not too "burdensome."

The Lost Promise of Earth Day

On that far-off Earth Day in 1970, Americans reclaimed the water, air, land, and forests that belong to all of us and to our descendants. We reclaimed the promise of government of the people, where people and our representatives would weigh, debate, and decide the balance of private and public, corporate and human. Since that spring day in 1970, we have pushed resources and the ecological systems on which life depends to the breaking point. Even as the oil, gas, and coal corporations mimic the strategy of the cigarette corporations to create a fraudulent "controversy" and "open question" about the global warming "hoax," we have ripped past the point of no return on climate pollution.

While the evidence of national and global environmental destruction at a level that will challenge our civilization and way of life is more compelling now than in 1970, our leaders in government are not even debating, let alone enacting, possible solutions. Incredibly, the current debate in Congress is not what we can do to save our world but whether Congress should strip the Environmental Protection Agency of its authority to regulate pollution that causes the global climate crisis.

Corporate media might tell you that the reason for inaction is that Americans oppose environmental regulation and oppose drastic changes to address the energy and environmental crisis. Yet there is little reason to believe that this is true. In fact, try an experiment. Find a moment to talk seriously in a nonpolitical, nonconfrontational way with your friends, neighbors, or family members, regardless of what political party or philosophy they may favor. I bet that you will find that they too think that we cannot continue to rely on corporations to protect freedom for us and that corporate business as usual will condemn us to disastrous energy, economic, and environmental policies and ensure that we pass to our children a very bleak and weak nation and world.

This basic understanding of the connection between our state of decline and crisis on one hand and our corporate-driven energy, environmental, economic, foreign and military policy on the other, is one of the many points of consensus among the American people that the corporatist political elite ignores. According to an independent, nonpartisan 2010 Pew Research poll, for example, huge majorities of Americans favor better fuel efficiency standards for cars and trucks (79 percent), more funding for alternative energy (74 percent), more spending on mass transit (63 percent), and tax incentives for hybrid or electric vehicles (60 percent).

Similarly, for years, most Americans have supported, and still support, stronger, not weaker, environmental and energy policies. This is true even in times of recession, terrorism, and deep concern about budgets.[26] From 1995 to 2008, when the independent multiyear Gallup poll was last done, through every variety of political environment, from good economies to bad, from terrorist attacks to war, the American people have been consistent in the response. More than twice as many Americans say we need "additional, immediate, and drastic action" to prevent major environmental disruption, compared to those who say "we should just take the same actions we have been taking on the environment." The percentage of those identifying a need for "drastic, immediate action" was 35 percent in 1995, 38 percent in 2007, and 34 percent in 2008. When you add in those who say "we should take some additional action," the range of Americans who want better, stronger, tougher environmental protection has stayed between 80 and 90 percent over the past ten years. The percentage of those who chose the status quo answer ("we should just take the same actions we have been taking on the environment") has ranged from 13 to 20 percent.

For years, most of us have known that the gathering and urgent environmental and energy crisis cannot be ignored, but what has our government done? Maintain the status quo, more or less, and usually much less as the global environmental crisis has worsened and the demand for fossil fuel exploitation soars.

Polls are not infallible, but I suspect that these results would be duplicated in most family discussions around the dinner table. And I believe that we would see a similar disconnect between what people know about the state of our nation and the world and what the corporate-dominated government does. Whether the issue is the environment, the economy, the decades-long wars in the Middle East and bloated military budgets, agri-corporate subsidies and industrial food systems, or corporate welfare, what most people think or want out of our government does not matter much anymore.

We have become accustomed to thinking that we cannot change, that our problems are too big, that our government cannot be effective. This was not always so, and it does not have to be so now. The choice we face in America now about whether to succeed or fail begins with our choice about whether we agree with Lewis Powell, the U.S. Chamber of Commerce, and the corporate rights movement that massive, global corporate entities are the same as people.

Chapter Two
Corporations Are Not People—and They Make Lousy Parents

If the tobacco companies really stopped marketing
to children, the tobacco companies would be out of
business in 25 to 30 years because they will not
have enough customers to stay in business.

—Bennett Lebow, cigarette corporation CEO[1]

"**F**#*k you." That (except without the sanitizing symbols) is what Bad Frog Brewery, Inc., a corporation chartered under Michigan law, demanded the Constitutional right to say on its labels. In the mid-1990s, the corporation wanted to market its beer to the young and rebellious with a foul-mouthed frog who, as the label said, "just don't care." The corporation offered a mascot on the label, a large cartoon frog elevating its middle finger. Because New York law prohibits alcohol labels that are "obscene or indecent" and "obnoxious or offensive to the commonly and generally accepted standard," the state liquor authority refused to approve the label for sale in New York. The corporation balked at complying with the law and filed a lawsuit against the New York State Liquor Authority and the people who served on it.

At first, Bad Frog insisted that the up-yours gesture really was a "symbol of peace, solidarity, and goodwill." Three judges of the United States Courts of Appeals in New York were assigned to the case and gravely noted its "significant issues." Despite the earlier claim that the up-yours gesture meant peace and solidarity, Bad Frog now admitted on appeal that its beer label conveyed, "among other things, the message 'f#*! you.'" (The court's opinion helpfully explains that this was "presumably a suggestion of having intercourse with yourself.") The court of appeals ruled in Bad Frog's favor and voided the New York law, leaving the people powerless to stop corporations from spewing vulgarities from every beer shelf in the land.[2]

OK, it's not the most serious case in the world. Maybe most people don't really care if lewd beer labels fill the shelves, although the people of New York cared enough to have a law preserving some decency in the beer aisle. Still, the case of the finger-waving frog reflects the hallmarks of the new corporate rights era: the shameless ("honest, the finger means peace, solidarity, and goodwill"), the irresponsible ("he just don't care," placed beside the health warning label), and the display of power over the people ("we will do whatever sells, and your law can't stop us"). These themes now run through far more serious areas of our national, community, and family life than beer labels.

Beyond Beer Labels

The fabrication of corporate constitutional rights has not only changed our politics and law; corporate rights and corporate power affect everything: the water we drink, the air we breathe, the food we eat, what our kids learn in school (and what they buy on the way home), what kind of health care we get, the wars we fight, and the taxes and debt we and generations to come will carry.

Do you want to know if your food is safe? Do you want to be able to choose milk, cheese, and yogurt that come from cows that are not injected with a genetically engineered drug that is banned in most of the world? Do you want to know if your water supply has been contaminated with diesel fuel, toxic chemicals, and radiation so that global energy corporations can "frack" natural gas? Do you want to stop toxic-pesticide manufacturers from claiming that their products are "safe for kids" in big letters on the label? Do you want the school to which you are required to send your kids to be inundated with youth-targeting advertisements? Do you want college education to be available without Wall Street corporations sucking billions of dollars of tax money into Ponzi-like for-profit student-debt schemes? In the new corporate rights era, the corporations say you can't.

The Right to Addict Kids

What should we do when a wealthy, suit-clad drug pusher sidles up to children and uses cartoon images and tricks to exploit teen insecurities and risk-taking to get kids hooked on a fatal drug? What kind of person would hang around a schoolyard trying to get teens and preteens hooked on an addictive drug known to kill hundreds of thousands of people a year? That's exactly what Philip Morris and the other cigarette corporations did for decades. When parents, lawmakers, prosecutors, and judges tried to stop them, the cigarette corporations self-righteously insisted on the corporate "free speech right" to say, well, to say what Bad Frog Brewery likes to say.

In the late 1990s, the people of Massachusetts tried to protect school kids from the cigarette companies' "youth-targeting" campaigns, banning cigarette ads within 1,000 feet of a school or playground. The U.S. Supreme Court struck down the law in 2001, calling it a violation of the speech rights of the cigarette corporations. In many ways, this case shows how much our courts and our Constitution have shifted away from the people and to corporations in the years since the 1970s, before the Powell–Chamber of Commerce campaign began.

Back in 1971, Lewis Powell, as a private lawyer for the cigarette companies, argued that the corporations had a First Amendment right to spread corporate lies in response to what the corporations called "propaganda" about smoking and health. He and the cigarette industry were essentially laughed out of court.[3] Back then (and in the two hundred years before that), the corporate legal foundations and the Supreme Court had not grafted the new concept of corporate speech into the Bill of Rights. Thirty years later, though, everything had changed. In 2001, the Supreme Court did exactly what the cigarette corporations asked, striking down the Massachusetts law that required cigarette advertisements to stay 1,000 feet away from schools and playgrounds.

Why Did We Need a School Playground Cigarette Law?

Inside the tobacco corporations, they referred to children as "replacement smokers." Corporate marketing plans and sales documents analyzed the need to replace smokers who died; children under eighteen years old were prime targets. The cigarette corporations did studies showing that if kids did not start smoking by the time they were eighteen, they probably never would become regular smokers. For decades, the cigarette corporations studied and researched nicotine, smoking, and the habits of teenagers. They spent millions of dollars on teenager tracking, marketing, and manipulation. The cigarette companies secretly called the strategy of addicting teens to cigarettes a "key corporate priority."

For decades, cigarette corporations tried to dispute allegations like these. They can do so no more after the Court of Appeals affirmed the 1,000-plus-page decision of Judge Kessler, the federal judge who oversaw the 2006–2007 racketeering trial of the cigarette corporations. Judge Kessler concluded: "The evidence is clear and convincing—and beyond any reasonable doubt—that Defendants have marketed to young people twenty-one and under while consistently, publicly, and falsely denying they do so."[4] The judge quoted Bennett Lebow, the president of a cigarette manufacturing holding corporation, who testified, "If the tobacco companies really stopped marketing to children, the tobacco companies would be out of business in 25 to 30 years because they will not have enough customers to stay in business."[5]

Judge Kessler's judicious reference to "young people under twenty-one" actually gives the cigarette corporations more credit than they deserve. Inside the cigarette corporations, the term "younger adult" was a euphemism. The terms *younger adult* and *YAS* (standing for "younger adult smoker") are corporate-speak for *child* or *teenager*. Corporate marketing studies of YAS in the tobacco companies included children as young as ten years old, and the cigarette corporations studied the percentage of "twelve- to seventeen-year-olds" who "smoked at least a pack a week." They called teens aged 15 to 19 the "new-smoker age group," and they noted with encouragement that "the thirteen-year-old age group 'shows the most dramatic increase in proportion of smokers.'"[6] The cigarette corporations knew that "YAS are the only source of replacement smokers—[fewer] than one-third of smokers start after age 18," and the companies spent hundreds of millions of dollars to increase sales to children between the ages of twelve and seventeen.[7]

According to Judge Kessler, "Defendants realize that they need to get people smoking their brands as young as possible in order to secure them as lifelong loyal smokers." She quoted dozens of internal corporate documents, including an "opportunity analysis" weighing how to exploit teen insecurities:

> *Socially insecure, they gain reinforcement by smoking the brands their friends are smoking, just like they copy their friends' dress, hairstyle, and other conspicuous things. To smoke a brand no one has heard of—which all new brand names are—brings one the risk of ostracism. It's simply not the "in" thing to do.*[8]

What drives so many people to go to work each day, year after year, trying to figure out how to hook children on smoking? A cigarette corporate executive provides the answer in a long-concealed internal corporate document: the possibility of billions of dollars in corporate profit. "If we hold these YAS for the market average of 7 years," he wrote, "they would be worth over $2.1 billion in aggregate incremental profit. I certainly agree with you that this payout should be worth a decent sized investment."[9] By the 1990s, the "decent-sized investment" targeting kids for cigarette sales had succeeded in ensuring that 72 percent of six-year-olds in America recognized the cartoon symbol of Camel cigarettes.[10]

This is why government needed to step in. Several states, including Mississippi, Washington, and Massachusetts, had begun law-enforcement actions against the cigarette conspiracy by the mid-1990s. These cases began to uncover the truth about the conduct of the cigarette corporations, and by 1998, Massachusetts banned outdoor cigarette advertisements within 1,000 feet of a playground, elementary school, or secondary school.[11] Massachusetts Attorney General Scott Harshbarger said the law was needed "to stop Big Tobacco from recruiting new customers among the children of Massachusetts."[12]

In response, the tobacco corporations went on offense; they cried "free speech!" and sued Harshbarger to block the law. They turned to the Powell-Chamber corporate rights theory that by 2000 had become a very potent tool for corporations to evade responsibility, accountability, and public oversight. The corporate "legal foundations" imagined by Lewis Powell and the Chamber of Commerce back in the 1970s were now fully funded by millions of corporate dollars and rushed into the fray. They filed briefs alongside the tobacco corporations, demanding that the Supreme Court protect the "vital role in American society" of the cigarette corporations. They quoted Henry David Thoreau and Justice Benjamin Cardozo, and they weirdly complained that during World War II, "commercial speech became a casualty as surely as Veronica Lake's 'peekaboo' hairstyle."[13]

The corporate lawyers and legal foundations repeated the now familiar refrain that corporations are the same as people. They said that restricting the cigarette corporations' advertising around playgrounds and schoolyards violates corporate speech rights under the First Amendment.[14] The Supreme Court, by this time fully shaped by the corporate power legacy of Lewis Powell, who had retired in 1987, agreed and struck down the Massachusetts law.[15] The law keeping Joe Camel and the cigarette ads away from schools and playgrounds was dead.

Cigarette Corporations Aren't People

Sometimes First Amendment cases can be infuriating because the freedom at stake is often the freedom to say things that are unpopular, cause offense, challenge or undermine government policy supported by many, or inflict emotional pain. Infuriating though that can be, people usually appreciate that the Supreme Court's protection of someone's unpopular free speech also protects a core American value and benefits all of us. But when the Supreme Court saved the "right" of cigarette corporations to advertise around playgrounds and elementary schools, was a single human being made any more free? Was our public debate and state of knowledge any more enriched?

When the government suppresses real speech, the speech of real people, we all lose some of our freedom. Our ability to govern ourselves is compromised when ideas and information are restrained, even bad ideas and unpleasant information. But when we regulate corporate economic conduct, what rights of anyone are lost? Is speech even at issue at all?

The Massachusetts law regulated corporate, commercial conduct, not speech. If the Massachusetts law curtailed the youth-targeting strategies of cigarette corporations, sales might have dropped, but how does that create less freedom of speech for anyone? Any human being who had something to say about cigarettes and youth smoking remained free to say or write whatever that person wanted, wherever and whenever he or she wanted, about cigarettes, youth smoking, or anything else. The Massachusetts law about cigarette advertising had nothing to do with people or groups of people speaking, writing, or expressing their point of view in any way. Even if someone wanted to stand outside a public park or school with a sign saying, "I love cigarettes and kids should, too," the Massachusetts law did not touch them.

In the unlikely event that a real person actually did that, though, what would happen? Perhaps we would see how free speech is supposed to work in America: other people would talk with the miscreant and ask him or her to consider whether that was a decent thing to do. The creep might respond, and debate would ensue. At some point, the cigarette enthusiast or his or her opponents would get tired and move along. If the smoking advocate really had strong views about the merits of smoking, the debate might continue the next day when the person came back again or in writing, interviews, meetings, or wherever people wanted to talk, listen, and debate. The Massachusetts law prevented none of that.

Try talking or debating with Joe Camel; it doesn't work. It doesn't work because Joe Camel and the corporation that spawned him are not people. Corporations never get tired, and they never move along until the money stops or the law steps in. People speak. Corporations do not speak. With the Court's new corporate speech theory, corporations won a dangerous immunity from the law and from the will of the people, while we the people gained nothing. Indeed, we lost freedom and we lost a tool of self-government.

Monsanto's Genetically Modified Drug

While the cigarette child-targeting fight was going on in Massachusetts, the people of Vermont were in a fight of their own. They were trying to preserve the right to know how our food is grown and made and the right to choose what kind of farming we want to support. As with the people in Massachusetts and the cigarette corporations, the people of Vermont were about to learn that winning the debate and overcoming corporate lobbyists and the likes of Monsanto Corporation in the legislative process are not enough. Monsanto now holds the corporate constitutional trump card.

Monsanto is a transnational chemical, biotech, and industrial corporation with more than $11 billion in annual global sales of chemicals, pesticides, herbicides, and genetically modified seeds and animal drugs. Some of Monsanto's products have included DDT, saccharine, aspartame, sulfuric acid, Agent Orange, and various plastics and chemical products. Monsanto's recent products include genetically engineered food and agriculture products that are variations of animal and plant pesticides and herbicides.

In response to questions about the safety of its "biotech food," Monsanto's spokesperson says, "Monsanto should not have to vouchsafe the safety of biotech food. Our interest is in selling as much of it as possible. Assuring its safety is the FDA's job."[16]

In the 1990s, Monsanto started selling a genetically engineered drug to be injected into the blood of dairy cows to force them to produce more milk. The drug was rBST (also called rBGH by some and labeled Posilac by Monsanto). Monsanto had used recombinant (meaning artificially created) DNA to fabricate rBST. *BST* stands for bovine somatotrophin, a naturally occurring hormone in cows, and *BGH* refers to "bovine growth hormone." The *r* in *rBST* and *rBGH* stands for "recombinant DNA" and refers to the Monsanto drug, which is not natural.

Most democratic countries in the world banned the use of rBST in any dairy product intended for human consumption. Canada prohibited the drug after "more than nine years of comprehensive review of the effects of rBST on animal and human safety, and consideration of the recent findings by two independent external committees."[17] All twenty-seven countries of the European Union, as well as New Zealand and Australia, also banned rBST. In the United States, Monsanto got its way. The Food and Drug Administration approved the use of rBST at the end of 1993. The FDA brushed aside the farmers, mothers and fathers, scientists, and other people around the country who raised serious questions about rBST.

Many people opposed the use of the Monsanto's drug, including Dexter Randall, a sixty-five-year-old dairy farmer who has lived and worked in Vermont all his life. Randall and others got involved in an organization called Rural Vermont and tried to stop the FDA from approving the Monsanto drug. They presented studies showing elevated antibiotic residues in milk (increased antibiotics were needed because rBST increased disease in cows).

They pointed to other studies showing higher levels in rBST milk of an insulin-like growth factor linked to breast cancer in humans and other dangers. They cited the absurdity of forcing cows to produce more milk, driving milk prices lower, at a time when family dairy farms all over the country were failing and taxpayers were paying millions of dollars to keep milk prices high enough to prevent a collapse of farm communities.

"Organic dairy farmers were already not getting paid enough for their milk, and when rBGH went on the market they suffered even more," says Randall. "But in addition to these economic concerns there were the health impacts of the product—the possible harm it could cause to livestock and humans. No long-term studies had been done. None of the truth was brought out. Our government let corporations override everything that made sense to the people."[18]

The Vermont farmer says, "Zillions of studies were presented to the FDA, but anything they saw they just turned the other way." The FDA claimed that it lacked the authority to consider "social" or "economic" factors or to require a label on rBST dairy products. The FDA, though, reported that "a State that has its own statute requiring food labeling based on a consumer's right-to-know would not be preempted by FDA from requiring rBST labeling."[19]

Randall and many other people in Vermont went to work to ensure that Vermont law would protect the people's right to know. "We lobbied our state senators and representatives, sent letters to the editor, talked all over the place, made people aware of the problem," Randall says. "There was lots of involvement. We basically held a protest in front of the statehouse, just to get our legislators and the public to take notice. We tried talking to our commissioner of agriculture and to other officials there."

Monsanto pushed back, and progress was slow. Randall says, "There was always money overriding us—the industry rules. The

Grocers' Association was screaming bloody murder, having to put labels on their products. Is it such a crime? People were still going to buy their products, but now they had a choice. I've always been a person for choice—you need to choose what size pants you're going to buy, don't you?"

Finally, after organizing, researching, testifying at hearings, and letter writing, the people persuaded the Vermont legislature to pass, and the governor to sign, a law to protect the right to know about our food. The 1994 Vermont law said, "If rBST has been used in the production of milk or a milk product for retail sale in this state, the retail milk or milk product shall be labeled as such."[20]

In deciding how to implement the law in a balanced way, the Vermont Department of Agriculture held four hearings around the state, including one with interactive television. Ninety-nine speakers took the time from work and home to participate in the hearings, and 152 written comments were filed.[21] Monsanto and the industrial dairy and grocery groups certainly weighed in, but according to the commissioner of agriculture in Vermont, "most individuals expressed that they felt they had a right to know what they wanted to purchase for themselves and their families."[22]

Monsanto and the industrial dairy corporations lost the public debate, lost the debate in the legislature, and failed to persuade the commissioner of agriculture to keep people in the dark about rBST. They weren't done, though. Monsanto had Covington & Burling, a corporate law firm in Washington, D.C., to lead the attack.

For years, Covington & Burling had serviced the drive to shelter corporations from public oversight by creating new theories of "speech." According to Judge Kessler in the federal racketeering trial of the cigarette corporations, Covington & Burling even took a leading role among corporate lawyers in furthering the illegal cigarette industry scheme: "Two of those law firms," she said, "in particular Covington & Burling, became the guiding strategists for the Enterprise and were deeply involved in implementation of those strategies once adopted." She added, "What a sad and disquieting chapter in the history of an honorable and often courageous profession."[23]

In Vermont, Covington & Burling represented the interests of Monsanto and the industrial dairy lobby in trying to stifle knowledge and disclosure about milk products derived from rBST-treated cows. They claimed that corporate speech rights entitled the industry to disregard the new right-to-know law. They insisted that Monsanto and the industry could refuse to disclose when milk and dairy products came from cows treated with Monsanto's genetically engineered rBST.

During the lawmaking process, the industry complained about costs and claimed that giving information to people would only cause "fear and uncertainty."[24] Employing odd euphemisms, the corporate lawyers called cows injected with the Monsanto drug "supplemented cows," while natural cows became "unsupplemented cows." Covington & Burling explained why "fear and uncertainty" would result from the truth: "Mandatory labeling of milk products derived from supplemented cows will have the inherent effect of causing consumers to believe that such products are different from and inferior to milk products from unsupplemented cows."

What about farmers or dairies that did not want to inject the Monsanto genetically engineered drug into the blood of their cows; they should be free to tell people about the natural way they make their milk, right? Oh, no, said the corporate lawyers: "The industry's experience in recent months demonstrates that voluntary 'rBST-free' type labeling of milk and milk products has a high potential for misleading consumers and for sowing the seeds of uncertainty, distrust, and fear about the quality and safety of milk and milk products." Thus, according to Monsanto and Covington & Burling, it is your right to know about your food—not Monsanto and its drug that is banned in most of the civilized world—that sows the "seeds of uncertainty, distrust and fear."

Monsanto and the industrial dairy corporations not only threatened to sue Vermont but also began to intimidate and silence farmers, dairies, and stores that tried to sell "rBST-free" milk.[25] Monsanto would even file a federal lawsuit against a Maine dairy that used its labels to tell people that the dairy would not use rBST. The dairy label that Monsanto sued to eliminate stated, "Our Farmers Pledge: No Artificial Growth Hormones."[26]

Nevertheless, people like Dexter Randall stood up to the corporate intimidation, and Vermont went ahead with its right-to-know law. Covington & Burling and the industry then followed through on their threat to sue. Now that Vermont law supported the people's right to know about rBST, the cry of "free corporate speech!" became the cry of "corporations are like people and have the right *not* to speak!" Covington & Burling argued that the "public right to know" must fall to "a manufacturer's right to decide when to speak and when to remain silent." According to a Covington & Burling brief filed in court, "Corporations have the same rights to remain silent as individuals."[27]

At first, Vermont had some success in the case. The chief judge of the federal court in Vermont, J. Garvan Murtha, concluded that corporate rights do not overpower the people's right to know:

Apparently, a majority of Vermonters do not want to purchase milk products derived from rBST-treated cows. Their reasons for not wanting to purchase such products include: (1) They consider the use of a genetically-engineered hormone in the production unnatural; (2) they believe that use of the hormone

*will result in increased milk production and lower milk prices,
thereby hurting small dairy farmers; (3) they believe that use of
rBST is harmful to cows and potentially harmful to humans;
and, (4) they feel that there is a lack of knowledge regarding the
long-term effects of rBST.*

According to Judge Murtha, "the First Amendment . . . does not
prohibit the State from insuring that the stream of commercial
information flow cleanly as well as freely."[28]

The industry appealed to the same federal court of appeals
that had decided the Bad Frog case. In the Vermont milk case,
the court of appeals again sided with corporations and struck
down the Vermont law. The court of appeals said that Judge
Murtha had "abused his discretion" by failing to agree with
the corporations that the law violated corporate speech rights.
According to the court of appeals, the people of Vermont had
caused a "wrong" to the industrial dairy manufacturers' "constitutional right *not* to speak."[29]

That was the end of the line for the Vermont law and for disclosure laws around the country. "It was a long, hard battle getting
the legislation passed, and it wasn't in place for any length," says
the dairy famer Dexter Randall. "We saw the end coming before
it happened. I learned a lot about the power of corporations—
about Monsanto's power."[30]

Corporate Rights Weaken People and Citizenship

Look again at how the court of appeals labeled what dairy farmer
Dexter Randall and so many other Vermont people had done by
deciding to participate in our government of the people. According
to the court, by passing a right-to-know law, the people of Vermont

committed a "wrong" to the constitutional rights of others, specifically, to the industry's "constitutional right *not* to speak."

This is how the fabrication of corporate rights hollows out American citizenship. A successful demand by a person or class of people for rights amounts to a declaration that such a person or class is equal to everyone else and has an equal share of sovereignty in our nation. Government then is accountable to that person, rather than the other way around. When we accept that people have constitutional rights, we quite properly have disdain for those who deprive our fellow people of rights, and we will resist. At a minimum, we are careful, or should be, not to press for government action that might hinder rights of others. After all, in a society of people with equal rights, when the government violates the rights of any of us, none of us is secure.

When courts strike down laws where they conflict with constitutional rights, they make a statement about who we are as a people and as a country. As we come to accept these judgments of the courts (or when we do not), our culture and politics, and even our way thinking and acting, can change. *Brown v. Board of Education* ruled that segregation violates the equality rights of African Americans; that helped transform who we are and how we act. *Reed v. Reed* ruled for the first time in 1971 that laws that discriminate against women are wrong; that contributed to a transformation of how we view gender in America. Court cases about rights may reflect and accelerate, rather than cause, movements and change. Yet when the courts rule, an insistent proposition about American life begins to become a fact.

The same phenomenon tends to occur when courts declare corporations to hold constitutional rights, as Dexter Randall found out. Lewis Powell's advice to the Chamber of Commerce in 1971 sought not merely to propose policies but to change American society. As Powell made clear, the creation of corporate rights is an "instrument for social, economic, and political change."[31]

These corporate rights cases, then, mean much more than allowing the Bad Frog Corporation to say whatever it wants on its product labels or the cigarette corporations to target children for addiction to a fatal product or Monsanto to deprive people of information about food. All of that would be bad enough. The impact of these cases goes beyond their specific facts; they push people back from exercising vigilance about corporate power. Even mild proposals that might serve the public good, from environmental stewardship to disclosure and transparency in the financial system, now get buried under savage attacks from corporate interests. Those who might serve as potential public champions are accused not merely of being "wrong" but of violating constitutional principles. Public champions retreat into defensiveness and uncertainty. As with other major developments of previously unrecognized constitutional rights, the fabrication of corporate rights is changing American culture.

The new metaphor of corporations as people in our understanding of the Bill of Rights and self-government threatens to erode, perhaps we can say "corporatize," the American character. We can see this in many areas of American life, from the state of our media to declining civic participation and voting. What was public for generations, from the sublime, such as mountains or groundwater, to the utilitarian, such as prisons, is shifting away from us. A combination of political, economic, and legal corporate power is shifting not only the law and not only our public assets but even how we think about ourselves and what we teach our children. Perhaps the most poignant effect on our culture and society of the corporate power campaign is what we now seem willing to tolerate in the education of children and young adults.

Learning to Be Corporate

Education in America has long been linked to our egalitarian vision of a free, democratic people who govern a republic. Thomas Jefferson wrote, "Of all the views of this law [for public education], none is more important, none more legitimate, than that of rendering the people safe as they are the ultimate guardians of their own liberty."[32] The Supreme Court has relied on Jefferson's view of public education "as a bulwark of a free people against tyranny" in concluding that "providing public schools ranks at the very apex of the function of a State."[33]

Now schools and children have joined the Constitution, legislatures, and courts as subjects for increasingly aggressive assertions of corporate power and influence. The critical civic function of our schools—teaching equality, citizenship, the critical thinking and competence needed to participate in a vibrant, free society—is deteriorating to make room for corporate access to children's minds and wallets. More corporations seek to turn schools into marketing outlets; more corporations seek to teach children, regardless of the views of their parents, to be consumers rather than citizens; and more corporations seek to make the curriculum itself reflect the corporations' position on public issues. As corporations increasingly "embed" in education, will the next generation recognize when the promise of American self-government has evaporated, let alone summon the will to restore it?

Joe Camel was not lurking alone outside the playground and school gates. In fact, compared to some other corporate child-targeting efforts, Joe Camel was downright shy by waiting *outside* the gate. The McDonald's Corporation, a Fortune 150 global corporation in 117 countries, with $24 billion revenue in 2010, sends employees or contractors dressed up as clowns with enormous shoes, bright clothes, and glistening red grins (the ubiquitous "Ronald McDonald") into schools to talk to children about "character education" and "fitness."[34] In 2008, some schools in Florida began "branding" report cards with the McDonald's logo and the clown-costumed pitchman promising a free "happy meal" to reward student performance.[35] Eight thousand middle and high schools in the country have contracted with the Channel One Corporation. Channel One beams into classrooms ten minutes of video "news" and two minutes of mandatory advertisements, which children are compelled to watch. The Channel One contracts require that the advertising content "must be shown when students are present in a homeroom or classroom (i.e. not before school, after school or during lunch)" on at least 90 percent of the days in which school is in session.[36]

Most schools, to which we are required by law to deliver our children each day, now serve as corporate marketing outlets. In 1983, corporations spent $100 million per year on child-targeted marketing; they now spend $17 billion per year.[37] Virtually every school in the land now carries corporate advertising.[38] School districts such as Los Angeles negotiate corporate naming rights, logo placements, and "school visits" during which corporate representatives can pass out samples to the children.[39] One Los Angeles school board member reluctantly voted for the corporate plan in 2010 but he knew that "the implications of doing this are really disconcerting and really bother me to the core."[40]

Since 1998, the National Education Policy Center at the University of Colorado (previously at the University of Arizona) has issued an annual report on "schoolhouse commercialization trends." The 2010 report, titled *Effectively Embedded: Schools and the Machinery of Modern Marketing*, reveals that corporations now spend billions of dollars on "embedding" advertising into the schools, including into the curriculum. They do so because "students are generally unable to avoid these activities; moreover, they tend to assume that what their teachers and schools present to them is in their best interest." According to the National Education Policy Center, "Advertising makes children want more, eat more, and think that their self-worth can and should come from commercial products. It heightens their insecurities, distorts their gender socialization, and displaces the development of values and activities other than those associated with commercialism."[41]

Revenue-desperate schools also are turning to "exclusive" contracts with Coke, Pepsi, and other corporations to sell and advertise their products in schools. These corporations do not only target older children. Even near-infants are not out of bounds. Coca-Cola denies that it markets to children under twelve but still "sells toys such as *Coca-Cola Uno* for children as young as eight, *Coca-Cola Checkers in a Tin* for children as young as six, and a *Coca-Cola Wipe-off Memo Board with Coke Magnets & Dry Erase Markers* for children as young as three."[42]

In school and out of school, corporations now spend billions of dollars to make kids fat and unhealthy. The U.S. food and beverage industry spends over $12 billion per year to market to children, and the vast majority of advertisements on television shows watched by children are for snacks, fast food, and candy.[43] "Nearly 20% of caloric intake among 12-to-18-year-olds comes from fast food, compared with 6.5% in the late 1970s."[44] Since 1980, as those billions of dollars in youth targeting got spent, the number of overweight children and adolescents has soared.[45] In 2005, Congress requested that the Federal Trade Commission (FTC) conduct a study of food and beverage marketing to children and adolescents. The FTC found that forty-four companies alone spent $1.6 billion in a single year to advertise fast food, soda, snacks, and other food and beverages to children as young as two years old.[46]

The FTC mission is to ensure that people are not hurt by unfair business practices; so why doesn't the FTC do something to stop the unfair practice of exploiting children and undermining parents? Because Congress passed a law in 1980 saying that the FTC is *not allowed* to do something. The law says, "The Commission shall not have any authority to promulgate any rule in the children's advertising . . . on the basis of a determination by the Commission that such advertising constitutes an unfair act or practice in or affecting commerce."[47]

Increasingly, corporations influence and embed marketing into the actual curriculum itself. BP and other corporations participated in the writing of California's environmental curriculum.[48] Materials provided to schools by Chevron suggest that global warming may not exist, while the American Coal Foundation class materials state that increased carbon dioxide levels in the earth's atmosphere could be beneficial.[49] The American Petroleum Institute (API), with four hundred corporate members, offers "lesson plans" for kindergarten through twelfth grade, including "Progress Through Petroleum."[50]

Kindergartners and elementary school kids will learn that "most of our energy needs are being met by nonrenewable energy sources—oil, natural gas, coal, and uranium (nuclear). This is because these energy sources are more reliable, affordable, and convenient to use than most renewable energy resources."[51] The API lesson plan does not mention climate change, oil spills, toxic wastes, or any air, land, or water pollution issues. The lesson plan offers an "Environmental Progress Report" that promotes the industry's investment in "improving the environmental performance of its products, facilities, and operations—$11.3 billion in 2006 alone." What about offshore drilling and the environment? Didn't BP's Deepwater Horizon oil disaster in April 2010 nearly destroy the Gulf of Mexico? Yes, kids can learn about offshore drilling and the environment: "Floating platforms, anchored to the ocean floor, allow energy companies to recover oil and natural gas reserves located under deeper parts of the ocean—and have proved to be valuable habitats for marine life."[52]

The Council for Corporate-School Partnerships says nothing is wrong with corporations embedding into children's education. Then again, the council was founded and funded by the Coca-Cola Company, a corporation under Delaware law that operates in two hundred countries with over $35 billion in annual revenue. One need not be too cynical to think that the council's opinion might not be a good-faith assessment made with due regard for the American interest.[53]

On to College: The Subprime Student Loan Game

In the age of corporate bailouts, the Wall Street financial system privatizes huge profits and socializes big risks. That model of enriching a very few at the expense of the many has created a new "industry" of for-profit colleges. For-profit corporations now own more than two thousand colleges or universities. The number of students enrolled in for-profit colleges has increased 500 percent in the past several years, to 1.8 million.[54] These operations effectively transfer hundreds of millions of dollars in federal student loans and government guarantees from the American taxpayers to corporate executives and shareholders.[55]

Most of these students (1.4 million) attend for-profit colleges that are owned and controlled by fourteen corporations. Wall Street values the publicly traded corporations at $26 billion, due to huge revenue flows based on high tuition, minimal standards, and government backing for tuition payment. In 2009 alone, American taxpayers provided these corporations and others that operate for-profit colleges with more than $4 billion in Pell Grants and $20 billion in guaranteed student loans.[56]

Among corporate schools examined by a United States Senate investigation, "over 87 percent of total revenues came directly from the federal government, but 57 percent of the students who enrolled between 2008–2009 have departed without a diploma but with a high probability of debt."[57] The sixteen largest for-profit schools had profits of $2.7 billion in 2009, with some corporations doubling profits between 2009 and 2010 alone.[58] In 2011, when the Department of Education proposed to apply minimal performance standards (based on actual student graduation rates) to corporations that take billions of taxpayer dollars, the corporations threatened a lawsuit challenging the constitutionality of such action.

A recent U.S. Senate committee investigation focused on one school owned and operated by Bridgepoint Education, Inc., a Delaware corporation traded on the New York Stock Exchange. In 2005, Bridgepoint Education used financial backing from a global private equity firm called Warburg Pincus to acquire a religious college in Clinton, Iowa. Bridgepoint bought the school, Franciscan University (originally Mount Saint Clare College), from the Sisters of Saint Francis. At the time, the Bridgepoint CEO announced, "Bridgepoint Education and the Sisters of Saint Francis have much in common. We believe in quality academic training and in service to others."[59]

The new corporate owner then changed the name to Ashford University. Before the corporate acquisition, Franciscan University was spending $5,000 per student on instruction. After the buyout by Bridgepoint, Ashford University spent $700 per student on instruction. The savings were not passed on to students, who now are charged as much as $46,000 in tuition and fees. Most of the tuition payment actually comes from taxpayer-funded federal programs. In the 2009–2010 school year, Bridgepoint's Ashford University received $613 million in federal student aid funds. Most of the revenue (86 percent) at the university comes directly from the United States government— in other words, from all of us. With all that revenue, how did instruction spending per student fall from $5,000 before corporatizing the school to $700 after?

From three hundred students at Franciscan University in 2005, enrollment (including online students) at the newly corporatized Ashford University zoomed to nearly seventy-eight thousand by 2010. Bridgepoint Education spends $2,700 per student to recruit new students (who need new federal loans). Bridgepoint directed $1,500 per student to corporate profit. Most of the students who enroll quickly drop out. Fully 84 percent of students who enroll in an associate degree program at Ashford University are gone by the following year, and 63 percent of students in the bachelor's degree program do not return the next year. Bridgepoint employs more than seventeen hundred people to recruit new students; it employs one person to help students with job placement.[60]

Bridgepoint paid its CEO, Andrew Clark, $20.5 million in 2009, and another $11.5 million to four other top executives. The CEO refused an invitation to testify at the Senate hearing.

Despite these depressing statistics, the Higher Learning Commission accredited Bridgepoint's Ashford University. Called to the Senate to explain, the president of the commission did not defend the decision. Instead, she confessed that the commission was "behind the curve" on corporate schools and failed to do "good peer review." She described the explosion of Wall Street–backed corporate for-profit universities as "a new phenomenon on the face of the earth."[61]

Government programs that help students and families pay for college become a very different phenomenon when they can be exploited by for-profit corporations, backed by Wall Street capital, willing to hire thousands of recruiters to keep the loan revenue flowing while cutting academic and guidance programs. As citizens, parents, leaders in government and education, and taxpayers who provide the revenue to enable $20 million CEO salaries, we ought at least to have a chance to engage in discussion and consideration before Wall Street unleashes a "new phenomenon on the face of the earth" on unsuspecting students and loan-strapped families.

Corporate university companies are unapologetic about the betrayal of students and virtual theft of tax money. When the Government Accountability Office (GAO) simply reported facts about the for-profit corporate education industry, its corporate lobby group sued the GAO for "negligence" and "malpractice." They claim that the report is "biased" and "erroneous." When the government proposed reform that would require some actual education performance before the taxpayers sent billions of dollars to Wall Street investors and CEOs, the industry sued to block the Department of Education reform. The case remains in court, where the corporate lobby argues that the rules are unconstitutional because they are "vague."[62]

No one can doubt that education is challenging and no model is perfect. But why would corporations rush into a Wall Street model of university education that so clearly fails far too many students and costs American taxpayers far too much money? Why would corporations in this business pay their CEOs $20 million for such awful performance? Why does our government not stop this?

The answer to all three questions lies in the massive profit that a corporation can reap from recruiting thousands of unwary students, taking the proceeds of government-backed student loans, and shaving costs from the educational program. That was the "play," in Wall Street parlance, the opportunity. A CEO who executes the play and delivers that massive corporate profit has accomplished what the corporation was designed to do. So from a corporate perspective, the CEO's performance was not awful, even if debt-burdened students drop out by the thousands and the transfer of government money to Wall Street and executives runs into the billions of dollars.

As currently designed, large public corporations (meaning those with shares that are actively traded on the stock exchanges) seek profit above all. The design has not required ethics, morals, values, shame, or other human values. Yes, socially responsible investing, responsible corporate conduct, and many efforts to "hardwire" corporations with ethical behavior matter a great deal. Nevertheless, the "market judgment" of global corporations measures profit into the share price and little else. And at least so far, we have not required a "character test" or imposed other responsibility requirements for corporate conduct.

Can we design a different corporation, an entity that engages in economic activity with more responsibility and ethical conduct? Can we conceive of corporations as holding public duties rather than constitutional rights? Or are we destined to become a corporate nation of underpaid hucksters in clown suits, trying to juice corporate profit and executive compensation by pushing school kids around?

I don't think Americans will accept such a fate, at least not for long. When we begin to insist that corporate money is not "speech" and that corporations are not people, we begin to take back power. Addressing the complex problem of corporate power requires, of course, more than recognition that corporations are not people. We also need a shared understanding of what corporations are and what they should and should not be doing in our national life.

This is the topic for the next chapter. A corporation is not a person, nor is it an association or a group of people. A corporation is a creation of law, a *public* tool of economic policy. If we appreciate this point, corporate "rights" are exposed as unconstitutional folly. Moreover, we can decide to create better corporations. We can require that corporations be much more effective, useful, and supportive instruments for the American people and our economy.

Chapter Three
If Corporations Are Not People, What Are They?

Metaphor . . . is the peculiarity of a language, the object
of which is to tell everything and conceal everything, to
abound in figures. Metaphor is an enigma which offers
itself as a refuge to a robber who plots a blow,
to a prisoner who plans an escape.

—Victor Hugo, *Les Miserables*[1]

What is a corporation? One might expect to find a good description of of a corporation in *Citizens United* or the other corporate rights cases, but the Supreme Court is strangely silent on that point. Instead, corporate rights decisions from the Court come packaged in metaphorical clouds. It is not corporations attacking our laws; it is "speakers" and "advocates of ideas," "voices" and "persons," and variations on what Justice John Paul Stevens called in his *Citizens United* dissent, "glittering generalities."

Corporations are economic tools created by state law; corporate shares are property. Yet the majority decision in *Citizens*

United did not explain even the most basic features of a corporation, an entity created and defined by state laws. The Court did not examine why Congress and dozens of state legislatures thought it made sense to distinguish between corporations and human beings when making election rules. One reading the *Citizens United* decision might forget that the case concerned a corporate regulation at all; the Court described the timid corporate spending rule it struck down as a "ban on speech," government "silencing" of some "voices," some "speakers," and some "disadvantaged classes of persons."[2]

Metaphor Marches On

The use of the "speaker" and "speech" metaphor in *Citizens United* follows the playbook dating back to the corporate rights pioneer, Justice Lewis Powell. In 1978, Powell wrote the *First National Bank of Boston* decision that created the new corporate rights theory to strike down a Massachusetts law banning corporate spending in citizen referenda. He sidestepped the question of what a corporation is, saying, "If the speakers here were not corporations, no one would suggest that the State could silence their proposed speech."[3] The people of Massachusetts, however, *did* suggest exactly that because corporations are not "speakers." And the corporations did not propose "speech." Rather, the corporations proposed to spend corporate money to influence a citizen referendum vote. A law prohibiting this did not "silence" anyone; it defined a prohibited activity of corporate entities in elections.

In a 1980 corporate rights case, Justice Powell described the Consolidated Edison Corporation as "a single speaker." The Court struck down a New York law regulating this corporate monopoly because, according to Powell, the law "restricts the speech of a private person."[4] Later that year, Justice Powell wrote the *Central Hudson* decision creating a "right" of utility corporations to promote energy consumption in defiance of a government policy of conservation. Justice Powell identified "the critical inquiry in this case" as whether or not the First Amendment allowed the state's "complete suppression of speech."[5] (Who's for the complete suppression of speech? If that's really the question, the answer is pretty easy: the Court struck down the law.) In a 1986 decision using the corporate speech theory to strike down regulation of utility corporations, Justice Powell identified the corporation as a "speaker," with an "identity" seeking to make "speech."

Justice Powell's successors on the Court have followed this pattern of euphemism and distortion. In the 2001 *Lorillard* v. *Reilly* case about cigarette advertising directed to schoolchildren, Justice Clarence Thomas explained that corporations selling cigarettes and targeting children are no different from "advocates of harmful ideas. When the State seeks to silence them, they are all entitled to the protection of the First Amendment."[6]

Justice Thomas wrote the Court's 1995 decision in *Rubin* v. *Coors Brewing Company*, which ruled that the Coors Brewing Company has a First Amendment right to ignore a federal law banning the display of alcohol levels on beer labels. Coors, now part of Molson Coors, is an international conglomerate of corporations with billions of dollars in sales around the globe. At the time of the 1995 corporate speech case, Coors Brewing Company was, among other things, a Colorado corporation; a subsidiary corporation of a larger corporation listed on the New York Stock exchange; one of a web of corporations with international operations, including alcohol products in Spain and Korea, and a joint venture among corporations for an aluminum processing operation; it had sales of nearly $2 billion and had its corporate name on the largest sports stadium in Colorado.[7]

Writing the 1995 corporate speech decision in *Rubin* v. *Coors Brewing Company*, Justice Thomas set out to describe exactly who or what it was that came before the Court claiming a free speech right to strike down a law passed by Congress and on the books for more than fifty years. Here is Justice Thomas's complete description: "Respondent brews beer."[8]

It is true enough, I suppose, that Coors "brews beer," but that is hardly the only relevant fact about a corporate entity created by the law of Colorado that demands that the Court invalidate a federal law. Why is the fact that Coors is a corporation relevant? Before the justices or the rest of us reach any conclusion about that question, it would seem useful first to define *corporation*. A definition would certainly seem in order before we attribute to the entity any capacity for "speech," participation in elections, and the constitutional rights with which humans are born.

What Is a Corporation?

A corporation is a government-defined legal structure for doing business. A corporation is created and defined by state legislatures to advance what the state deems to be in the public interest. Corporations as entities are government policy tools; only government makes incorporation possible.[9] Unlike other associations or ways of doing business, a corporation cannot exist by private arrangement.[10]

Many good reasons support state laws that permit ready incorporation of enterprises. The corporate legal entity is supremely effective at bringing together and channeling ideas, capital, and labor to make a productive, growing enterprise. The corporate form streamlines the making and enforcement of contracts; it encourages, secures, and rewards investment; it enables risk-taking as well as sustained operations, expansion, and innovation over long periods of time; and it can efficiently spread risk (and reward) over many diverse shareholders. All this and more makes incorporation a very useful tool to encourage and reward investment, innovation, job creation, and economic growth. That's why my business, Clements Law Office, LLC, is a corporation, why the publisher of this book is a corporation, and why thousands of businesses choose to incorporate their operations.

Because the corporate entity is so useful and so prevalent, we can forget that it is a legal tool created by government to advance government policy. People can start and run businesses without government permission or a government form of organization. People can form advocacy groups, associations, unions, political parties, clubs, religious organizations, and other institutions without incorporating and without the government's permission or involvement. But people, or even "associations of people," cannot form or operate a corporation unless the state enacts a law authorizing the formation of a corporation and provides rules for operations in corporate form.

The attributes of a modern corporation include limited liability, perpetual life, and legal identification as a unitary actor so as to encourage simplicity and efficiency in making and enforcing contracts, suing and being sued, and so on. State law defines these attributes. That law offers, but does not require, a useful vehicle for the individuals involved in doing business. No one is required to use the corporate form, with its relative benefits and burdens, but if people decide to do so, the privilege of incorporation is a package deal. They cannot decide to comply with some of the law to get the benefits and defy the parts of the corporate laws they find inconvenient.

Some people mistakenly call corporations "associations of people" or a "product of private contract."[11] This is incorrect. Corporations are not private matters, and they are not mere "associations of citizens."[12] Corporations exist only because states enact laws defining exactly what a corporation is, what it can do, and what it cannot do. In virtually every state, it is illegal for people to do business as a corporation unless the corporation is incorporated or registered under the laws of that state.[13]

Most transnational corporations are incorporated under the law of Delaware. Three hundred of the mega-corporations listed on the Fortune 500 list are incorporated under Delaware law, as are more than half of all publicly traded companies in the United States.[14] The reason for this is a matter of some debate. Some say that giant global conglomerate corporations such as BP, Dow Chemical, and Goldman Sachs incorporate under the law of Delaware, where the corporations do little business, to ensure low corporate standards that benefit the few at the expense of the many.[15] Others say that Delaware offers a rich body of corporate law. In any event, as with the law of every state, none of the features of the Delaware corporation law are "required." Rather, they are policy choices made by elected legislatures.

Take shareholder limited liability, for example. The concept of limited liability for corporate shareholders means that if you invest in a company, you might lose your investment if things go badly, but you will not be responsible for paying all of the debts of the corporation or for compensating victims of any misconduct or neglect by the corporation. Imagine that you owned some shares in the BP Corporation in April 2010 when the Deepwater Horizon oil well exploded in the Gulf of Mexico. If the corporation cut corners on safety, resulting in the death of eleven people and a catastrophe that ruins a vast ecosystem and fishery that had sustained millions of people for eons, are you as a shareholder to blame? If BP is liable for this death and destruction but the corporation runs out of money to pay its debts, why are the shareholders who own the company and who profited in the safety-cutting years not forced to sell their personal property, their houses, their cars, and their kids' college savings accounts to pay BP's bills? After all, the shareholders own and are presumed to control the corporation that caused so much damage in the pursuit of their profit. Why are the shareholders not held to account?

The rule of limited liability, that's why. Limited liability of corporate shareholders did not come down from on high. Only because people in the state of incorporation (in BP's case, Delaware) decided to include limited liability in their corporate laws, the shareholders are not responsible for the debts of the corporation. Here's how the elected state representatives in Delaware put limited liability into the law, which they call the Delaware Corporations Code: "The stockholders of a corporation shall not be personally liable for the payment of the corporation's debts except as they may be liable by reason of their own conduct or acts."[16]

As with many other features of incorporation law, I think limited liability is probably good policy because it encourages efficient, effective capital investment in economic activity that benefits all of us. Others may disagree and can make strong arguments that limited liability encourages excessive risk, "externalizes" losses and damage of all kinds onto society, and directs profits only to a few individuals. Whether limited liability is good policy or bad policy, though, it is public policy that we decide on. It is not a private arrangement among people involved in the corporation.

The same is true of the other basic features of a corporation. How is it possible that GE Corporation keeps going on, decade after decade, long after every shareholder, director, executive, and other human being involved in forming and building GE has long since died? How does something called GE Corporation sign contracts, go into court, or prove to a creditor or a bank that it exists as an entity that will pay its bills, no matter how the people involved in the corporation may come and go? GE and other corporations can do that because we the people in our states elect representatives in government who decide to make corporate "perpetual life" possible. Again, we very well could decide otherwise if we chose to do so.

Let's look at Delaware law again, by way of example. GE and all other corporations incorporated under Delaware law have "perpetual existence" because the Delaware legislature said so. Here's how the legislature of Delaware wrote the law: "A provision [may limit] the duration of the corporation's existence to a specified date; otherwise, the corporation shall have perpetual existence."[17] Notice that the Delaware law does say that "the duration of the corporation's existence" can be limited "to a specified date." This used to be the norm with corporate law. Years ago, traditional American distrust of concentrated power and caution about corporate dominance of government led most state laws to limit the life span of corporations. The period in which a corporation could exist was usually limited to a defined term of years, often twenty years.[18] Is it not strange that a thing that exists only by the policy of the state, a thing as to which the state can decide "the duration of the corporation's existence," can successfully take control of the people's Bill of Rights to strike down the state's laws?

Delaware Cannot Rewrite the Constitution

This brings us to the notion that some call "corporate personhood," the idea that under the law, corporations are treated as "persons." As with perpetual existence, limited liability, and other features of corporations, the source of this concept of a "corporate person" is not particularly complicated. We came up with it, or rather, our state and federal legislatures did, because treating the corporation as a legal "person" makes sense for certain purposes. That policy choice, though, is our choice and has nothing to do with the constitution or corporate "rights."

There are lots of good reasons why states and the federal government enact laws that say, in some instances, that the word *person* includes corporations. For example, the Clean Water Act prohibits unpermitted discharge of toxics and pollutants into the waters of the United States by any person. Congress wrote the Clean Water Act to create civil and criminal penalties for "any person" who violated the law. Obviously, we want to make sure those penalties apply to corporations that violate the Clean Water Act. For that reason, here's what Congress said in section 502 of the Clean Water Act: "The term 'person' means an individual, corporation, partnership, association, State, municipality, commission, or political subdivision of a State, or any interstate body."

Congress and the states take the same approach to include corporations when we say "no person shall violate another person's trademark" or "no person shall sell drugs that have not been approved by the FDA." Similarly, it makes sense as a matter of policy to treat a corporation like a "person" when a corporation makes a contract or is sued or brings a lawsuit or engages in any one of many activities that state law may authorize a corporation to do. We do this because we have decided as a matter of state law that the "person" metaphor can help make the corporation better as a tool of public policy. Yes, corporations create private wealth, and shareholders own shares as private property, but the corporation as an artificial entity, and the rules that define it are public choices.

The Constitution is different from state laws and federal statutes. Our Bill of Rights is not a "policy choice" that government can decide. Rather, the Bill of Rights defines the relationship between us as human beings and our government. The First Amendment and our other rights in the Constitution are the natural human rights that we insist on ensuring to ourselves when we consent to the Constitution's plan of government.

When we decide, as we might, that under our state or federal laws, corporations are "persons" that can be prosecuted (or that can contract or be sued), that decision cannot transform corporations into "persons" under the Constitution's protections of rights. We can change state laws of incorporation anytime we can muster a majority in the legislature for a particular change. We do not change the meaning of the Constitution anytime a legislature, let alone the legislature of Delaware alone, decides it might be efficient to do so. The rights in our Constitution, including the rights of "life," "liberty," "property," and "equal protection" for all "persons," are human rights.

The Constitution cannot be changed by state or federal laws or majority vote; it can be changed only by the process of amendment as set forth in Article 5 of the Constitution. The people have never added corporations to the definition of "persons" in the Constitution by using the amendment process (a vote of two-thirds of Congress, ratified by three-quarters of the states, or a constitutional convention). As the Supreme Court declared in the 1800s when rebuffing early corporate efforts to create corporate rights, "State laws, by combining large masses of men under a corporate name, cannot repeal the Constitution."[19]

To appreciate the distinction between "person" under state or federal law and "person" under the Constitution, consider Delaware law again. Recall that Delaware law declares that corporations can exist for a defined period of years or may have "perpetual existence." If a majority of the Delaware legislature wanted to delete that last part of the law and simply declare that corporations may exist for a period of twenty years, they could do so. In contrast, neither Delaware nor any other state or federal legislature in America can decide that people shall have a limited period of existence. No matter how good the policy justification for such a law, that law obviously would violate the Constitution's due process clause protecting the life of all persons.

The Right Thing in the Wrong Place

Corporations, then, are policy tools; they are not people or holders of constitutional rights. As economic tools, corporations are highly effective. Yet the same traits that make corporations such useful economic policy tools can also make them dangerous to republican government and democracy if people and lawmakers do not watch and restrain abuses. Corporations can aggregate immense power, corrupt government, drive down wages, trash public resources, concentrate markets to squeeze out competitors, and more. As Justice William Rehnquist said in one of his many dissents from the corporate rights decisions in the late 1970s and the 1980s, a "State grants to a business corporation the blessings of potentially perpetual life and limited liability to enhance its efficiency as an economic entity. It might reasonably be concluded that those properties, so beneficial in the economic sphere, pose special dangers in the political sphere."[20]

As with all tools, use of the corporate entity requires oversight and care. Gasoline is fantastic. It is also dangerous. I love working with a chainsaw or taking out guns for hunting or practice, but I know that care and rules are necessary to prevent potentially disastrous consequences of using either one. Great tools, but we would not hand them out to anyone without having some clarity about how they will be used.

The problem of corporate power is not the personal failings of the many good and decent people who work for corporations, often creating wonderful products or services that benefit us all. Rather, corporate power is now subverting our democracy because we have forgotten that corporations are just tools, and we have forgotten our duty to keep an eye on them. Until the corporate rights offensive of recent years, the idea of restraining corporate power was a mainstream, basic American proposition, not a fringe viewpoint.

The *Southern Pacific* Case

Americans always have had the responsibility to keep corporate power in check, just as we keep government power in check. It is true that the Supreme Court sometimes references the 1886 case of *Santa Clara County* v. *Southern Pacific Railroad Company* to claim that corporations are constitutional "persons" with rights. In that case, the Southern Pacific Railroad Company tried to claim that it was a "person" under the recently adopted Fourteenth Amendment to the Constitution. The Fourteenth Amendment was enacted after the Civil War to ensure that freed slaves and all people in America had equal rights to due process, liberty, property, and equal protection of the law. Southern Pacific Railroad sued Santa Clara County, California, trying to avoid a tax assessment on railroads. The railroad corporation argued, among other things, that it was a "person" under the Fourteenth Amendment and that the tax assessment on railroad property was not "equal" with taxes applied to other "persons." The Court decided the case in favor of the railroad, but not for the reasons for which the case became known. In fact, in the *Santa Clara* decision, the Court did not discuss Southern Pacific's Fourteenth Amendment argument at all.

Though the Court likes to cite this case even today to shore up its creation of corporate rights, a first-year law student would be chastised and embarrassed for citing that decision for the proposition that corporations are persons under the Constitution. In fact, the decision says no such thing. The Supreme Court's *Santa Clara* decision rested on California law and did not even decide a constitutional question.[21] Nevertheless, the Gilded Age Supreme

Court, almost as corporate-oriented as today's Court, repeatedly used *Santa Clara* to fabricate corporate rights and strike down economic regulations.[22]

The response of the American people in the Progressive Era that followed is instructive for our time. Following *Santa Clara* in 1886, the Supreme Court faced a wave of cases in which large corporations and the infamous corporate monopoly "trusts" demanded constitutional rights to shield them from the growing movement for laws to protect employees (including child labor), the environment, fair taxes, and other public interests. On several occasions in the 1890s and early 1900s, the Supreme Court agreed with the corporations. The cases stated, without any explanation whatsoever, that "a corporation is a person under the Fourteenth Amendment," as if saying that with a straight face would make it true.[23] Could it be true?

Not a chance. Absolutely no evidence suggests that corporations were intended to be included in the Fourteenth Amendment or in the Constitution generally. Indeed, the evidence is exactly to the contrary. Since the beginning of our country, virtually every generation of Americans has acted to prevent corporate power from being leveraged into political power at the expense of the people. During the colonial era, only "a handful of native business corporations carried on business . . . four water companies, two wharf companies, two trading societies, and one mutual fire insurance society," and only twenty business corporations were formed by 1787, when the American people convened the Constitutional Convention in Philadelphia.[24] Legislatures, however, increasingly permitted the creation of corporations in the new republic to facilitate and expedite all kinds of public purposes, such as the building of roads, dams, and bridges.[25] Yet it remained clear that corporations were legal instruments of the state, defined and controlled by the state, with limitations on their purposes and their duration.[26]

It would be bizarre if the generation that defiantly declared to the world that "all men are created equal" and that "they are endowed by their Creator with certain unalienable Rights" and who wrote a constitution opening with "We, the People," would have tolerated corporate constitutional rights. Founders such as Thomas Jefferson and James Madison could not have been more clear about the danger of unregulated corporations and the need for, as Madison put it, "proper restraints and guards." Another founder, James Wilson, a Pennsylvania man who signed the Declaration of Independence, served in the Continental Congress, helped draft the Constitution, and was nominated by George Washington to be one of the first six justices on the Supreme Court, agreed. He well expressed the prevailing view of the time that corporations can be useful tools of the state but must always be controlled by the people:

> A corporation is described to be a person in a political capacity created by the law, to endure in perpetual succession. . . . It must be admitted, however, that, in too many instances, those bodies politick have, in their progress, counteracted the design of their original formation. . . . This is not mentioned with a view to insinuate, that such establishments ought to be prevented or destroyed: I mean only to intimate, that they should be erected with caution, and inspected with care.[27]

The Supreme Court at the time knew that any "rights" of corporations come from the state charter, not from the Constitution (let alone from our Creator). That is because corporations are "creatures of law." The corporate legal form today is not fundamentally different than when Chief Justice Marshall explained in 1819 that a corporation, as a "mere creature of law . . . possesses only those properties which the charter confers upon it, either expressly or as incidental to its very existence."[28] A corporation today is chartered from the state just as in 1809 when a unanimous Supreme Court held that "a body corporate as such cannot be a citizen within the meaning of the Constitution."[29]

For nearly two hundred years, the Supreme Court rejected the argument that corporations were entitled to the rights of citizens under the Constitution's "privileges and immunities" clause. In 1839, the Court said, "The only rights [a corporation] can claim are the rights which are given to it in that character, and not the rights which belong to its members as citizens of a state."[30] Fifty years later, the Court said that the term *citizens* in the Constitution "applies only to natural persons, members of the body politic owing allegiance to the state, not to artificial persons created by the legislature, and possessing only such attributes as the legislature has prescribed."[31]

At least until recently, the vigilance of American leadership about corporate power did not waver as corporations became more dominant in our economy. "Corporations, which should be the carefully restrained creatures of the law and the servants of the people, are fast becoming the people's masters," warned President Grover Cleveland.[32] Theodore Roosevelt sought to end "a riot of individualistic materialism" and successfully called for a ban on corporate political contributions: "Let individuals contribute as they desire; but let us prohibit in effective fashion all corporations from making contributions for any political purpose, directly or indirectly."[33] President Roosevelt said he "recognized that corporations and combinations had become indispensable in the business world, that it is folly to try to prohibit them, but that it was also folly to leave them without thoroughgoing control."[34]

This vigilance did not mean that powerful corporations simply accepted or cooperated with the public's "thoroughgoing control." As those who came before us well understood, concentrated power and aggregated wealth in corporations have always led corporations to seek "rights." An assertive, vigilant citizenry and leadership has always been needed to push back.

Until the success of the Powell–Chamber of Commerce plan, the *Santa Clara* line of "corporate person" cases was rendered largely meaningless by the people's rejection of corporate rights throughout the twentieth century. The Republicans under Theodore Roosevelt restrained corporate power with effective antitrust enforcement, labor laws, environmental laws, and laws banning corporate political spending. In Roosevelt's words, "There can be no effective control of corporations while their political activity remains."[35] Democrats under Woodrow Wilson and Franklin Roosevelt likewise regulated corporate power to ensure the strength of the people and the country as a whole. And Republicans, Democrats, and Independents came together to amend the Constitution in 1913 to weaken the corporate hold on government by requiring senators to be elected by the people rather than appointed by state legislatures.

Finally, in a 1938 dissenting opinion, Justice Hugo Black, a former Alabama senator, demolished the idea that corporations were "persons" with rights under the Constitution's Fourteenth Amendment. While he wrote in dissent, the clarity of his expression about corporations and persons sounded a warning to any justice who might try to slip corporate rights into the Constitution with "glittering generalities" and glib citation of *Santa Clara*. His lengthy dissenting opinion examined the words, history, meaning, and purpose of the Fourteenth Amendment:

> *I do not believe that the word "person" in the Fourteenth Amendment includes corporations. . . . A constitutional interpretation that is wrong should not stand. I believe this Court should now overrule previous decisions which interpreted the Fourteenth Amendment to include corporations.*

> *Neither the history nor the language of the Fourteenth Amendment justifies the belief that corporations are included within its protections.*
>
> *Certainly, when the Fourteenth Amendment was submitted for approval, the people were not told that the states of the South were to be denied their normal relationship with the Federal Government unless they ratified an amendment granting new and revolutionary rights to corporations. . . . The records of the time can be searched in vain for evidence that this amendment was adopted for the benefit of corporations.*[36]

With Justice Black's warning shot that there would be no more free rides for corporate rights on the Supreme Court, *Santa Clara* "corporate personhood" was a dead issue for decades. Indeed, the Court said little more about corporations' "rights" until Justice Lewis Powell and his Chamber of Commerce plan came to the Supreme Court following the death of Justice Black in September 1971. Through most of the twentieth century, the Court returned to the basic American understanding that corporations were economic, not political, entities.

For example, in rejecting the claim of corporations for privacy rights in 1950, the Supreme Court said:

> *Corporations can claim no equality with individuals in the enjoyment of a right to privacy. They are endowed with public attributes. They have a collective impact upon society, from which they derive the privilege of acting as artificial entities. . . . Law-enforcing agencies have a legitimate right to satisfy themselves that corporate behavior is consistent with the law and the public interest.*[37]

For more than a century until *Citizens United*, most states and the federal government banned corporate political contributions and spending. Some states, such as Kentucky, even made the control of corporate political activity part of their state constitutions.[38] With the exception of Justice Powell's early foray into corporate rights in the 1978 *First National Bank of Boston* case, this basic understanding of the place of corporations in American democracy guided the Supreme Court, even as Justice Powell's "corporate speech" cases worked away at creating the new corporate rights doctrine.

The one time before *Citizens United* when the Supreme Court went off the rails with respect to corporate political spending occurred with Justice Powell's maiden corporate rights decision in *First National Bank of Boston*, striking down a state law banning corporate spending in referendum elections. That exception should have proved the rule, in large part because of the force of Justice Rehnquist's dissent. Rehnquist concluded that the "Fourteenth Amendment does not require a State to endow a business corporation with the power of political speech."[39] Instead, Rehnquist forcefully pressed the truth that corporations are not people with rights but are entities defined by the states, with restrictions that the legislatures find appropriate. Congress, he wrote, and numerous

> States of this Republic have considered the matter, and have concluded that restrictions upon the political activity of business corporations are both politically desirable and constitutionally permissible. The judgment of such a broad consensus of governmental bodies expressed over a period of many decades is entitled to considerable deference from this Court.[40]

Again, the different opinions of these two Richard Nixon appointees—William Rehnquist and Lewis Powell—showed the stark gap between the corporatist and the conservative understanding of our American republic. For a time, the conservative

Rehnquist was able to form a majority on the Court. In 1990, the Chamber of Commerce in Michigan attacked a law restricting corporate political spending and lost. The Court upheld the right of the people to keep corporations out of politics. In that case, *Austin v. Michigan Chamber of Commerce*, Justice Rehnquist's dissenting views in the corporate speech cases became the majority view.[41]

Rehnquist joined the liberal Thurgood Marshall, who wrote for the Court in affirming Michigan's regulation of corporate spending in elections. Marshall's words for the Court were drawn from the earlier Rehnquist dissents:

> *State law grants corporations special advantages. . . . These state-created advantages not only allow corporations to play a dominant role in the Nation's economy, but also permit them to use "resources amassed in the economic marketplace" to obtain "an unfair advantage in the political marketplace."*[42]

Even as late as 2003, before Chief Justice John Roberts and Justice Samuel Alito replaced Chief Justice Rehnquist and Justice Sandra Day O'Connor, the Court agreed that the same corporate election spending law that the Court would later strike down in *Citizens United* was perfectly fine under our Constitution. In that 2003 case, *McConnell v. Federal Election Commission*, the Court affirmed that the people's representatives in Congress were entitled to "the legislative judgment that the special characteristics of the corporate structure require particularly careful regulation."[43]

Citizens United: Corporations Back on the Track, People to the Back

We then come to *Citizens United* a mere seven years later, posing again this fundamental question of American democracy: Can Congress and state legislatures make laws distinguishing between the American people spending money in politics and corporations spending money in politics? What had changed since 2003, 1990, the New Deal, Theodore Roosevelt's presidency, the 1800s, or the days of Madison, Jefferson, and President Washington's Supreme Court justice and national founding father James Wilson?

Is *Citizens United* different because that case involved a nonprofit corporation? Although that point may have been worthy of examination, it made no difference to the Court. The Court in *Citizens United* made very clear that its decision applied to all corporations (or, as Justice Kennedy's decision called them, all "voices" and "speakers"). That is why Koch Industries, Target, News Corporation, and other global, for-profit corporations funneled hundreds of millions of dollars into the November 2010 elections and are gearing up to do even more in the 2012 elections.

While sympathy for a nonprofit corporation seeking to express the views of its members is understandable, corporations, whether for-profit or not-for-profit, are creatures of the state. Take Citizens United, for example. Citizens United is a corporation organized under Virginia law. It exists as a nonprofit corporation because the people of Virginia passed an incorporation law. Under this law, people may create a nonprofit corporation only if they file with the state a set of articles of incorporation containing elements that the state requires, pay a filing fee of $75, designate a registered agent to deal with the state's annual assessment packet, and comply with record-keeping and other requirements set out in the Virginia law.

Without all of these steps, Citizens United (or any other nonprofit corporation) does not exist. In fact, the state provides the equivalent of the corporate death penalty for noncompliance with these laws. No one forced people to incorporate their activity as Citizens United, the nonprofit corporation, but once they chose to do that, is it too much to ask that the corporation comply with the laws on the books?

That does not mean that the people who support Citizens United, who work there, or who believe in its mission lose any rights whatsoever. They have all the same rights they had before they decided to incorporate and the same inalienable rights of all Americans. The corporation, however, does not, and we are not required to pretend that the corporation is the same as the people.

Once we recall that the rules for corporations come from us, for the betterment of our nation, the idea of "corporate rights" will be exposed as ridiculous. If we return to recognition that corporations are policy tools, rather than people with constitutional rights, we can then begin to realize many possibilities to improve the tool so that it better serves the purposes for which we Americans permitted the corporate entity in our laws in the first place. We can begin to rethink and reinvigorate our incorporation laws.

We might decide that the 306 million Americans who do not live in Delaware should have as much say about corporate law as the 900,000 people who live in Delaware now have. We might decide to create new and better corporate entities under the law, such as for-benefit "B Corporations," and options for sustainable "low-profit" hybrids between for-profits and nonprofits. We can change the rules to make real shareholder democracy and to make corporations justify their corporate charters and show how they have served the public and complied with the law. We can use the corporate chartering and charter revocation process and other features of corporate law to prevent and punish corporate crime and misconduct. We can insist on accounting for externalities—the dumping onto society of costs from pollution, destruction of our global ecosystem, and financial bailouts.[44]

That's not all. When people—voters, legislators, businesspeople, everyone—take responsibility for the public tool of incorporation, we are not only saving our republic; we may also be saving our economy. With new corporate rules, we can make corporations more effective at business, protect innovation and competition, create more jobs, and free human creativity.

In Chapter Seven, I will explore these ideas in more detail, along with the tools to enact a constitutional amendment and many more things you can do to take back our rights, our republic, and our democracy. This will succeed because more and more Americans know just how badly unbalanced corporate power and the Powell-Chamber vision of a "corporate marketplace" country has corroded our political system and how costly that corrosion has become. In the next chapters, I will examine more closely how these costs are imposed on the nation as a whole and on so many people who can no longer count on their government and elected representatives to stand up for them.

Chapter Four
Corporations Don't Vote; They Don't Have To

The strength of America is in the boardrooms, country clubs and Lear jets of America's great corporations. We're saying to Wal-Mart, AIG and Pfizer, if not you, who? If not now, when?

—Murray Hill Inc., Candidate for United States Congress[1]

Not long after the *Citizens United* decision, a corporation chartered under Maryland law announced its campaign for Congress. Leading with the slogan "Corporations Are People Too," Murray Hill Inc.'s statement explained: "Corporate America has been driving Congress for years," and now "it's time for us to get behind the wheel ourselves." Proposing to "eliminate the middleman," the corporation promised "an aggressive, historic campaign that puts people second, or even third." The corporation explained that it would use Astroturf lobbying, avatars, and robocalls to reach voters, concluding, "It's our democracy. We bought it, we paid for it, and we're going to keep it."[2]

The satirical Murray Hill congressional campaign was the inspiration of a real person, the company's president, Eric Hensal. As with all good satire, the jest works because it hits so close to the truth.

Corporate Money Changes Everything

Transnational corporations now dominate our government. That statement should shock us, yet it is now a commonplace with which few Americans would disagree.[3] Uncontrolled corporate money and power in politics are fast transforming our republic of people into what may better be described as a corporate state. People may no longer need precise numbers to appreciate the government takeover by narrow corporate interests, but the numbers still appall (see Table 1). The top twenty spenders alone spent close to $4 *billion* over the past decade to gain or keep advantage in Washington. Those numbers do not include the massive lobbying in the states, campaign spending, or the massive funding of corporate "grassroots," "foundation," and "think tank" front groups.

Corporations spend these billions of dollars not to advance any "special interest," at least if "special" is meant in any ideological sense. The interest is not "business," "jobs," "free market," or anything quite so noble. Corporations spend those billions of dollars to block reforms or enact favors for the profit interest of a very few specific corporations and the people who control them.

Take the U.S. Chamber of Commerce, which is the biggest spender by far. Despite the innocuous name and its self-description as a "business" lobby, the Chamber of Commerce does not promote a positive American business environment or conservative points of view. In large measure, the U.S. Chamber acts for and is funded by a few global corporations. It is far removed from the local chamber of commerce in any American town.

The U.S. Chamber brags that it is a $200 million "lobbying and political powerhouse with expanded influence across

Table 1
Top Twenty Spenders on Lobbying in Washington, 1998–2010

Lobbying Client	Total
US Chamber of Commerce	$770,655,680
American Medical Association	252,037,500
General Electric	251,940,000
AARP	207,432,064
Pharmaceutical Research and Manufacturers of America (PhRMA)	204,433,920
American Hospital Association	203,648,736
Blue Cross/Blue Shield	169,655,236
National Association of Realtors	166,150,553
Northrup Grumman	164,845,253
ExxonMobil	156,692,742
Verizon Communications	158,014,841
Edison Electric Institute	154,005,999
Business Roundtable	150,550,000
Boeing	147,884,310
Lockheed Martin	142,374,763
AT&T	126,449,336
Southern Co.	124,130,694
General Motors	121,899,170
PG&E	119,190,000
Pfizer	114,757,268

Source: Center for Responsive Politics, "Lobbying: Top Spenders, 1998–2011," *Open Secrets,* http://www.opensecrets.org/lobby/top.php?indexType=s; data from Senate Office of Public Records as of January 31, 2011.

the globe." Its president, Tom Donohue, says the Chamber is "so strong that when it bites you in the butt, you bleed."[4] This biting is not done to benefit most American businesses or communities but to promote the interests of the largest transnational corporations in the world. The bleeding is for the rest of us.

In some recent years, 83 percent of the Chamber's contributions were $100,000 or more; 40 percent came from just twenty-five contributors; the top three contributors provided 20 percent of the Chamber's dollars—anonymously.[5] In 2009, a single contribution accounted for 42 percent of all contributions to the Chamber. That came from the health insurance corporate lobby, which funneled $86.2 million to the Chamber to make sure no public option or other reform would hurt insurance company profit.[6] A former Federal Election Commission member explained why the insurance groups would use the Chamber as a front: "They clearly thought . . . it would appear less self-serving if a broader business group made arguments against it than if the insurers did it."[7]

Self-serving? Ten of the for-profit health insurance corporations paid their CEOs a total of $1 billion in compensation between 2000 and 2009.[8] One "nonprofit" health insurance corporation, Blue Cross and Blue Shield of Massachusetts, fired its CEO in 2011 with a $12 million severance and compensation package. CEOs of the ten largest publicly traded health insurance corporations earned a total of $118.6 million in 2007.

Meanwhile, back in the public sector, "the Administrator of the federal Center for Medicare and Medicaid Services, who manages the health care of forty-four million elderly Americans on Medicare and about fifty-nine million low-income and disabled recipients on Medicaid," is paid $176,000.[9] It is hard to see how the Chamber serves the interests of America's businesspeople and employees who pay towering health insurance premiums to help fund massive executive salaries and multimillion-dollar lobbying campaigns to block "government" health care.

In addition to protecting bloated health insurance companies, the Chamber works in other areas to protect the few and hurt the many. Bailed-out Wall Street corporations use the Chamber to block financial reform. Subsidy-collecting fossil fuel corporations pay the Chamber to block energy reform. In fact, the U.S. Chamber of Commerce opposition to any effort to address the climate crisis is so extreme that even other global corporations such as Apple, Nike, and PG&E have resigned from the Chamber in protest.[10]

What About Union Spending?

"What about unions?" Anyone who questions the impact of staggering amounts of corporate money in our democracy will hear that from time to time. The question makes sense: Americans distrust excessive concentrations of power and potential corruption, regardless of the institution in which the power is concentrated. We should seek transparency and accountability, checks and balances for any institution that has concentrated power, whether governmental, corporate, union, or otherwise. But we also should consider some facts about unions before accepting false equivalency with corporations.

The Chamber of Commerce says not to worry, *Citizens United* "provided unions with the same political speech rights as corporations."[11] David Bossie, who brought the *Citizens United* case, says the "newfound freedom" for corporations makes a "level playing field" with unions and interest groups.[12] Perhaps they think that unions will somehow balance out corporate power.

Unfortunately, they won't. First, the federal law that the *Citizens United* case struck down had assumed a level playing field; corporations *and* unions were covered by the same restrictions on election spending. That had been true since 1947. If you are concerned about union political spending, then *Citizens United* is a disaster for you, too, since *Citizens United* blocks Congress and the states from restricting union election spending. In that sense, David Bossie is correct: *Citizens United* means that democracy is for sale to any and all that have the cash to bid.

Behind this vision of a pay-to-play democracy is a deeply flawed premise that Americans are supposed to be spectators rather than governing citizens as corporations and unions throw money around to decide our elections. That assumption, however, is not the only thing wrong with the "level playing field" viewpoint about unions. In real life, there is no such thing as equality between unions and corporations, just as there is no equivalence between most people and the CEOs of large corporations.

First, a union is very different from a corporation. A union is an organization of employees. The employees agree to be represented by an elected leadership of the organization. The leadership negotiates with employers to reach terms of employment on behalf of all of the workers, terms that are approved by the workers, as well as by management of the business. People who decide to form unions may choose to incorporate the union, or they may not. Some unions are corporations, but many other unions are not. Unincorporated unions are simply voluntary associations of workers or federations of local "chapters." The largest labor organizations, such as the AFL-CIO, are federations of smaller unions.

That does not make unions perfect, and it's true that union corruption has been a problem at times, as in any human institution. When they worked well, though, as they usually did and continue to do, unions offer some counterbalance to corporate power. They provide an employee voice into the question of how corporate profits should be allocated among all of the people who contribute. In the long-gone heyday of unions, when corporations profited, everyone did well. Shareholders still gained, and CEOs and executives still made a fine living, but unions helped employees get a fair share, too.

Strong unions helped create the middle class. In the 1950s, when unions represented more than 35 percent of American workers in the private sector, wages rose. More people who worked hard had a chance to have health insurance and to retire in something better than poverty. For a variety of reasons, though, including corporate union suppression tactics, the rate of union membership declined steeply. By 1970, only one in four private sector workers was in a union. This number kept falling until today, when unions represent only 7 percent of private sector employees.[13] That means that 93 percent of private sector employees are *not* in unions.

So one answer to the question "What about unions?" is "What unions? They don't count anymore." That's not a complete answer, however. While private sector unions have declined significantly, public sector unions have grown over the same years. About 35 percent of public sector employees now belong to unions. Though the data are mixed, unions in the public sector have probably helped those employees retain slightly more of what all Americans seek—a decent wage, health care, some possibility of retirement, and some level of security.

Also, it's true that public and private union members spend money to influence government and policy. Union members pool contributions through political action committees (PACs), and unions do have political influence, particularly in the Democratic Party. In 2010, members of SEIU (a union representing service employees) contributed over $11 million, members of teachers' unions contributed $15 million, and the teamsters, electrical workers, and carpenters all contributed millions of dollars. So unions should not be exempt from any examination of the influence of money in politics.

Upon examination, however, the falsity of assertions about union-corporation parity is apparent. Unions do not have the membership, money, or influence to come anywhere close to balancing corporate power. The high ground for union members in politics comes at election time. Apart from the PAC spending (which itself is dwarfed by corporate money), unions can mobilize members to help get out voters and rally for favored candidates. But then the election is over, and regardless of the winner, corporate influence in government overwhelms unions as much as it overwhelms every other interest.

If you go back and look at that top-twenty list of lobbying spenders, you will see not a single union or federation of unions on the list. Not one. If we pull back from the top-twenty list to see *all* lobbying spending, including unions, corporate industries, and "special interests," the corporate domination remains clear (see Table 2).

In summary, corporate spending on lobbying came to more than $20 billion; union spending on lobbying, $0.4 billion. The financial industry alone spent $4 billion more than all of the unions combined, in every field, in the public and private sectors. Even by Wall Street's accounting, $20 billion and $0.4 billion are not close to equivalent.

Apart from the overwhelming magnitude of corporate money, the type of money from a union is different. Jon Youngdahl, national political director of the SEIU, explains where that $11 million that SEIU put into elections last year came from:

> About 300,000 janitors, nurses' aides, child-care providers and other members who voluntarily contribute on average $7 per month to SEIU's Committee on Political Education (COPE). . . . We are a union of working people, and the money we spend on politics is money donated by workers.[14]

Finally, in lobbying spending as elsewhere, the outputs reflect the inputs. If unions are using whatever power they have to drive into our government the union agenda—enlarged union membership, better wages, health care and pensions for union members, and in the private sector, a more equitable division of corporate

Table 2
Lobbying Expenditures by Industry (1998–2010)

Sector	Total
Finance, Insurance, Real Estate	$4,405,909,610
Health	4,369,979,173
Miscellaneous Business	4,352,728,292
Communications, Electronics	3,611,482,885
Energy, Natural Resources	3,233,636,465
Transportation	2,323,450,594
Other	2,271,149,632
Ideology, Single-Issue Lobbies	1,514,021,745
Agribusiness	1,317,839,638
Defense	1,261,711,454
Construction	482,824,245
Labor	441,259,274
Lawyers, Lobbyists	348,111,867

Source: Center for Responsive Politics, "Lobbying: Top Spenders, 1988–2011," *Open Secrets*, http://www.opensecrets.org/lobby/top.php?indexType=s; data from Senate Office of Public Records as of January 31, 2011.

earnings among executives, shareholders, and employees—they have failed miserably. By contrast, transnational corporate spending to dominate government has been a very good investment for the largest corporations.

What Corporations Get for the Money

Virtually every significant issue now reflects a corporate agenda, with the possible exception of social issues of limited economic impact, such as abortion, lesbian and gay rights, and the role of religion in public life. Consider two macro issues: spending versus debt; and energy and the environment. Whether Americans can find a way to manage these two issues wisely may have the most impact on whether we face precipitous decline as a nation and as a world. On both, the well-financed corporate agenda overwhelms the public national interest.

Corporate Power Drives Deficits and Debt

Admiral Michael Mullen, chairman of the Joint Chiefs of Staff, has identified the growing national debt as one of the most significant national security issues.[15] The national debt, approximately $10 trillion, is now at the highest point, as a percentage of gross domestic product (GDP), since 1946, in the aftermath of the Great Depression and World War II.[16] If current Congressional Budget Office (CBO) projections hold, that debt will rise to $16 trillion in ten years.

The biggest contributing factors to the rapid debt increase since 2001 are (1) trillions of dollars in "temporary" tax cuts enacted in 2001 and 2003 that remain in place, (2) the costs of the wars in Iraq and Afghanistan (the latter alone was costing $10 billion per month in 2011), (3) the enactment of a massive prescription drug benefit called Medicare Part D without funding the program, and (4) the collapse of the global financial system in 2008, followed quickly by the government bailouts to Wall Street and financial firms.[17]

The national debt reflects accumulated borrowing over the years. The budget deficit, on the other hand, reflects the amount of government spending in excess of government revenue in any given year. Continued deficits contribute to rising national debt.

In 2010, by official measures, the $3.5 trillion federal budget broke down as follows: Medicaid and Medicare, 21 percent; military, 20 percent; Social Security, 20 percent; "mandatory" spending (veterans' compensation, unemployment, food stamps, and so on), 17 percent; "discretionary" spending (law enforcement, roads, student aid, energy, and the like), 16 percent; and interest payments on the national debt, 6 percent.[18] More accurate measures that include all government spending for military purposes, not merely that counted in the Pentagon's budget, show federal spending on the military and war much closer to 50 percent of the budget.[19] On the revenue side, in 2010, tax revenues fell to the lowest level since 1950.[20] For 2011, the nonpartisan Congressional Budget Office has projected the budget deficit to be $1.4 trillion. The CBO projects cumulative deficits of $6.7 trillion between 2012 and 2021.[21]

What does any of this have to do with corporations? The corporate stranglehold on Washington drives huge corporate subsidies and earmarks. Diverse organizations from Public Citizen to the Cato Institute calculate "corporate welfare," defined as unnecessary federal spending and subsidies for specific corporations, at $92 billion to $125 billion per year.[22]

The Cato Institute describes subsidies for corporate agribusiness ($26 billion in 2006, as much as $30 billion in 2010) as, "a long-standing rip-off of American taxpayers."[23] The vast majority of agriculture subsidies do not go to "family farms" but to the biggest corporate producers. These subsidies could not be justified on any measure of public policy merit; they are bad for the health of the American people and an unfair business advantage for large corporations over small business. Taxpayer subsidies for corn production and industrialized by-products make unwholesome and fattening foods and drinks artificially cheap and place locally grown, organic, and otherwise healthy unprocessed food in an unfair competitive position.

Why does a practice that is bad for people and the country continue? Look back at Table 2; "agribusiness" is one of the largest lobbying machines in Washington, spending over $1.3 billion in the past decade.

The trillion-dollar bailouts after the 2008 financial crisis may be the champion of corporate welfare programs. Government bailouts to corporations after the financial crisis add up to $562 billion as of March 2011 ($256 billion has been returned), including loans to Fannie Mae and Freddie Mac ($154 billion); AIG ($68 billion); General Motors and other auto companies ($80 billion); and Citigroup, Bank of America, Goldman Sachs, and other banks ($245 billion).[24] Estimates that include additional federal assistance set bailout spending at $4.7 trillion, with $2 trillion returned to date.[25] I explore the financial sector and its impact on our economy in more detail in Chapter Five.

Our military spending, the largest component of the federal budget, is as big as all of the defense budgets of every other country in the world combined. The budget includes billions of dollars of corporate handouts, weapons systems that the Pentagon does not want, and a troubling expansion of corporate contractors for every aspect of military activity, from supply to mercenary corporations like Haliburton or Blackwater (now called XE, after its name became infamously associated with corruption in Iraq). In 2000, the military budget was $294 billion. For 2011, the military budget is $710 billion, the largest contributor to the deficit this year.

Consider General Electric's "alternative engine program" for the F-35 fighter jet. The engine is called "alternative" because it is not really the engine for the F-35. Pratt & Whitney, not GE, already makes the F-35 engine. The Pentagon says GE's proposed engine is not necessary. For years, the military has said that it does not want the "alternative" engine and that the money spent on it is a waste. President Bush urged Congress to kill the program in 2007, and President Obama did the same in 2009. That has not mattered. GE keeps spending political money, and Congress keeps approving spending for the "alternative" engine program. The cost to taxpayers so far for the unnecessary "alternative" F-35 engine has been $3 billion. If you go back to Table 1, you will find GE near the top, spending more than $230 million on lobbying in the past decade.[26]

Corporate power also drives deficits in indirect ways. Corporate lobbyists ensure that even programs intended to benefit the public interest must be designed for corporate profit, at the expense of the government and the American people. This is usually accomplished by writing the law to require hundreds of billions of dollars in corporate revenue, such as health care reform that mandates customers for health insurance corporations or that prohibits the government from negotiating pharmaceutical prices.

Health care costs are among the primary drivers of the deficit. While domination of government by corporations is partly a fiscal issue, the health care area also shows the terrible price many people pay in their personal lives for the disconnection of our representatives from the interests of the people.

Health Care Corporations Block Reform to Preserve Profits

The reason our government spends so much on health care is not because we are unduly generous for too many of our fellow citizens. Exactly the opposite: We are the only developed country in the world that relies on an expensive, wasteful, private sector, employer-sponsored health insurance system that leaves millions of citizens with nothing. Our health care costs include billions of dollars of CEO pay and corporate profit that other countries do not need to add into the bill. We pay twice as much on health care as other developed democracies—about 17.4 percent of GDP versus 9.3 percent—with less to show for it.[27]

When President Clinton tried to change this unsustainable system in 1993, the health insurance and pharmaceutical companies spent hundreds of millions of dollars to defeat reform. The system only got more dysfunctional over the next fifteen years, and the corporate lobby got stronger, spending even more in 2009 and 2010 to block effective health care reform again.

Although a version of reform passed in 2010, the corporate-dominated approach to that reform has serious consequences for long-term deficits and continuing financial drain on American businesses and people. What is mainstream and conventional throughout the world—cost-effective single-payer health care—was never given a second of consideration, despite the fact that a majority of Americans favor that approach.[28] The so-called public option, which at least would have allowed people to choose to take our business from profit-driven corporations to a government pool to help keep costs down, never had a chance, despite support from three-quarters of the American people. Even after months of assault by corporate money and lobbyists, most Americans did not think the health care reform went too far; they either supported it or thought it did not go far enough.[29]

We saw a preview of this type of corporate-dominated health care lawmaking in 2003, when Congress enacted and President George W. Bush signed the Medicare "Part D" prescription drug program for senior citizens. The law provided no means for paying for this expensive program, which effectively transfers hundreds of billions of dollars of (borrowed) money from the federal government to global pharmaceutical corporations. Much worse, the 2003 Medicare law actually made it illegal for the government to negotiate fair drug prices. The law also banned the import of cheaper drugs from Canada and made generic alternatives more difficult to obtain.[30]

According to a House of Representatives committee report, the federal government now pays 30 percent more for pharmaceuticals as a result of the 2003 law, resulting in overcharges to the government of billions of dollars per year. How did this happen? A Republican congressman from North Carolina explains: "The pharmaceutical lobbyists wrote the bill."[31]

A few months after the Medicare Part D law was enacted, the leading congressman who worked on the bill, Representative Billy

Tauzin, who had been both a Democrat and a Republican over the years, left Congress. He took a job as president of the pharmaceutical corporations' lobby group, the Pharmaceutical Research and Manufacturers of America (PhRMA), at a salary of more than $2 million a year. "As a member of Congress, Billy negotiated a large payout to the pharmaceutical industry by the federal government," said another congressman. "He's now about to receive one of the largest salaries ever paid to any advocate by an industry."[32]

Olga Pierce, a journalist for *ProPublica*, reviewed what had happened to others in government who worked on that 2003 payout to the pharmaceutical corporations:

- Former Sen. John Breaux, D-La., . . . fought against allowing drug prices to be negotiated in Medicare Part D. A year after the bill passed, he left the Senate to begin his lobbying career. He now has his own lobbying firm, Breaux Lott Leadership Group, which this year has received $300,000 to lobby for the pharmaceutical industry.

- Former Sen. Don Nickles, R-Okla., who helped negotiate the final version of Part D, then left to form his own lobbying firm. Bristol Myers-Squibb paid the Nickles Group $120,000 this year to lobby for, among other things, "health care reform issues related to Medicaid and Medicare."

- Thomas Scully, the former Medicare chief who helped design Part D, . . . obtained a waiver allowing him to discuss job offers before he left his government post. Less than two weeks after the bill passed, he went to work for the lobbying firm Alston & Bird, where he works on behalf of drug companies.

- Raissa Downs . . . a top legislative aide in the Department of Health and Human Services . . . helped spearhead the agency's efforts to shape Part D. Now she's a partner at Tarplin, Downs & Young consulting firm, where she is lobbying against changes to Part D.

- Michelle Easton has gone through the revolving door several times, working for Breaux, then the industry, then for Senate Finance Chairman Max Baucus, the Montana Democrat who is a key player in the current reform debate. Now Easton works in Downs' firm.

- John McManus, . . . staff director of the House Ways and Means health subcommittee when Part D was created, now has his own lobbying firm. Between 2004 and June 2009 the McManus Group earned about $6 million lobbying for PhRMA and various drug companies.[33]

To move reform forward in 2009, the White House secretly negotiated a deal with the pharmaceutical lobby, headed by the former Representative Billy Tauzin. The Obama administration promised not to touch the ban on the government's negotiating fair Medicare pharmaceutical prices. In exchange, the international drug corporations promised not to block other reforms and offered some unspecified "savings" of $80 billion over the next decade.

Apart from the grotesque elevation of a corporate lobby into a branch of government requiring negotiation with the White House, the deal was bad: If Medicare simply paid the same price that the government pays for the same drugs under the Medicaid program, taxpayers would save $150 billion.[34] As former Secretary of Labor Robert Reich says, "Perhaps the White House deal with Big Pharma is a necessary step to get anything resembling universal health insurance. But if that's the case, our democracy is in terrible shape."[35]

The Human Cost

The impact of the corporate takeover of government lawmaking in health care contributes to huge deficits and drains small business capital, but we should also remember the human cost. Health care is about lives of real people. Those who advance the corporate interest at the expense of the people's interest should do what one health insurance executive did: look into the eyes of Americans who suffer the consequences.

Wendell Potter had been a high-level public relations executive for the CIGNA health insurance corporation. As Potter describes in his book *Deadly Spin*, after more than two decades in the health insurance industry, he quit in a moment of conscience. His life was changed by his visit to a "health fair" at a county fairground in Tennessee, where Potter had grown up. A nonprofit medical group that usually brings needed health care to Third World regions had made its eighth annual trip to the fairgrounds to help Americans who had no other option for treatment.

Potter's description of stepping into what he calls a "war zone" at the health fair is haunting. Hundreds of soaking-wet Americans waiting all day in lines to be examined and treated in barns and animal stalls; teeth being pulled in open-sided tents; people "lying on gurneys on the rain-soaked pavement"; hundreds more turned away at the end of the day before they could be treated.

These are Americans. They were not waiting all day to be treated in animal stalls because they are shirkers. Two-thirds of them had jobs but no health insurance because, as Potter explains, they worked for small businesses that could not afford for-profit health insurance or, in many cases, the health insurers had "purged" unprofitable small business coverage from their rolls.[36]

Bill Moyers calls Potter's book "an exposé of corporate power that reveals why real health care reform didn't happen, can't happen, and won't happen until that power is contained."[37] He's right, and the problem goes beyond health care.

Beyond Health Care

American strength has come from resiliency coupled with practicality, determination coupled with distrust of zealotry. Our eighteenth-century republic has prospered into its third century because we have been able to endure and adapt to tremendous changes and challenges. Now *Citizens United* and the buildup of corporate power is ossifying government, blocking reform, and preventing adaptation to fundamentally new circumstances in the world.

Citizens United turns *uncontrolled* corporate lobbying and corruption of government into *uncontrollable* corporate lobbying and corruption of government. Any attempt to control that problem, now says the Supreme Court, violates the right of free speech. The dynamic that culminated in *Citizens United* of corporate rights feeding corporate power, and of corporate power building corporate rights, makes the practical balancing effect of a political process that represents all interests increasingly difficult or even impossible to achieve.

This danger is particularly acute in the energy sector. Just as we can have no real health care reform until we contain corporate power, we can have no real energy reform. That has catastrophic consequences, given our dependence on fossil fuels. Multibillion-dollar oil, coal, and gas subsidies grow, our costly ensnarement and overextension in the Middle East further weakens our own country, alternative technologies are developed elsewhere, and the resources and environment that we need to sustain life and security are rapidly destroyed.

As Jared Diamond reminds us in *Collapse: How Societies Choose to Fail or Succeed*, empires and societies often fail not because of a sudden, surprising blow but because of a long-term unwillingness or inability to adapt. Decline proceeds apace, as all can see the plainly perilous conditions, but candor and action are blocked by zealotry, denial, or force. What can it mean except fatal, corporate-fueled zealotry when the rallying cry of a major political party in America becomes "drill, baby, drill" after all we know the dangers of our reliance on oil?

Corporate Power: Energy, Deficits, and the National Interest

In a real sense, our entanglement in seemingly endless wars in the Middle East (Iraq-Kuwait, 1990–1991; Iraq no-fly zone, 1991–2003; Iraq War, 2003–2009; Afghanistan, 2001–present; Libya, 2011; Yemen 2010–2011; ongoing near-war with Iran; billions of dollars in military aid to Pakistan, Israel, Egypt, Saudi Arabia, and others in the region) is a multitrillion-dollar subsidy to protect the oil on which we have depended for too long. We expend so much in that region because it is highly strategic for one main reason: because we depend on its oil.

Apart from the indirect subsidy of our military, fossil fuel corporations are among the biggest corporate welfare recipients. They receive billions in tax subsidies, liability caps, and other government assistance, not to mention the subsidy of massive highway funds and minimal funds for transportation other than auto and truck. Between 2002 and 2008, the government provided more than $100 billion in direct subsidies to the energy sector. Approximately $72 billion of that went to the fossil fuel industry, while only $29 billion went to alternative energy programs. Half of that alternative energy support went to the inefficient corn-ethanol industry.[38]

Do the global oil companies need these handouts to obtain oil? Oil corporation profits are extraordinarily high and keep setting new records, so that seems unlikely. Take it from a Texas oilman, George W. Bush: "I will tell you with $55 [per barrel] oil, we don't need [to provide] incentives to oil and gas companies to explore."[39] With oil now costing nearly twice as much per barrel, it is insane to subsidize oil companies, which already have the massive built-in subsidy of benefiting from the price-fixing of the global OPEC cartel.

We know we have to change. Here's what the president has said: "At the end of this decade . . . the United States will not be dependent on any other country for the energy we need to provide our jobs, to heat our homes, and to keep our transportation moving." The president also said: "My program was designed to conserve the energy we now have, while at the same time speeding up the development and production of new domestic energy." And the president said, "We must start now to develop the new, unconventional sources of energy that we will rely on in the next century."

Actually, three presidents said those things, nearly four decades ago: the first was spoken by Richard Nixon in 1974; the second, by Gerald Ford in 1975; and the third, by Jimmy Carter in 1977.[40] It is a tradition as reliable as the Thanksgiving turkey pardon ceremony and the White House lawn Easter egg roll to promise change, conservation, and development of alternative energy, and yet little changes.

Ronald Reagan said this a quarter-century ago:

"My goals in this area are to . . . continue conservation and progress toward diversification of our energy resources."

George H. W. Bush, twenty years ago:

"[I've] prepared a detailed series of proposals that include . . . a comprehensive national energy strategy that calls for energy conservation and efficiency, increased development, and greater use of alternative fuels."

Bill Clinton, thirteen years ago:

"Our overriding environmental challenge tonight is the worldwide problem of climate change, global warming. . . . We have it in

*our power to act right here, right now. I propose $6 billion in
tax cuts and research and development to encourage innovation,
renewable energy, fuel-efficient cars, energy-efficient homes.*

George W. Bush:

*"America is addicted to oil, which is often imported from unstable
parts of the world." "Our security, our prosperity, and our
environment all require reducing our dependence on oil."*

Barack Obama:

*"We have known for decades that our survival depends on
finding new sources of energy, yet we import more oil today than
ever before. . . . We know the country that harnesses the power of
clean, renewable energy will lead the twenty-first century."*[41]

By 2006, we imported 60 percent of our oil, compared to 35 percent in 1973. Two-thirds of the known oil reserves are in the Persian Gulf. OPEC cartel countries have 70 percent of the world's oil reserves; the United States has 2 percent.[42] "Drill, baby, drill" will not change these facts. We have compromised our national security, our military is overstretched, our trade deficit is exploding, and our republican values and commitment to democracy for all are undermined by our unshakable commitment to profit for global fossil fuel corporations.

The rising costs of our fossil fuel dependence for the environment, families, and communities have moved from inconvenient to dangerous and are approaching catastrophic. When crises occur, as in the Gulf of Mexico when BP's Deepwater Horizon oil rig exploded in 2010 or when the Exxon *Valdez* ripped open in Alaska or when oil refineries exploded as in Texas and Washington State in recent years or when another war in the Middle East begins or an old one enters its second decade, we see the death of people, ecosystems, businesses, and livelihoods. What we sometimes fail to see right in front of us is the growing and terrible price that we place on families, communities, and our environment everywhere, every day. In some ways, oil is not the worst of it.

According to the coal lobby, we burn what the lobby calls "clean coal" for half of our electricity.[43] But there is no such thing as "clean coal." Coal-burning utilities emit toxic pollution. Coal causes tens of thousands of premature deaths each year in the United States, as well as many thousands more cases of lung and other cancers, asthma attacks, upper respiratory illness, heart attacks, and hospitalizations.[44] Coal combustion pushes 48 tons of mercury, a neurotoxin, into the air each year.[45] Mercury and other coal pollutants contaminate the air we breathe and are deposited with the rain into our rivers, lakes, and streams. Thousands of water bodies where people used to fish are poisoned. Forty-five states now have fish advisories.[46]

Coal is not cheap, either. The coal industry, like other nineteenth-century industries that leverage improper political power from their old economic power, takes billions of dollars each year from American taxpayers. As with oil, massive government subsidies prop up outdated coal energy, while Arch Coal, Peabody Energy, Patriot Coal, Massey Energy, and Alpha Natural Resources take record profits for themselves. Since 1950, the coal industry has received direct subsidies of $72 billion from the U.S. government. Congress added $9 billion in subsidies as recently as 2005. The so-called stimulus bill in 2009 added another $3.4 billion to help the coal industry figure out—so far unsuccessfully— how it could stop emitting massive amounts of carbon pollution.[47]

Coal corporations pass on, or to use the economists' term, "externalize," huge costs onto American society. Annual costs of thousands of coal-caused disease, land devastation, and destroyed water resources are conservatively estimated at $333 billion.[48] Coal, along with oil, is the principal cause of the very real climate crisis. Fossil fuel emits polluting greenhouse gases such as carbon dioxide, which trap heat in the atmosphere due to absorption of sunlight. The climate change we now face is due to human-caused emissions, 80 percent of them stemming from the burning of coal, oil, and natural gas. The increased emission of these gases, based on thermometer measurements going back to 1880, has led to an average global rise in temperatures of 1.5 degrees Fahrenheit—twice as much in the Arctic—and an additional warming of 2.0 to 11.5 degrees is predicted over the next century if emissions go unabated. Likely effects of this rise include diminished water supplies; vanishing of snow and ice; rising sea levels endangering coastal populations; increased frequency of droughts, floods, and more devastating hurricanes and storms; and long-term decline in agricultural production and increased incidence of malaria, cholera, and other disease.[49]

Corporate Power Blocks Alternatives

Are we unable to change and adapt because we have no alternative? No, alternatives are available now. If all we did was allow the Environmental Protection Agency (EPA) to do its job and proceed with proposed auto standards, we could reduce oil imports by billions of barrels, save every American thousands of dollars each year, and eliminate millions of pounds of carbon pollution. Alas, oil-funded politicians are pushing laws to strip the EPA of its authority to do this and in 2011 came within minutes of shutting down the federal government in a budget standoff caused in part by their zeal to neuter the EPA.

We do next to nothing to tap the vast energy resources in our buildings and homes, where 70 percent of energy is consumed, much of it wasted. For a small fraction of the cost of new power plants, we could have national retrofit programs for insulation, windows, electricity-saving devices, and other efficiency steps that would save many more billions of barrels of oil, pounds of coal, cubic feet of gas, and American dollars. People may want that, but in contrast to oil, coal, and gas, we do not have a string of multibillion-dollar corporations lobbying to get our government moving on that.

We are falling farther behind. Denmark and Spain generate 21 percent and 14 percent of their electricity demand, respectively, from wind power alone. Spain is on target to generate an additional 10 percent of its electricity from solar power and has a large export business in solar technology, though behind the leaders in this lucrative business—China and Germany. Three states in Germany generate 40 percent of their electricity from wind power. Scotland recently moved its 2020 target of 50 percent of power from wind up to 80 percent. The Philippines derives 28 percent of its energy needs from geothermal sources. In the United States, we generate less than 3 percent of our electricity from solar, wind, biomass, geothermal, and the like (an additional 6.5 percent comes from hydropower).[50]

Why do we fail to do what we know we need to do and what other countries seem fully capable of doing? We do not change because old-line corporations that profit from preventing change have extraordinary and growing power to resist. After all, those first "corporate free speech" cases involved power struggles between the people and utility corporations such as Central Hudson, Consolidated Edison, and PG&E, and with the Supreme Court's creation of corporate rights, the people lost.

Thanks to the successful efforts of the Chamber of Commerce and Lewis Powell and his allies to enlist the power of the Supreme Court, it is now illegal—a violation of "free speech"—to prevent utility corporations from promoting energy consumption. After *Citizens United*, it is illegal for us to regulate corporate spending in politics and elections.

The energy industry spent $3 billion in federal lobbying expenses from 1998 to 2010. The oil, gas, and coal companies have been some of the biggest corporate spenders to gain and keep corrupt political influence in Washington and state capitals. Oil and gas corporations set a record for lobbying spending in 2009, topping $154 million. Electric utilities spent $134.7 million. Alternative energy companies combined managed to come up with $29 million to lobby in 2009.[51]

After *Citizens United*, the American Petroleum Institute announced that it would spend millions of dollars to support friendly candidates and attack perceived opponents of the oil companies. "This is adding one more tool to our toolkit," said an API official. "At the end of the day, our mission is trying to influence the policy debate."[52]

Symbolic of Our Fall: Mountaintop Removal

To fully appreciate the ecological, moral, and social disaster of corporate domination of government, you should go to Appalachia and see the impact of mountaintop removal coal mining. You should hurry, though, if you want to see mountains; they are going fast. To get coal more cheaply than it would cost to hire more miners, vast swaths of Kentucky, West Virginia, Tennessee, and Virginia, with some of the richest, most diverse ecosystems in the world, have been destroyed.

More than five hundred mountains have been blown up and flattened, the toxic debris dumped into valleys and obliterating more than two thousand of miles of headland streams—literally, they no longer exist. As Robert Kennedy Jr. points out, if you filled 25 feet of a stream in your town, you could go to jail.[53] Coal corporations have filled 2,500 miles of streams in Appalachia. Towns and communities have been destroyed, drinking water poisoned, disease incurred, and local economies ruined by this most destructive, irresponsible, and shortsighted form of extracting energy in the history of humanity.[54]

If you cannot go to Appalachia, you can still see and hear some of the brave people working to stop this by going to Web sites for organizations such as I Love Mountains, a coalition campaign to end mountaintop removal, or Appalachian Voices, the Kentucky Riverkeeper, or the Waterkeeper Alliance.[55] The I Love Mountains Web site has a "see your connection" function that lets you type in your ZIP code and see how the destruction of Appalachia connects to you.

I live in Concord, Massachusetts, and felt good that our lower-cost municipal utility pursues alternative energy and conservation. However, when I put in my ZIP code at the I Love Mountains Web site, I discovered that when I turn on a light, coal from obliterated mountains in Appalachia is burned in the AES Thames power plant in Connecticut, which feeds into the New England grid and into the Concord Light & Power system.

Knowing this makes it hard to visit the people in West Virginia and Kentucky who cannot drink what used to be clean mountain water, whose coal-dust-covered homes shake with explosions, whose children go to schools and get sick from the toxic dust settling over them; the people who are pitted against one another by coal companies who destroy jobs and threaten to destroy the rest of them if anyone complains.

I did visit, and one must see it to believe that this is happening in America. Bill Haney, a businessman and film director, has documented the terrible crime going on across Appalachia in the film *The Last Mountain*. To watch it is to understand the sad, dangerous consequences of unchecked corporate power. Or watch Robert Kennedy Jr.'s speech from Blair, West Virginia, in June 2011, in which he explained the connection between mountaintop removal extraction, *Citizens United*, and the destruction of American democracy.[56]

Or you can hear online the voice of Elmer Lloyd, a retired coal miner in Harlan County, Kentucky.[57] After he retired, Elmer

Lloyd built a fish pond because the local streams had been ruined. "When I was small, kids could go down to the river to fish; I could go down to the river, put a line in, and catch all the fish I wanted. But over the years, I mean, it become where you couldn't even find a minnow, or a fish, or nothin' in the river, because they were all gone. So I figured I'd build me a pond, you know, you'd have something in the area where the kids could fish."

When the mountaintop removal started, "people told me, when they start stripping behind your house, they're going to destroy your home. I said no, I believe there's enough laws out there to make 'em do it right. Well, they said, you wait and see." Toxic runoff from the operations destroyed the stream and the fish pond, killing all the fish. When Lloyd complained, the coal company sent people over: "They were kinda laughing about it. Saying, there's one that might make it. There's one that didn't make it. And they were saying it like they thought it was funny."

Lloyd called the Kentucky Department of Fish and Wildlife, which told him to fill in the pond because with mountaintop removal coal mining, there was no hope for it. Lloyd says, "It just ain't right for companies to try and come in here and get a dollar and destroy the place, destroy people, and leave because they don't have to worry about it next year because they're gone looking for something else to make money on and destroy."

Lloyd's right when he says, "I believe there's enough laws out there to make 'em do it right." Many of those laws are the laws that we demanded after the first Earth Day in 1970, such as the Clean Water Act, which the government once vigorously enforced. The Clean Water Act has a "citizens suit" provision so that when the government fails to do its job, people can bring a case of their own. People in West Virginia, Kentucky, and Tennessee did this, exposing widespread illegality by the coal corporations, from Clean Water Act violations (twelve thousand violations by one company at one mine alone) to falsified water-monitoring reports. Joe Lovett, a West Virginia lawyer who brought one of the first cases, says he "naively believed that we would just go to court, point out what was wrong, and that the United States government would fix it."[58]

In four different cases, a federal judge in West Virginia found that the coal corporations, and the government that was supposed to regulate the coal corporations, were violating the law. Mountaintop removal mining had "cracked the walls" of nearby homes and "made the air so dusty that [people] cannot sit out on the porch comfortably." Even inside, people "cough from dust particles and their furniture is constantly layered with dust." Judge Haden also heard testimony from kayakers who could no longer travel up a favorite tributary "because it no longer existed, having been covered and destroyed by mining activities."

Judge Haden flew over southern West Virginia and saw the impact himself:

> *Mined sites were visible from miles away. The sites stood out among the natural wooded ridges as huge white plateaus, and the valley fills appeared as massive, artificially landscaped stair steps. Some mine sites were twenty years old, yet tree growth was stunted or non-existent.*
>
> *If the forest canopy of Pigeonroost Hollow is leveled . . . and aquatic life is destroyed, these harms cannot be undone. If the forest wildlife are driven away by the blasting, the noise, and the lack of safe nesting and eating areas, they cannot be coaxed back. If the mountaintop is removed, . . . it cannot be reclaimed to its exact original contour. Destruction of the unique topography of southern West Virginia, and of Pigeonroost Hollow in particular, cannot be regarded as anything but permanent and irreversible.*[59]

Four times, the court of appeals reversed Judge Haden's decisions and allowed the mountaintop removal and valley fills to continue. The court noted that the coal corporations, United Mineworkers, and "the West Virginia State political establishment" all were allied against the citizens groups and the Environmental Protection Agency.[60] When Judge Haden again ruled that mountaintop removal and the obliteration of streams violated the Clean Water Act, the Bush administration rewrote the rules to try to make what was illegal "legal." Judge Haden ruled that maneuver, too, was illegal because only Congress has the authority to rewrite the Clean Water Act, and "the rule change was designed simply for the benefit of the mining industry."[61] The court of appeals reversed that decision, too.

The power that leads government to encourage illegal activity is not because of the great number of jobs and livelihoods at stake. Coal corporations favor mountaintop removal precisely because it requires *fewer* jobs and is therefore more profitable. There are fewer than 20,000 coal-mining jobs in West Virginia today, compared to 145,000 in the 1950s. Underground mining requires many more miners than mountaintop removal mining.

The political force that obliterates the very Appalachian Mountains themselves is not driven by the people of Appalachia demanding the destruction of their homes, communities, woods, mountains, and streams for all time but from the power of corporate money. The vast majority of the people in West Virginia want mountaintop removal mining stopped now, yet not a single West Virginia politician will stand for them because of the political power of the coal corporations.[62]

Recently, the Environmental Protection Agency said it may begin to enforce the Clean Water Act on mountaintop removal. The coal corporation executives and hired hands went ballistic, calling this possibility a "regulatory jihad," a "regulatory assault," and "out of control." Indeed, if you search the Internet on "EPA out of control," you will encounter a well-funded corporate campaign spread out across the land, the blogosphere, the "think tanks" and "foundations," and the airwaves.

After *Citizens United*, according to a leaked letter from a coal corporation executive to other coal executives, the coal corporations moved in for the kill. The letter said, "With the recent Supreme Court ruling, we are in a position to be able to take corporate positions that were not previously available in allowing our voices to be heard." (There are those corporate "voices" again.) He suggested that representatives of the corporations meet to discuss "developing a [political-spending] 527 entity with the purpose of attempting to defeat anti-coal incumbents in select races, as well as elect pro-coal candidates running for certain open seats." He proposed "a significant commitment to such an effort."[63]

This is what government of, for, and by the corporations looks like. If we want to live with it, the American experiment in freedom and government of the people is doomed. Fortunately, millions of Americans, from the mountains to the prairies and to the oceans, too, are saying "enough!" To win change, though, people will need to be prepared for the implicit blackmail of corporations threatening "jobs" if we try to restrain or balance corporate power. For that reason, the next chapter looks more closely at the idea that we must quietly accept corporations as rulers if we want to make a living.

Chapter Five
Did Corporate Power Destroy the Working American Economy?

Crony capitalism is usually thought of as a system in which those close to the political authorities who make and enforce policies receive favors that have large economic value. . . .

[In such a system] the intermingling of economic and political elites means that it is extremely difficult to break the implicit contract between government and the privileged asset holders.

—Stephen Haber, "The Political Economy
of Crony Capitalism"[1]

Since the *Citizens United* decision in 2010, hundreds of business leaders have condemned the decision and have joined the work for a constitutional amendment to overturn expanded corporate rights. These include entrepreneurs such as Yvon Chouinard, founder of Patagonia; Ben Cohen and Jerry Greenfield, founders of Ben & Jerry's Ice

Cream; Amy Domini, founder of Domini Social Investments; Gary Hirschberg, founder of Stonyfield Farm; Nell Newman, founder of Newman's Own Organics; Wayne Silby, founder of Calvert Social Investment Fund, and many more.[2] These business leaders are doing this because they believe that democracy, freedom, and a sustainable world depend on a bill of rights for people, not corporations. They know that *Citizens United* and corporate domination of government are terrible for American innovation and business.

The Hoover Institution and others have probed the problem of "crony capitalism" and how it hampers economies in other parts of the world. These studies tend to associate pay-to-play crony capitalism with Indonesia, Russia, Egypt, and other countries with less of a tradition of freedom and democracy. It may be time to look closer to home. Stephen Haber's description of crony capitalism as an economy where "those close to the political authorities who make and enforce policies receive favors that have large economic value," increasingly fits the American economy.

Now, even the most gifted economists probably could not definitively answer the question that titles this chapter. Nevertheless, I would suggest that two propositions are worth serious consideration: First, the *Citizens United* vision of American government as a corporate marketplace, where citizens are reduced to consumers, rewards old, entrenched corporations that can leverage their last-generation economic muscle to delay and obstruct new rivals. Innovative businesses and nascent industries waste precious capital trying to keep up politically, rather than economically. As with the unions, however, new businesses, small businesses, or disfavored businesses do not have a prayer in the multibillion-dollar corporate lobbyist playground or in the corporatized courts. As a result, opportunity wanes, private costs in the favored corporations are shifted out to the public or onto potential competitors, and economic vitality declines.

Second, *Citizens United*'s elimination of the last modest restraint on corporate power—the limitation on spending in elections—is likely to be the endgame of the transformation of our economy into one where only a few people, rather than most people, have a shot to prosper. In our present corporatist era, good wages, benefits like health care or pensions, and such notions as craftsmanship and job stability have become bad things that should be crushed. They are costs to be reduced, avoided, or eliminated altogether, rather than good things to which society might aspire. It may be hard to remember, but we used to think that higher wages with more benefits for working people was a worthy goal rather than a problem to overcome so that corporations can be more "competitive." Now CEOs who find a way to eliminate jobs and benefits or destroy a union are celebrated and paid tens or even hundreds of millions of dollars, while the stock price rises and the analysts and media cheer.

Entrenched Corporations Gain Inefficient Advantage

If we accept the false metaphor of corporate money as a "voice" and the fantasy that big corporations are no more of a threat to our political life than big people, you can count on coal and oil corporations prospering and solar, wind, tidal, and geothermal energy corporations struggling. When you call government for help after coal corporations crack your walls and poison your fish pond, you can count on being told to fill in your pond and move on. And we all can count on a low-wage, low-benefit economy with a great divide between the rich and everyone else.

In crony capitalism, distorted policies corrupt and tilt markets to favor connected, rather than good, businesses. Too often the "free-market" advocates concerned about "government" or "excessive regulation" propose the elimination of regulations on even the most complex and potentially destructive businesses.[3] If this argument ever made sense, it no longer does. Eliminating regulations, or obtaining regulatory advantage, is the essence of inefficient, pay-to-play corrupt capitalism.

The perceived absence of regulations is neither the absence of government nor the presence of a market economy. The choice is not between regulation and no regulation; the choice is between a government that regulates in service of the public interest or one that regulates in the service of powerful corporate interests. Sometimes it's *more* regulation (as in the case of laws prohibiting Medicare from negotiating with pharmaceutical companies for market rates), *less* regulation (as in passing a law prohibiting regulators from regulating the derivatives market), or *different* regulations (as in expanding the rights of patent protection to delay increased competition and lower prices). Under any of these scenarios, government action shifts public assets and benefits to a favored slice of powerful people and interests while allocating huge costs to powerless people and interests.

Unremitting hostility to regulation that serves the public does not create more efficient business—just the opposite. Weak government oversight of transnational corporations rewards bloated enterprises that use political power to dump their inefficiencies off their balance sheets and onto society, at the expense of new and more efficient enterprises.

Coal is a good example. Corporate and investor calculations about energy production will differ if the cost of coal does not include the cost of preventing the destruction of what belongs to other people—water, air, mountains and valleys, fish ponds, and house foundations. Coal appears "cheaper" than wind, solar, or other sources of power only if its costs do not include the very large costs—externalities—that coal corporations and coal burning utilities can, in the absence of effective regulation, displace onto others outside of the business. This is the corporate "externalization" problem.

Robert Monks, a businessperson, investor, and former chair of the Republican Party in Maine, says, "The corporation is an externalizing machine in the same way a shark is a killing machine."[4] That is just what it does. If it is legal to dump untreated waste or toxic pollutants into a river or the air, corporations will do so. They will do so not because corporations are evil or because the people who work for corporations are bad; they will do so because it is legal. If it is legal to dump pollution onto others, then the market price assumes "free" pollution disposal. If one corporation does not do that, another will. The one that dumps wastes and emits pollutants may have lower costs than the one that spends money to treat or prevent pollution. The one with higher costs will go out of business because it cannot compete, and "the market" then will require dumping waste into rivers and toxins into the sky.

In theory, this is a human problem, not a corporation problem. In the real world, it is a corporation problem. Corporations fund campaigns against the "out-of-control EPA" and "regulatory jihad" because they seek more profit. If allowed, coal corporations pour money into electing whomever they consider "friends of coal" and to defeating whomever they regard as enemies, because the corporations seek more profit. Without government regulation to control greenhouse gas emissions, the destruction of mountains, the poisoning of streams, and so on, we can be sure that someone else (or everyone else) will bear the cost while the corporation reaps the profit.

What makes the hostility to regulation more perverse is that those problems—global environmental catastrophe, for instance—are caused in large measure by government's creation of the corporate entity and its advantages. Without the laws permitting incorporation, conferring limited liability and other advantages, it would be difficult to marshal the scope of investment and operations capable of eliminating five hundred mountains in a few years (unless the government itself coerced the capital for such operations, as in the Soviet Union or other state-enterprise regimes). Would you invest in Massey Energy or the Alpha Natural Resources coal corporation if you were personally held responsible for its actions?

That is not to say that we should not have corporations. Rather, we should not pretend that corporations are natural products of "the market" and that government has no business regulating them. As Theodore Roosevelt wrote about corporations a century ago, it is "folly to try to prohibit them, but . . . also folly to leave them without thoroughgoing control."[5]

So crony capitalism may be un-American, but do not fall for the idea that "government" or "regulation" is un-American. A true libertarian might not want any government or any regulation, but such a libertarian would not stoop to ask government for a corporate charter and would not hide behind limited liability and other government favors. Maybe we could live with a true libertarian society if we could get there, but we cannot live with a government that creates, protects, and serves corporate power but leaves corporations unsupervised and unregulated.

Jobs, Taxes, and Wealth

A lot of data suggest that the success of the corporate drive to power in our country over the past three or four decades has helped transform our economy from a broad-based growth engine for all into a plutocracy. It now is very difficult for any but the rich to prosper in healthy, strong communities.[6]

In the corporate era, most Americans no longer make enough money. Per capita income is now around $27,000, and "household" income (i.e., husband and wife both working in many cases) is around $50,000.[7] Wages for most people have been flat for three decades. Personal savings have plummeted, and debt has soared.

This was not true in the previous thirty years: from 1950 through 1980, when the economy was growing, wages for most people grew too. The average income for nine out of ten Americans grew from $17,719 to $30,941 in that period, a 75 percent increase in constant 2008 dollars. Since 1980, however, the economy continued to grow but the gains went overwhelmingly to the top fraction of Americans. The top 1 percent received 36 percent of the income gains between 1979 and 2008. The top sliver (again, 1 percent) received 53 percent of income gains from 2001 to 2006.[8] Wealth now is more concentrated in the top 1 percent of American incomes than at any time since 1928.[9]

For average Americans, income went from $30,941 in 1980 to $31,244 in 2008, a gain of only $303 dollars in twenty-eight years.[10] Total household income rose a little more than that, but only because most households required two paychecks and more women entered the workforce.[11]

The top 1 percent of income-earning Americans now takes a larger share of income—24 percent of the total—than ever before, and they own a larger share of total net worth—34 percent—than ever before. Ninety percent of Americans own just 29 percent of total net worth.[12] Between 1993 and 1997, "corporations enjoyed double-digit profit increases for five years in a row. . . . Meanwhile, over the 1990s, hourly wages fell for four of every five workers."[13] CEO pay rose 600 percent in the same decade.[14]

In the past decade, the United States has lost thousands of factories, and thousands more are on the precipice.[15] By 2009, fewer Americans worked in manufacturing jobs than at any time since 1941.[16] Most other measures of the American middle class are just as bad. Hours worked? Since 1979, married couples with children are working an additional five hundred hours (equivalent to more than sixty-two eight-hour days).[17] Vacation time? We have by far the lowest standard for vacation time in the developed world. Debt? With incomes stagnating, savings rates are near zero, and most Americans live under pressing burdens of credit card, mortgage, auto, school, and other debt. Affordability of housing? Ability to pay for college? Retiring with a safe pension? Health care? Most people have it much worse on these measures than thirty years ago.

Some people say that this steady decline is just the way it is, due to "globalization and all that," as if globalization were a meteor from outer space rather than a trend that democratic societies can shape. The intentional offshoring of American jobs to low-cost countries has taken a terrible toll. An accountant in India makes $5,000 per year, compared to an American accountant's average salary of $63,000. And as one well-paid CEO noted, "If you can find high-quality talent at a third of the price, it's not too hard to see why you'd do this."[18] Even if that is true as a mathematical calculation, should our government really enable, encourage, and reward so richly those who "do this"?

Could the struggles of American workers be a productivity problem? That might be an explanation; if American productivity (how much is produced per unit of labor, capital, and other inputs) steadily declined in those years, then noninflationary income gains for American workers would be unlikely. The problem with that explanation is that American productivity did not decline but instead continued to improve. Productivity continued to rise after 1979, but we distributed the gains from that rise differently in the corporate era than we did before. According to a 2005 analysis of data from the Bureau of Labor Statistics, between 1947 and 1973, productivity and the median income rose by almost exactly the same amount (productivity increase, 100.5 percent; median income increase, 100.9 percent). Between 1973 and 2003, however, things changed. Now, even though productivity continued to increase (71.3 percent), median incomes increased much less (21.9 percent). In other words, the gains were no longer going to all Americans but were increasingly going disproportionately to a very few people at the top.[19]

This did not "just happen." Gains from economic growth that used to be widely shared now go disproportionately to the extraordinarily wealthy because government chooses that outcome. The crony capitalist "intermingling" of political and economic elites and the corporate campaign envisioned by Lewis Powell have built an antiregulation, antigovernment theology that works to enrich a very few individuals and to prevent choices that previously distributed wealth and opportunity more evenly. Tax policy is a good example.

Corporations, People, and Taxes

Although corporations are not people, people control corporations, and a very few people control the largest, richest corporations. As Stephen Haber noted regarding crony capitalism elsewhere in the world, "The intermingling of economic and political elites means that it is extremely difficult to break the implicit contract between government and the privileged asset holders." That intermingling is on full display in Washington and state capitals when government allocates the tax burden.

The idea that the United States of America is a place where people can work hard and have a chance at getting rich is very strong, but so is the idea that people should pay their fair share and that graduated, progressive tax rates fairly balance the burden of funding the nation's continued progress. Indeed, we have a progressive income tax only because Americans of all parties came together to amend the Constitution in 1913 to overturn a Supreme Court case that struck down the federal progressive income tax law.

Gross income disparities are an enemy of successful market economies.[20] Nevertheless, shifting income to the very top lies at the heart of the corporatism agenda. In fact, the first of the modern corporate rights decisions arose from organized corporate opposition to a modest proposal in Massachusetts to tax the wealthy at a slightly higher rate than the middle-class and the poor. The 1978 decision in *First National Bank of Boston v. Bellotti* (written by Justice Lewis Powell) struck down a Massachusetts law banning corporate funding for or against citizen referendum campaigns. The referendum at issue in that case would have allowed Massachusetts to have a progressive, graduated income tax instead of one where the poor paid the same rate as the rich. That was the question that galvanized corporations such as Bank of Boston, Gillette, and Digital Corporation to sue for corporate speech rights to block a citizen referendum.

These corporations demanded that the Supreme Court guarantee them the right to spend as much corporate money as their executives decided was necessary to block the citizen tax referendum. Otherwise, the people might vote for progressive income taxes. According to the argument used by the corporations in the case, progressive income taxes would make it more difficult for corporations to recruit talented executives in Massachusetts. The corporations won. Now, thirty years later, Massachusetts still does not have progressive income taxes.[21]

What happened to the companies that got the Supreme Court to give corporations "speech" rights to spend unlimited money to defeat a citizen vote in Massachusetts? They presumably went on to recruit those talented executives whom the corporations claimed would not have come to Massachusetts if the state had progressive income taxes—right?

Massachusetts should have been so lucky. Here's an update since the 1978 *Bellotti* decision. Gillette sold itself to Procter &

Gamble in 2005, with the loss of more than one thousand jobs.[22] The Gillette CEO who engineered the deal, James Kilts, made $188 million on the sale.[23] Bank of Boston sold itself to Fleet (five thousand lost jobs; $25 million for the CEO), which then sold itself to Bank of America (thirteen thousand lost jobs; $35 million for the CEO).[24] Digital sold itself to Compaq in 1998 (fifteen thousand lost jobs; $6.5 million for the Digital CEO who sold the company).[25] The tax rate for those CEOs and the laid off employees remains equal.

CEO Pay, Political Spending, and Corporate Government

It approaches a state of what Robert Kerr has called "cognitive feudalism" to imagine that there are no connections among corporate power, wealth disparity, and the erosion of democracy.[26] The same CEOs and executives who decide to spend corporate lobbying money and corporate "independent" campaign money also make substantial personal contributions directly to candidates. They also decide how much to pay themselves, advised by a sympathetic board compensation committee. In the corporate era of today, that pay is now much, much more than it used to be, so that millions of dollars in CEO personal campaign contributions are relatively easy to make.

Between 2000 and 2008, CEO pay ranged from 319 to 525 times the average employee's pay. In 1980, the average CEO made only 42 times the salary of the average employee.[27] Even after the 2008 financial meltdown, the average CEO salary (nearly $10 million) remains 263 times higher than the average employee salary.

The nonpartisan Center for Responsive Politics (CRP) has pulled together data showing contributions to candidates and political parties from individual "heavy hitters." The CRP defines a heavy hitter as someone who has given federal political candidates and parties more than $50,000 during a single election cycle. That $50,000 giveaway to politicians is more than the annual income of 75 percent of Americans.

The CRP heavy hitter list includes dozens of CEOs and executives of global financial corporations that received billions of dollars in taxpayer-funded bailouts or other government aid during the recent financial crisis, including Goldman Sachs, Citigroup, AIG, JPMorgan Chase, UBS, Credit Suisse, Wachovia, Merrill Lynch, and Bank of America. The list of $50,000 campaign contributors also includes executives from global energy, media, tobacco, telecommunications, and pharmaceutical corporations that benefit from government policy decisions (or inaction) to the tune of billions of dollars in corporate profit.[28]

These "investments" seem to pay off for the companies *and* for the executives. Both receive coddling tax treatment that makes no sense from the perspective of national interest or sound fiscal policy in times of high deficits. Despite large profits and multi-million-dollar executive payouts, bailed-out Bank of America has paid zero taxes since 2009. GE ($14 billion in profits) paid zero taxes and instead claimed a $1 billion tax credit. The wars go on, Medicare and school budgets are cut, and "temporary" tax cuts for those making more than $250,000 (2 percent of American households) remain sacrosanct.

Then there's the "hedge fund loophole." In 2009, twenty-five hedge fund managers paid themselves a total of $25.3 billion— yes, that is *billion*, with a *b*. If these twenty-five billionaires paid income taxes like everyone else, one would expect those billions in earnings to be taxed at 35 percent, the federal income tax rate for the highest-paid Americans, or at 38 percent if the "temporary" tax cut enacted after the September 11 attacks had been allowed to expire in 2010. As the late billionaire Leona Helmsley famously said, however, "Only the little people pay taxes."

Hedge fund managers do not pay income taxes like other people do. Hedge fund managers take a fee in the form of a "carried interest" in the performance of the fund or, in other words, a designated percentage of the profits from investing other people's money. Hedge fund managers call this a "gain" rather than "income" and hence claim the right to pay a low capital gains tax rather than a normal income tax. The top capital gains tax rate is 15 percent, the same as the *lowest* income tax rate possible, available only to those with income of $34,000 or less. To put this in perspective, 75 percent of Americans make less than $50,000 per year. Say you are doing much better than most or have a high combined income with your spouse, and you make $100,000 per year. You would pay federal income tax at a 28 percent rate. Yet if you are a hedge fund manager who makes $1 billion, you pay a 15 percent tax. That's the hedge fund loophole.

Unsurprisingly, this loophole outrages regular taxpayers (that is, almost everyone). Perhaps good arguments may be made, as a general proposition, for taxing capital gains at a lower rate than general income taxes. Lower capital gains taxes may encourage investment, generating economic growth, jobs, and wealth. The lower rate reflects risk-taking: investments might result in a gain, but they might also result in a total loss. But do hedge fund managers who make billions of dollars need the additional encouragement of a tax discount to do what they do? Are they going to stop making billions of dollars unless we promise not to tax them at more than 15 percent? Hedge fund managers do not have a risk of loss because they are investing other people's money, not their own. Hedge fund managers' compensation is in fact much closer to income than it is to investment gain.

Congress considered proposals to close the hedge fund loophole in 2007, 2009, and 2010. Each time, people thought that the loophole did not have a chance to survive because it is so indefensible. Undaunted, the hedge fund and private equity industry drove millions of dollars in lobbying expenses, up 800 percent and 560 percent, respectively.[29] The U.S. Chamber of Commerce rushed out "studies" claiming that economic disaster would befall America if the hedge fund managers paid taxes like other people, and corporate-funded front groups with names like American Crossroads and Crossroads GPS shouted "liberty" and inveighed against "taxes and wasteful government spending." With that snap of the leash, Congress did nothing.[30] At the end of 2010, a hedge fund manager paid himself $5 billion for the year's work or, as he would prefer, a year's "gain."

The Intermingled Elite and the Economic Crisis

Perhaps nothing illustrates the "intermingled elite" of crony capitalism and its devastating consequences for the American economy better than the creation of the Citigroup financial conglomerate in 1998 and its decadelong dance into financial apocalypse.[31] Citigroup is the largest and perhaps the most dysfunctional of the "too big to fail" financial conglomerates. In 2007, it fired its CEO but paid him $105 million.[32] In 2009, the federal government bailed out Citigroup with a $306 billion guarantee of its toxic assets and a $20 billion cash infusion.

Citigroup is a monument to virtually every component of corporate misconduct that wiped out millions of jobs, homes, retirement funds, and other assets of middle-class America in the 2008 financial crisis. These components include incestuous relationships with high government officials, subprime mortgage scams, unregulated derivatives and credit default swaps, misleadingly inflated assets, securities packed with junk loans and stamped with bogus ratings, wildly excessive and irresponsible CEO and executive compensation, billions in government bailouts, unapologetic resistance to regulation or oversight, and millions of dollars in lobbying and campaign spending to continue the flow of government favors. Almost as a bonus, Citigroup has also been a leader in corporate outsourcing of thousands upon thousands of American white-collar jobs to what it calls "lower-cost locations" such as India.[33]

Back in April 1998, Citigroup, at the time one of the largest bank corporations in the world, announced its merger with Travelers Group, also a large financial and insurance conglomerate. The merger would create the largest financial company in the world. According to reports at the time, "Much of Wall Street liked the deal," and the share price of both companies soared.[34] There was only one problem: the corporate conglomerate they had in mind was illegal.

The law of the United States for at least fifty years had banned this kind of financial conglomerate. The law, known as Glass-Steagall, was passed after the 1929 stock market collapse and the ensuing financial panic that led to the Great Depression. Requiring separation of commercial and investment banks, Glass-Steagall created "firewalls" that had successfully prevented a repeat of the financial panic and Great Depression for half a century.

Illegality, though, was no deterrent. The CEOs and leaders of Citigroup and Travelers privately consulted with President Bill Clinton, Federal Reserve Chairman Alan Greenspan, and Treasury Secretary Robert Rubin (former chair of Goldman Sachs) before going public with the merger, confident that they would change the law.[35] Announcing the merger, Sanford Weil, CEO of Travelers, said that the corporations could take time to "divest" the illegal pieces of the business if they must but did not think they would need to do so. "We are hopeful that over that time the legislation will change."[36]

They were right; the legislation did change. Congress dutifully repealed Glass-Steagall with the Financial Modernization

Act of 1999 soon after the merger. A few days after Secretary
Rubin's Treasury Department and the White House paved the way
for Citigroup by supporting the repeal of Glass-Steagall, Rubin
announced that he would be leaving government to become a top
official and "senior adviser" at Citigroup. In the next decade, Citigroup paid Rubin $126 million.[37] Upon leaving the company in the
midst of the meltdown and bailout in 2009, Rubin said he regretted
that he did not "recognize the serious possibility of the extreme circumstances that the financial system faces today."[38]

At least Rubin acknowledged regret. The same cannot be
said for former Senator Phil Gramm, who as chair of the Senate
Banking Committee drove the repeal of Glass-Steagall and was a
longtime antiregulatory zealot. In Congress from 1983 to 2002,
Gramm, like the corporate pharmaceutical lobbyist Billy Tauzin,
was flexible enough to be both a Democrat and a Republican,
depending on the winds. Gramm led the way to repeal Glass-
Steagall's stabilizing regulation for Wall Street and the financial
industry. A year later, he led the way to enact a law to exempt
derivatives from government oversight.[39] Consensus opinion,
apart from Phil Gramm, links the financial meltdown in 2008
directly to this rash abandonment of responsible government.
Congress essentially surrendered the country's fortunes to the
"years-long, massive lobbying effort by the banking and financial
services industries to reduce regulation in their sector."[40]

Economists say this deregulation of the financial services
industry and the related failure of oversight created a "less competitive and more concentrated banking system" that directly
contributed to the financial crisis of 2008.[41] Conservatives and
libertarians like Robert Ekelund and Mark Thornton at the
Ludwig von Mises Institute say, "This 'deregulation' amounts to
corporate welfare for financial institutions and a moral hazard

that will make taxpayers pay dearly."[42] Investigative journalists at *Mother Jones* say:

> *Because of the swap-related provisions of Gramm's bill . . . a $62 trillion market (nearly four times the size of the entire U.S. stock market) remained utterly unregulated, meaning no one made sure the banks and hedge funds had the assets to cover the losses they guaranteed. In essence, Wall Street's biggest players (which, thanks to Gramm's earlier banking deregulation efforts, now incorporated everything from your checking account to your pension fund) ran a secret casino.*[43]

Where is Phil Gramm now? In 2002, while still serving in the Senate, he announced that at the end of his term he intended to join the UBS corporation, an international investment bank headquartered in Switzerland, as vice chairman. Since then, UBS has added a new twist to Citigroup's long list of misdeeds, the folly, greed, and misconduct that led to the financial crisis: in 2009, as a result of a federal criminal investigation, UBS admitted that between 2000 and 2007, UBS participated in a criminal scheme to defraud the United States by helping rich people hide assets so as to illegally evade taxes.[44]

Gramm, still with UBS, now lives in Texas with his wife, Wendy, who chaired the Commodity Futures Trading Commission (CFTC) from 1988 until 1993 and who herself is an intermingled corporate-government player. Back in 1993, just before leaving the CFTC office, she granted a "midnight order" that barred CFTC oversight of the trading in derivatives (called "weapons of mass destruction" by Warren Buffett). Mrs. Gramm then joined the board of directors of Enron, a major beneficiary of unregulated derivatives trading and a major financial supporter of Phil Gramm's political campaigns. She remained on Enron's board and its audit committee until the company's collapse due to systemic, repeated, and egregious accounting fraud in late 2001. Her Enron salary and stock income amounted to between $915,000 and $1.8 million.[45]

Phil Gramm is unrepentant. He says that he has seen "no evidence" that the financial crisis was caused by deregulation. In the summer of 2008, as the financial crisis began to unravel the nation and the world, he explained that the economy was not the problem. Rather, the American people were the problem. "This is a mental recession," he said. "We have sort of become a nation of whiners."[46]

Chapter Six
Corporations Can't Love

Only a virtuous people are capable of freedom.

—Benjamin Franklin

*No free government can stand without virtue in the
people, and a lofty spirit of patriotism.*

—Andrew Jackson

*Virtue may be defined as the love of the laws and of
our country. As such love requires a constant preference
of public to private interest, it is the source of all private
virtue. . . . A government is like everything else: to
preserve it we must love it. . . . Everything, therefore,
depends on establishing this love in a republic.*

—Thomas Jefferson

In America, we are equal and free not
because we have the same material goods,
power, and interests as each other but because we are people. We
believe that freedom and rights are our birthright. Now *Citizens
United* has reopened ancient questions: How can a republican
government of free and equal people survive in the real world of
massive inequalities of wealth and power? How can all Americans

participate in government on equal terms? How do we prevent the corruption of government and the destruction of liberty by what James Madison called "faction"?

Madison defined *faction* as "a number of citizens, whether amounting to a majority or minority of the whole, who are united and actuated by some common . . . interest, adverse to the rights of other citizens, or to the permanent and aggregate interests of the community." Madison and the other Founders well understood that faction was part of life. Because we are people, we might grasp for power and seek advantage for ourselves, for our families, and for our friends. The Constitution incorporates the truths of human liberty and equality and of human faults.

The Constitution seeks to increase the odds for the success of liberty and self-government by diluting faction, balancing powers, and declaring rights. Even with better odds, government of the people requires a trait that only people can seek: virtue. "To suppose that any form of government will secure liberty or happiness without any virtue in the people, is a chimerical idea."[1]

Americans have kept this improbable run of human possibility going one generation after another, overcoming grievous injustice and brutal challenge, because of love: love of country and family, of justice and freedom. As Americans and human beings, we cannot help but believe and sacrifice for this miracle that has nothing to do with the corporate marketplace. In *Citizens United*, the Court forgot this human underpinning of our Constitution and, in thrall to its imprecise corporate metaphors, forgot the essential relationship of speech and other human rights to a virtuous republic of people. Corporate money is *not* speech, and corporations do *not* have the capacity for virtue—nor are they designed for it.

This point lay at the heart of Justice Rehnquist's repeated objections to Justice Powell's creation of corporate rights in the 1970s and 1980s. Whether or not the states or Congress regulate corporate political spending, Rehnquist wrote, "all natural persons, who owe their existence to a higher sovereign than the Commonwealth, remain as free as before to engage in political activity." He added, "In a democracy, the economic is subordinate to the political, a lesson that our ancestors learned long ago, and that our descendants will undoubtedly have to relearn many years hence."[2]

Virtue, Patriotism, and the Corporation

We are relearning at last. Distorting our Constitution and its Bill of Rights to create corporate, rather than human, rights destroys virtue and strengthens faction. Rather than balance or dilute Madison's faction, the corporate rights doctrine promotes and strengthens the most formidable faction the world has ever known. Then it disables the constitutional mechanisms of controlling such faction by invalidating inconvenient laws and inserting corporate money between lawmakers and the people. That is why, in America, there can be no such thing as "corporate speakers," "corporate voices," or "corporate citizens."

Corporations do not have voices or rights; they have no virtue or shame; and they do not love America. I am not saying, and do not believe, that people who work at corporations do not love our country and would not sacrifice for the nation. But corporations are not people. People in the corporation come and go, but the corporation goes on and on (so long as it is making money). Corporations do not love (or hate) anything, including countries or humanity. It is not that corporations are disloyal to our country (and again, here I am speaking primarily of global, *Fortune* 500, extremely large corporations). Rather, it is more that they are "aloyal." Loyalty is not a trait that has any meaning or applicability to corporate charters or corporate entities or transnational corporate conglomerates, no matter how many flags General Motors or Anheuser Busch may use in advertisements. Indeed, despite its flag waving, Anheuser Busch and its "Great American Lager," Budweiser, are part of the Belgium-based global corporation called Anheuser Busch InBev.

After *Citizens United* ruled that Americans are not permitted to limit corporate spending in elections, some of the grave concern focused on "foreign corporations." But what does "foreign corporation" even mean today? The global corporations that dominate the Chamber of Commerce agenda and spend billions on lobbying are not American or any other nationality. They have trillions in revenues and profits from around the world. They operate everywhere but are citizens of nowhere. Their largest shareholders are institutions, extremely wealthy people, or even other countries, anywhere in the world. They may have a cluster of corporate charters out of Delaware (and in various countries), but to global corporations, including what we might think of as "American corporations," the United States is just another market to control and manipulate and, if possible, in which to eliminate government oversight.

By way of example, News Corporation, the parent corporation of Fox News, funneled millions of dollars into the November 2010 election. Prince Waleed bin Talal's Kingdom Holding Company of Saudi Arabia is the second-largest shareholder, with $2 billion in shares. UBS, the bailout recipient and employer of former Senator Phil Gramm, is headquartered in Switzerland, operates in fifty countries, and has as its largest shareholder the government of Singapore. Exxon, one of the biggest spenders on Washington lobbying, handing out more than $150 million from 1998 to 2010, operates in two hundred countries. Exxon derives most of its revenues outside of the United States, and fewer than 25 percent of its employees work in this country. BP, formerly known as British Petroleum, is based in London, operates in eighty countries, and has twice as many employees outside the United States as in the country. GE (which spent more than $230 million in Washington lobbying from 1998 to 2010) operates in one hundred countries and has more employees and more production plants outside the United States than here. Apple, which has experienced explosive growth and enriched its shareholders, assembles virtually every one of its products in China and other parts of Asia.

It would have been bizarre and dangerous indeed if the Supreme Court of earlier times had ruled that Rockefeller's Standard Oil Corporation or the Union Pacific Railroad Corporation had "free speech" rights to spend corporate money in elections, no matter what the people or Congress thought about that. Now, in the modern age of giant corporations with byzantine international structures and international institutional shareholders, the ruling in *Citizens United* borders on assisted national suicide.

We Americans may disagree vehemently on many things. We may lose our tempers and perspectives in political fights and say terrible things about each other, but at bottom, I think, most Americans know that we all love our country and we all want America to succeed. We share values. We are family members, sometimes literally, sometimes figuratively. Our children will live together. And we take the future, nature, patriotism, and other nonmonetary considerations into account when we vote, support parties or candidates, and do what people in a republic must do. We know we will not be here to see the America our grandchildren will grow old in, but we all hope to make decisions and live in ways that will leave a free, strong country and world behind for them.

Corporations do not, and cannot, do that. The owners and executives and other people in the corporation do that, as people, on their own behalf outside of work. Almost certainly, however, any decision to spend corporate money to influence an election or to make up a constitutional corporate right to eliminate a law regulating the corporation will not reflect these diverse human considerations but will reflect only a calculation of possible corporate profit.

The virtue that so concerned the founders of our nation is a human aspiration, if not always a human trait. We all know that no one is perfect, but it is impossible to observe a jury deliberate a case, or talk to people in polling places at election time, or watch cops, nurses, firefighters, teachers, and soldiers do their jobs, or go to a school parent meeting, blood drive, food kitchen, or any local volunteer group, and not see how strong virtue remains in America. That is civic virtue, and it happens because of human, not corporate, love.

Crime and Punishment: Conceiving of Corporations as "Speakers" or a Mere "Group" Is Foolhardy

No matter how forgiving we may be, it is very hard to think of those who commit crimes against people and against the community as virtuous. People may be rehabilitated, and eventually, in some states, former felons may participate fully in civic life again. We usually expect, however, some combination of jail time, shame, and repentance before someone can earn back the right to be a full participating member of the community after committing crimes against it.

Not so with corporations. Shame, repentance, community condemnation, and redemption are for people. Bank of America, General Motors, Credit Suisse, General Electric, Deutsche Bank, BP, Exxon, Boeing, WellCare Health Plans, Alcoa, Volvo, Pfizer, and many, many more large corporations are criminals.[3] I don't say that as a provocative insult. I say that as a fact for consideration in evaluating whether it makes any sense to conceive of corporations as bearers of the people's constitutional rights. Those corporations have all admitted crimes or, in the case of General Motors, have been convicted of crimes after trial. If these corporations were people, they might not be allowed to vote, coach Little League, or head a scouting troop. They would not be trusted. Yet after *Citizens United*, nothing restricts their dominating political influence in our national life.

These convicted corporations are not people, so they did not go to jail, feel shame, or let down their parents, children, or neighbors. They paid some money and went back to making more money. They went back to paying hundreds of millions of dollars to lobbyists to block laws, preserve tax breaks and subsidies, and otherwise ensure favorable government policy. In some instances, they went back to committing more crimes.

In most cases, the corporation itself suffers no lasting damage after pleading guilty to crimes and, indeed, may even profit from breaking the rules. In the corporatist era, some even claim that is just fine and is as it should be. As Kent Greenfield describes in *The Failure of Corporate Law*, some of the leading scholars argue that corporate managers "do not have an ethical duty to obey economic regulatory laws just because they exist. They must determine the importance of these laws. . . . The idea of optimal sanctions is based on the supposition that managers not only may but also *should* violate the rules *when it is profitable to do so*."[4]

BP, Crime, and the Corporate Charter

The constitution of Delaware, the state in which most of the largest corporations get their corporate charter, requires that corporate charters be subject to revocation if they have been misused or abused. Criminal acts are considered misuse and abuse under the law.[5] Virtually every state has corporate charter revocation laws because those who came before us recognized the danger of misuse of the advantages of incorporation and took seriously the public obligation to oversee the conduct of corporations. In our amoral age of corporate law and the careless transformation of corporations into metaphorical people or speakers, the charter revocation laws are widely ignored. This lack of responsibility and accountability helped create the environment in which the Powell–Chamber of Commerce campaign to transform corporations into holders of constitutional rights could succeed, and makes that success all the more dangerous.

The global oil giant BP illustrates like no other the lack of public accountability and control over the giant transnational corporations that now dominate so much of our lives. BP is a web of corporations. The corporation was founded in the United Kingdom as British Petroleum in 1909. The parent corporation is now called BP plc and maintains its headquarters in London. BP operates in the United States through numerous subsidiary corporations that have been granted corporate charters under Delaware law. These include BP America, BP America Production Company, BP Products North America, BP Corporation North America, BP Exploration (Alaska) Inc., BP West Coast Products, Standard Oil, BP Amoco Chemical Company, and more.

On April 20, 2010, BP's Deepwater Horizon oil rig in the Gulf of Mexico exploded and sank, killing eleven people. The resulting massive oil inundation into the Gulf waters created an environmental and economic catastrophe for people living and working in and along the Gulf. BP has concealed, evaded, or misrepresented the facts about the amount of oil that has poured into the Gulf. Even when scientists implored BP to allow them to monitor the flow of oil that created massive underwater plumes, BP stonewalled: "The answer is no to that. We're not going to take any extra efforts now to calculate flow there at this point."

A criminal investigation is under way relating to a whistle-blower disclosure that BP violated the law by not retaining key safety documents about the Deepwater Horizon oil rig. As BP tried to shift the blame and evade accountability, BP's CEO Tony Hayward whined, "I want my life back."

BP's reckless and illegal activity in American waters in the Gulf was only the latest of its crimes. On one day alone in October 2007, BP admitted to a virtual crime spree. First, BP Products North America Inc. pleaded "guilty to a felony" for causing a 2005 refinery explosion in Texas that killed fifteen people. BP admitted, "If our approach to process safety and risk management had been more disciplined and comprehensive, this tragedy could have been prevented." The criminal plea agreement required BP to pay a fine of $50 million and serve three years of probation.

Second, on the same day, BP admitted that it engaged in criminal conduct that caused "the largest oil spill ever to occur at Prudhoe Bay" in Alaska. As a result, BP Exploration Alaska Inc. pleaded guilty to a misdemeanor violation of the Federal Water Pollution Control Act. BP's plea agreement required BP to serve three years' probation and pay a fine of $12 million. BP admitted that its approach to "risk" was "not robust or systematic enough."

Third, BP also admitted that it engaged in criminal conspiracy, mail fraud, and wire fraud after BP America and several other BP subsidiary corporations "manipulated the price of February 2004 TET physical propane and attempted to manipulate the price of TET propane in April 2003." As a result of BP's criminal price manipulation, BP was required to pay $303.5 million in fines, penalties, and restitution. BP admitted that its "view of the legality of these trades changed as our knowledge of the facts surrounding them became more complete." BP admitted its "failure to adequately oversee our trading operations."

And these crimes by BP were not the first and not the last. BP's other recent admissions or convictions of crimes and misdemeanors include the following:

- A guilty plea in Alaska related to the illegal disposal of hazardous waste, including paint thinner and toxic solvents containing lead, benzene, toluene, and methylene chloride, on Alaska's North Slope

- $25 million in penalties in California due to "significant and numerous violations" at a BP refinery

- $900,000 in penalties after producing and distributing gasoline that threatened public health

- $87,430,000 in proposed penalties to BP Products North America Inc. "for the company's failure to correct potential hazards faced by employees." OSHA found that despite the death of 15 people and the injury of 170 in its Texas oil refinery explosion and despite its promises to change its ways, BP continued to commit "hundreds of new violations"

- $3 million in additional fines to BP North America when OSHA "found that BP often ignored or severely delayed fixing known hazards in its refineries"

- Thirteen "serious safety violations" at a BP refinery near Blaine, Washington. A Washington official stated in 2010 that "we are disturbed that more than ten years after the explosion that killed six workers at the Equilon refinery, our inspectors are still finding significant safety violations every time we inspect one of the refineries in the State of Washington."

BP's oil refinery operations account for 97 percent of all "egregiously willful" and "willful" violations found by government safety inspectors over the past three years. Despite (or perhaps because) of this record of crime and misdeeds, in the first quarter of 2010 alone, BP made $5.6 billion in profit. And what happened to Tony Hayward, the CEO who wanted his life back after BP ruined the Gulf of Mexico and killed workers on the Deepwater Horizon? BP gave him a salary and bonus of $6 million in 2010 and awarded him $18 million when he left the company.

In June 2010, an organization called Green Change filed a petition requesting that the attorney general of Delaware initiate an action to revoke the Delaware charters of BP, a serial criminal. More than five thousand people joined the call.[6] A year later, the attorney general has not responded to or commented on the detailed petition describing BP's crimes, let alone taken action.[7] We have had plenty of corporate "fraud, immorality, and violations of law" warranting charter revocation proceedings. We have not had nearly enough action by attorneys general and other state officials to enforce this law.

Too Big to Tell the Truth

Large corporations defy even mild controls of health, environmental, and consumer protection laws and then seek shelter from the Supreme Court's corporate rights regime. Not long before *Citizens United*, the corporate "speech" campaign reached the point of claiming the right of corporations to lie, or at least to have the constitutional right of "breathing space" to protect them from charges of lying.

A California law allowed people to bring consumer fraud charges alleging that Nike fraudulently launched a campaign of lies about why no shoes were made in America anymore and whether Nike's shoes were made by badly exploited poor people in brutal overseas sweatshops. Nike went all the way to the Supreme Court arguing that the transnational corporation had a "free speech right" to block the law. Again, the global corporations and corporatist "legal foundations" rallied to the cry that corporations are people, and the Constitution prevents any restriction on corporate "speech."

Covington & Burling (remember them from the cigarette child-targeting and Monsanto drug-created milk cases on pages 44–46?) filed briefs for ExxonMobil, Microsoft, Morgan Stanley, and GlaxoSmithKline to support "corporate speakers'" First Amendment rights to block laws holding corporations accountable for massive deceptive disinformation campaigns. Covington & Burling wrote, "If a corporate speaker must limit its factual statements on matters of public concern to statements that no one could possibly challenge, or that the speaker could be certain it could prove as 'true' in a court of law or before a regulatory body, the result will be a deterrence of speech which the Constitution makes free."[8] The Washington Legal Foundation brief went straight to the heart of the matter: the Court should not allow anything that might cause the corporate share price to fall. Washington Legal Foundation, one of the largest of the Powell-Chamber–inspired corporatist legal groups, argued that a corporation must be able to block a law like California's or otherwise it would risk a "shareholder suit alleging negligence for the drop in stock values resulting from its failure to defend itself in the court of public opinion."

The theme of all of these corporate arguments is only partly that corporations should have the same First Amendment "breathing space" as people do to debate public issues with passion, hyperbole, and even scurrilous attacks and arguable falsehoods. An additional theme is that global corporations are just too big, too powerful, and in too many countries to be subjected to judgments of state law when they launch false feel-good public relations campaigns in response to criticism or when they spew lies about cigarettes, global warming, sweatshops, the rainforest, or anything else.

In the Supreme Court brief, the global corporations argued that Nike could not possibly guarantee "truth" (the brief itself uses quotation marks around the word *truth*) when Nike has "736 facilities located in the 51 countries in which 500,000 workers are used by its subcontractors to manufacture its products."[9] In other words, Nike is too big, too global, and in too many countries exploiting cheap labor to possibly operate without potentially getting sued by someone for fraudulent statements. And we can't have that, can we?

Why can't we have that? If that really is a problem, it is an economic problem for Nike and its shareholders, not a constitutional problem for Americans. The slippery slope argument that the Court and the Constitution must step in to make sure that Nike does not find itself in court having to defend its false statements implies that Nike not only has a "right" to its corporate charter and privileges but also has a corporate "right" to operate in fifty-one countries and outsource jobs to impoverished areas of the world and the "right" to wage PR campaigns if people question the human impact of Nike's decisions. Each of those, however, is a corporate policy preference, not a right.

Nike's arguments state a business problem, not a constitutional problem. Nike could solve its business problem in a number of ways without fabricating constitutional rights to block the law. It could make its shoes in the United States. It could be smaller. It could price into its shoes the cost of defending itself from global human rights campaigns about its overseas sweatshops. It could ask the legislature to create an exception in the law for global corporations operating overseas sweatshops. Whether these options are unattractive or might raise the price of Nike sneakers or, God forbid, lower the share price has nothing to do with the Constitution. There is no constitutional right to cheap overseas labor and false marketing campaigns to make Americans feel better about lost jobs, human rights abuses, and immoral conduct. In the end, the Supreme Court declined to hear the Nike case, but we know how this story ends in *Citizens United*.

The Consequences of Corporate Amorality and Crime

Corporate crime and allowing corporate power to slip out of control of the people have consequences. WellCare Health stole millions of dollars from a children's health program in Florida. One of BP's many crimes killed fifteen people in a Texas refinery. Massey Energy (now owned by Alpha Natural Resources) committed thousands of violations and killed twenty-nine people in a mine explosion in 2010. Volvo supported Saddam Hussein's regime in Iraq by committing crimes to get heavy trucks and equipment around a United Nations sanction, and Credit Suisse criminally moved money around to evade American economic sanctions against dangerous regimes in the world.

Unchecked corporate power poisons food, water, and air, and people get sick and die. Workplaces are more dangerous, and people die. Markets are corrupted, and people lose their savings and jobs are wiped out. Taxes for most people are higher because corporations and the rich do not pay their share and hide money "offshore," abetted by criminal international bank corporations.

The Court's *Citizens United* decision failed to consider whether the problem of serial corporate crime and the reality of global corporate power exposed the fallacy of excess metaphorical thinking when it comes to corporations. Had the Court considered why Congress might have distinguished between corporations and people in the Bipartisan Campaign Reform Act and the 1907 law banning corporate money in politics (see page 11), the Court would have inquired into how corporations might be different from people.

In doing so, the Court might have connected "speech" to "virtue" as essentially human characteristics and recognized the relationship of both to a self-governing republic of free people. This virtue, as Jefferson and the other Founders knew, is not only "love of the laws and of our country" but also a love that "requires a constant preference of public to private interest."[10]

Corporations are incapable of virtue, not because they are bad but because they are mere tools. A hammer has no virtue either. And we would not call a hammer a "speaker." We could design a better tool, but for most of the large public corporations, the risk of crime and fraud runs high because we do not sufficiently conceive of the corporation as a tool to aid the progress of the many rather than as an enrichment machine for a few in control of the corporation.[11]

Sadly, the failure to control corporate power corrodes and destroys virtue itself in too many American people. Think of those CEOs who reaped millions to destroy jobs or the public servants who sell out the country for corporate dollars or position. Think of the self-effacing, kind Lewis Powell described by Sandra Day O'Connor and all those decent, patriotic, kind, hardworking people who went off to work each day on behalf of the long cigarette conspiracy to addict children and kill people. I do not intend sarcasm here. Decent, kind, patriotic, hardworking people *do* go off to work every day in corporations that create terrible consequences for the world, when allowed to do so. When we fail to keep corporations in their proper economic place and to protect our political space, we corrupt virtue in all of us.

The crimes of corporations, from trading with the enemy to stealing from children, as well as the political corruption caused by corporate power, happen because people make decisions on behalf of the corporation. Yet it is not because those people are evil. It is because government, crippled by corporate "rights" and corporate power, has abandoned its duty to control the powerful tool in which those people find themselves working. When we, the people, cannot control corporations because of fabricated constitutional rights and dangerous imbalances in lobbying and election spending, people making corporate decisions are rewarded for *not* exercising virtue and punished for exercising it. Corporate decisions then overwhelmingly favor the private, not the public, interest, and the corporate, not the American, interest.

As Thomas Jefferson wrote in his commonplace book more than two centuries ago, "everything . . . depends on establishing this love in a republic." The real people of America must overturn *Citizens United* and corporate rights and must assert the will of the people over the unchecked power of corporations. As in the past, we have the means and, I believe, the virtue to do exactly that.

Not long after the BP disaster in the Gulf of Mexico exposed how deeply and corruptly the oil corporations had insinuated themselves into our government, Senator Sheldon Whitehouse, former attorney general of Rhode Island and a former United States attorney, took to the Senate floor. He issued a warning and plea to the American people:

> *Have we now learned what price must be paid when the stealthy tentacles of corporate influence are allowed to reach into and capture our agencies of government?*
>
> *I pray, let us have learned this; let us have learned that lesson. I sincerely pray we have learned our lesson, and that this will never happen again. But let's not just pray.*
>
> *In this troubled world God works through our human hands; grows a more perfect union through our human hearts; creates his beloved community through our human thoughts and ideas. So it is not enough to pray. We must act.*

We must act in defense of the integrity of this great government of ours, which has brought such light to the world, such freedom and equality to our country. We cannot allow this government—that is a model around the world, that inspires people to risk their lives and fortunes to come to our shores—we cannot allow any element of this government to become the tool of corporate power, the avenue of corporate influence, the puppet of corporate tentacles.[12]

We are people. We love. We pray. We act. We are all on the same side. So let's get to work.

Chapter Seven
Restoring Democracy and Republican Government

This is a moment of high danger for democracy so we must act quickly to spell out in the Constitution what the people have always understood: that corporations do not enjoy the political and free speech rights that belong to the people of the United States.

—Maryland Senator Jamie Raskin[1]

Great corporations exist only because they are created and safeguarded by our institutions; and it is therefore our right and duty to see that they work in harmony with these institutions.

—President Theodore Roosevelt[2]

As President Theodore Roosevelt put it, we have the right and *the duty* to control corporate power to protect our institutions of self-government. So what can those who wish to fulfill that duty do now? Three key steps will lead the way back to government of the people, not of the corporations.

First and most important, we need to work for the Twenty-Eighth Amendment to the Constitution, a People's Rights Amendment, to reverse *Citizens United* and corporate constitutional rights. For thirty years, we have been in a power struggle over the Constitution and Bill of Rights, but only one side—the side of organized corporate power—has shown up to fight. It is time for the people to take the field. Without ending the corporate rights veto over our laws and without reforming the corporate domination of our government, elections will become more meaningless. Representative democracy will become a fading memory.

As the second step, we must insist, rather than beg, that corporations actually serve the public interest. Corporate law should ensure that corporations do not merely take benefits *from* the public; they must they also fulfill duties *to* the public. Reform of corporate law and enforcement of existing laws that have been ignored for too long, such as corporate charter accountability laws in virtually every state, will level the playing field on which responsible and irresponsible corporations alike now compete. No longer should socially responsible businesses be considered as "alternative" or "optional" approaches to doing business. Corporate law should no longer give advantages to socially irresponsible corporations. Unreformed nineteenth-century corporate thinking and the unfair, undemocratic dominance of Delaware corporate law no longer serve the nation or the world.

Third, we need to make election and lobbying laws that punish, rather than reward, corrupt crony capitalism and bribe-based politics. If we intend to control rather than be controlled by corporate power, we must reform how we elect our representatives and clean up the swamp of corporate bribery and corruption of government that we now quaintly call "lobbying." For elections and lawmaking—two of the most important public responsibility of citizens in a republic—we now rely on a sliver of rich people

146

and global corporations to fund campaigns and elections. They don't do it for nothing. Those who pay for campaigns and elections are those who get the most representation; we should not be surprised to find that corporations and the rich are now very well represented and everyone else is not. However, if all of us pay for campaigns and elections through public funding, all the people will be better represented in Congress and the state legislatures. And we will know which politicians are willing to rely on the people for election or reelection and which are cutting deals with the big funders.

While the amendment campaign is most important, these three steps are not mutually exclusive. They do not require a particular order of accomplishment. Indeed, pushing all of the steps forward at the same time will have a synergistic effect. Each step helps address the fundamental problem of corporate dominance over our government and the American people.

So pick up wherever you find you can do the most good, and join in this work. We will win. And we will leave a chance to the next generations of Americans and free people around the globe. Then they too can continue the work to ensure that government of the people "does not perish from the earth."

Step 1: The People's Rights Amendment

In mounting a constitutional amendment campaign to push back corporate power and to protect freedom and democracy, we must consider the people who will come after us. They will inherit the world we make, for better or worse. But let's not forget, too, to consider the people who came *before* us.

Much that is right about our democracy, and much that we now take for granted, exists only because Americans before us did the seemingly impossible. They amended the Constitution; they insisted on the people's having the "last word" over the Court and other branches of government. With successful amendment campaigns, they guaranteed equal voting and participation for all races; they insisted on voting rights for women, after the Supreme Court ruled that the Constitution provided no such thing; they demanded that all people eighteen and older have the right to vote after the Supreme Court ruled otherwise; they insisted that equality in voting cannot exist if poll tax barriers are placed in front of those with less money, property, or power; they insisted on election of United States senators by the people rather than by a corrupt appointment process; they rejected the Supreme Court's ruling that a fair federal income tax violated the Constitution; they made Congress accountable to the people when Congress raised its pay; they insisted that the states were not subservient to the federal judiciary when bondholders wanted to drag states into federal court. None of this happened without successful amendment campaigns by the American people.

Some scholars call the constitutional amendment process a "republican veto."[3] By that they mean that the American people, the real sovereigns in our system of government, retain the last word when egregious Supreme Court decisions undermine our understanding of democracy and the Bill of Rights. At least six times, Americans amended the Constitution to overturn Supreme Court decisions. *Citizens United* deserves the same fate.

Amendment campaigns, even campaigns like the Equal Rights Amendment that fall short, spur national conversations in times of crisis and doubt. They define our values and shape us as a people. They keep the Supreme Court honest and accountable to the people. They make government of and by the people real again.

The People's Rights Amendment will overturn *Citizens United* and settle once and for all what most people have always known: our Constitution protects the rights of people, not corporations.

Here's what the amendment says:

Amendment XXVIII

SECTION I. We the people who ordain and establish this Constitution intend the rights protected by this Constitution to be the rights of natural persons.

SECTION II. The words *people, person,* or *citizen* as used in this Constitution do not include corporations, limited liability companies, or other corporate entities established by the laws of any state, the United States, or any foreign state. Such corporate entities are subject to any regulation as the people, through their elected state and federal representatives, deem reasonable and as are otherwise consistent with the powers of Congress and the States under this Constitution.

SECTION III. Nothing contained herein shall be construed to limit the people's rights of freedom of speech, freedom of the press, free exercise of religion, and all such other rights of the people, which rights are inalienable.[4]

This is not radical; just the opposite. The People's Rights Amendment returns the Constitution to what it always has meant. The People's Rights Amendment makes clear, once and for all, that the Bill of Rights was created for and by the American people, not corporations, and that corporate abuse of the judicial power to declare laws unconstitutional must end.

A robust campaign for the People's Rights Amendment already is under way. Fully 82 percent of Americans—Republicans, Democrats, and Independents—already support a constitutional amendment to overturn *Citizens United*.[5] In the year after the *Citizens United* decision, nearly a million people signed resolutions calling for a constitutional amendment, and people are organizing in every state in the country.

As a cofounder of Free Speech for People, I traveled to Washington in late January 2011—the first anniversary of the *Citizens United* decision—to join others from Free Speech for People, as well as Public Citizen, People for the American Way, Move to Amend, the Backbone Campaign, and many people from across the country. We went to the Capitol to meet with staff of several senators and representatives, including Max Baucus, John Kerry, and Donna Edwards, about the People's Rights Amendment. We presented more than 750,000 signatures on petitions calling for the constitutional amendment to reverse *Citizens United* and corporate rights.

It was another cold January day, as it had been the year before when the Supreme Court announced the *Citizens United* decision. This time, though, the grass between the Capitol Building and the Supreme Court was filled with people of all ages, races, occupations, and political viewpoints, people who had come from all over the country to stand to object to *Citizens United* and to demand a constitutional amendment to reverse it. Similar meetings have taken place in state capitals, town meetings, law schools, colleges, religious institutions, and every sort of assembly.

Scores of leading law professors and lawyers have joined the call for Congress to consider a constitutional amendment to reverse *Citizens United*. Increasing numbers of American businesses are supporting the amendment campaign. Free Speech for People has partnered with the American Sustainable Business Council, representing more than seventy thousand businesses that stand as "Business for Democracy" to oppose corporate rights. Free Speech for People is also working with the American Independent Business Alliance and other business groups to organize the majority of American businesses that want nothing to do with crony capitalism and corporate rights.

As in Theodore Roosevelt's day, this cause is not partisan. Libertarians and tea party activists, conceding nothing of their concern about big government, are joining the battle to keep America free of dominating global corporate power. The Transpartisan Alliance, headed by the libertarian Michael Ostrolenk, is organizing conservatives who recognize the need to contain the government-created and -subsidized transnational corporations that wield such power over American lives and communities. Chuck Baldwin, the 2004 nominee of the conservative Constitution Party for the office of vice president, calls corporate America the greatest threat to freedom. "I will be even so bold as to say," said Baldwin in 2007, "that America has much more to fear from today's Chamber of Commerce than it does from al Qaida."[b]

Clearly, there is no reason to stay on the sidelines, but how do we win? Article V of the Constitution provides at least two approaches to amending the Constitution. Congress may pass a resolution with a two-thirds vote, and the resolution is then ratified by three-quarters of the states. Alternatively, amendments can be passed in a constitutional convention called by the states and then ratified by three-quarters of the states. The convention route has not been taken since the initial Philadelphia Convention of 1787. All twenty-seven amendments to date have been passed by a two-thirds vote of Congress and ratified by three-quarters of the states.

Achieving a vote of two-thirds of Congress and three out of four states sure sounds challenging, and it is. But don't buy the discouraged or cynical claims of those who say that the Twenty-Eighth Amendment will never happen or those who think that Americans cannot achieve dramatic constitutional reform anymore. That admission of weakness, masquerading as sophisticated political analysis, has never worked when Americans faced a fundamental challenge to the vision of liberty and equality that is our birthright.

It would be one thing if the constitutional amendment proposal were a novel or untested path, but it is not. We have amended the Constitution twenty-seven times, seventeen times since adopting the Bill of Rights. We have done this repeatedly, and not only back in the distant days of history. The Twenty-Seventh Amendment (requiring an intervening election before any congressional pay hike takes effect) became part of the Constitution only in 1992. Before that, the voting age amendment came in 1971. Indeed, going back to the Seventeenth Amendment in 1913, almost every subsequent decade in the twentieth century saw a new amendment become part of the Constitution. The only exceptions were the wartime 1940s and the 1980s. We're overdue.

We frequently hear of the emphasis in constitutional interpretation on the intent of the framers of the Constitution. That is certainly one important aspect of constitutional interpretation. We ought not to forget, however, how often and how actively Americans have updated the Constitution by using the amendment process as a basic tool of democracy. In the end, it is the American people who are the ultimate interpreters of our Constitution, and it is we who decide how to fulfill the framers' vision of equality, freedom, and justice for all.

If original intent is the guidepost, we can take comfort in two key facts. The framers intended the Bill of Rights to protect the liberties of human beings, not corporations. And the framers intended that Americans take responsibility for amending the Constitution when necessary to strengthen self-government and protect our liberties. Indeed, the Constitution itself might never have made it out of the Philadelphia Convention in 1787 and on to ratification by the people and states had Article V's procedure for amendment not been included.[7]

Road Map to Success

The road to the People's Rights Amendment goes through our communities and the states. In the end, Congress will need to vote out the People's Rights Amendment bill, and it is true that leaders in Congress have already introduced amendment bills that would overturn *Citizens United*. But if we stand back and wait for Congress to do the job, we will fail. Congress won't do it, not without a national movement.

This movement is growing. It is focused and increasingly organized by passage of amendment resolutions wherever Americans or our elected representatives assemble: state legislatures, town meetings, county and city councils, houses of worship, business associations and trade groups, advocacy and charitable organizations, and anywhere else people assemble. People who support the constitutional amendment campaign have lots of different views on other issues, ranging from limited government, balanced budgets, and local control to environmental protection, climate change, and open space; from labor unions to free marketers; from health care to healthy food; from bar associations to barkeepers. Passage of a critical mass of People's Rights Amendment resolutions throughout the country will bring decisive pressure on Congress to finish the job. Wherever you engage with other people, talk to your colleagues, pass a resolution, and ask your elected representatives to do the same. Resolutions are available in the Resources section of this book.

Help others who want to strengthen our country with the People's Rights Amendment connect to one another and bring in new people to join the effort. Sign up at Free Speech for People, and join the many other national, state, and local groups working together to move this forward. If you cannot find a group in your area, start one. Organize people, have a house party, form committees of e-correspondents, and do all of the varieties of old-fashioned and new-fashioned hard work of self-government and citizenship. Resources for doing this can be found in the Resources section. Help yourself to whatever you find useful.

The Resources section contains the People's Rights Amendment, a sample amendment resolution, sample petitions, frequently asked questions, talking points, and a long list of additional resources and connections to people and organizations that are already working to make this new American Revolution a reality. You can sign on to the amendment resolution, stay up to date, and download these and more tools at Free Speech for People.

Step 2: Reforming the Corporation

Who says corporations are accountable only to shareholders? Why should we not expect that those who accept the government-created privilege of incorporation balance that privilege with good standards for the livelihood of employees, our economy, and the health of the environment and of the communities in which they do business? And why should we allow multibillion-dollar global corporations to take shelter in the corporate law of Delaware? Should not the size and complexity of a corporation at some point warrant a federal charter rather than a state charter from the most corporate-friendly state that transnationals can find (or can pressure)? Why shouldn't all Americans decide what standards we expect from global corporations that choose to do business here? Why should the corporate status be perpetual, without some ability of the people to evaluate whether the corporation has complied with the law and served the public interest as intended?

In America, we are free, or should be, to answer these questions in the democratic way: we can debate and then vote to make whatever answers best serve the country. The rules of corporations come from us (see Chapter Three).[8] If we do not like how the corporate rules are working out, we need to change them. We need to dust off and use some of the rules that already exist, such as revocation of corporate status when corporations repeatedly violate the law.

At least two principles should guide corporate law reform to restore balance between large corporations and human beings and our government. First, incorporation is a privilege. Second, transnational corporations such as BP should not be able to use the corporate law of a single state, such as Delaware, without proper *national* corporate standards and safeguards.

Principle One: Incorporation Is a Privilege

The corporate charter is a privilege from the public; we should expect public accountability and benefit. Corporate law is a public matter, not a private one. Corporate law defines parameters of corporate conduct and shapes our world, our families, and our communities in profound ways. We cannot afford to leave it to corporate lawyers to decide what they think corporate duties and responsibilities should be. Corporate law may seem boring at first, but we need to care about corporate law as much as we care about any other law or issue, from the environment to the economy, from healthy communities to strong families, from energy to foreign policy and war. The consequences of corporate law, for better or worse, have as big an impact on those issues and others than any other law, and perhaps more.

Professor Kent Greenfield at Boston College Law School has laid out the kind of clear standard that we should expect our public incorporation laws to have at their core:

> No corporation, even one making money for its core constituents, should be allowed to continue unchallenged and unchanged if its operation harms society. . . . The corporation is an instrument whose purpose is to serve the collective good, broadly defined, and if it ceases to serve the collective good, it

should not be allowed to continue its operation, at least not in the same way. If we all knew that all corporations, or corporations of a certain type, or even an individual corporation created more social harm than good, no society in its right mind would grant incorporation to those firms.[9]

This commonsense standard is not new. It is rooted in traditional reasons why states allowed business corporations in the first place. Americans have always been suspicious of government-created advantages built into those corporations. We used to do a much better job at making sure that the public benefits of a corporate charter outweighed the public harms. Current corporate law still reflects remnants of this approach, and at a minimum we should insist that our public officials start enforcing that law again.

For example, as discussed, in virtually every state, even Delaware, the ability to operate as a corporation, or the corporate charter, is "subject to dissolution or the revocation or forfeiture of the corporate charter."[10] The Delaware Constitution (Article IX, §1) *requires* that the General Assembly "shall, by general law, provide for the revocation or forfeiture of the charters or franchises." The law authorizes the Delaware attorney general to file a petition in state court to revoke a corporate charter in cases of "a sustained course of fraud, immorality or violations of statutory law . . . ," or "misuse" of a corporate charter.[11] "Misuse" includes corporate crime: "Continued serious criminal violations by corporate agents in the course of the discharge of their duties could very well constitute the misuse of a charter."[12]

An example of a charter revocation request filed by Free Speech for People and Appalachian Voices concerning Massey Energy Company based on its criminal and immoral conduct as a corporation is included in the Resources at the back of this book.

The Resources section also contains links to frequently asked questions about charter revocation.

Remnants of nineteenth- and twentieth-century corporate law, though, are not enough. We need to modernize the corporation to serve our present needs. After *Citizens United*, for example, Kent Greenfield and others proposed that states change their charter laws to make clear that no corporation is authorized to spend corporate money to influence elections.[13] Others have proposed that once corporations reach a certain size, they must apply for a new charter every twenty years after showing how they have served the public interest over the past twenty years.

Some alternative incorporation laws emerging now offer an even better approach. Increasing numbers of states, including Virginia, Maryland, New Jersey, and Vermont, have recently enacted incorporation laws for "benefit corporations" or "B corporations." Under these laws, benefit corporations "must create a material positive impact on society and the environment, consider how decisions affect workers, community, and the environment, and publicly report their social and environmental performance according to third-party standards."[14] These and many other reforms would make corporations work well for their owners and employees, the public, the economy, *and* the earth. That is the least that we should expect when we grant the government favor of incorporation.

Principle Two: Incorporation Is a National or International Matter

No single state, be it Delaware or any other, should make the rules for multinational corporations. With Delaware making the rules for most global corporations, a few legislators and judges representing 900,000 people set the course for the lives of 310 million Americans and the rest of the world's people who bear the consequences of corporate power. That's not democratic, fair, or wise. When some states try to improve corporate law, large corporations play the states off one another to get the most corporate-friendly law. If Delaware decides that its corporate law requires managers to consider not only profit but also workers, community, the environment, or other criteria, corporations can reincorporate in another state with lower standards. The corporation does not even have to move its headquarters or offices; its lawyers simply file some paperwork.[15]

This kind of shell game should be outlawed. Once corporations reach a certain size and operate in countries around the world, why should we leave the rules of the road for the corporation to one state? Uncontrolled corporate power is methodically taking national and international treasures away from all of us: our government, our wealth, the Gulf of Mexico, the Appalachian Mountains, water in the ground from New York to Texas, the air, the land, and more. We should have national standards for large multinational corporations. This could be done either by way of a federal incorporation law or by federal law that sets minimum (but not maximum) standards for state incorporation laws used by corporations operating in interstate commerce.

Today, at least for publicly traded corporations, the Securities and Exchange Commission (SEC) provides some federal oversight of corporate affairs, but this limited oversight is focused on protecting shareholders rather than society. Still, providing shareholders with information and a say with respect to corporate political influence would help. Socially responsible investment firms and other shareholders are increasingly active as shareholders to demand disclosure of policies and accountability for corporations. This shareholder consciousness about the consequences of corporate conduct and active involvement in improving that conduct is essential.

"Shareholder democracy" has been difficult as a practical matter because of the control of large corporations by its executives and frequently too-cozy boards of directors. After *Citizens United*, some members of Congress proposed a shareholder approval requirement for any political expenditure by corporations. And the SEC recently developed a rule requiring publicly traded corporations to give shareholders a say in the nomination of board members, rather than be presented with a slate to rubber-stamp.[16] You may not be surprised by now to hear that this reform is going the way of so many others in our country. The U.S. Chamber of Commerce sued the SEC to block the rule, claiming that any requirement that corporations include shareholder-nominated directors in the corporations' proxy statement violates the corporations' First Amendment rights. The corporations won again: In August 2011, the U.S. Court of Appeals in the District of Columbia struck down the new SEC requirements.

So long as the rules for corporations are quietly made by corporate lawyers in Delaware, in arcane SEC rulemaking, or by overzealous judges imposing their own corporate policy preferences, necessary reform for the kind of sustainable economy that we need in the twenty-first century will be difficult to achieve. More businesses and people, however, are determined to change the rules, and the Resources section at the end of the book has links to groups working on corporate charter reform, corporate accountability, and new corporate rules that will work for everyone.

Step 3: Freedom and Fair Elections

The third action piece, after the People's Rights Amendment and corporate charter reform, might be referred to as "cleaning the swamp." You should be able to run for office without groveling to corporations and the rich. You should be able to vote for someone who does not have to grovel and owe allegiance to corporations and the rich. We expect and demand public financing of our roads, canals, airports, armed services, and schools because we want those to serve *all* of the people. Why should we not insist on public financing of our elections so that all of the people can participate?

That's what millions of Americans think, and that's why the Fair Elections Now Act nearly passed in the House of Representatives after *Citizens United*. Public financing of federal and state elections is essential if we do not want elected representatives owing fealty only to corporations and the top sliver of American wealth.

Several states, including Maine, Arizona, Wisconsin, and North Carolina, as well as cities and towns, already have some form of public financing. This has helped open up government and elections to people who might not make the "heavy hitter" list of donors who give $50,000 a year to politicians. Under most public finance approaches, when a candidate can demonstrate support by some significant number of people who may not have thousands of dollars to contribute but can pitch in small donations to a campaign, some public money is triggered to match the small donors.

Under Maine's Clean Election Law, for example, a clean-money candidate for governor can qualify for public funding only after meeting two conditions. First, the candidate must collect at least 3,250 contributions of $5 or more from registered Maine voters. Second, this "seed money" must amount to at least $40,000, it must come from individuals only, and no contribution can be more than $100.[17] The thresholds and funding are much less, of course, for state representative candidates. Lo and behold, candidates and elected officials are very interested in the views of thousands of Maine voters who might have only $5 or $50 to pitch in.

This public funding is available to any candidate, regardless of point of view or political persuasion. The result is that well-qualified people can run for office without pandering to the corporations and the rich, and they can offer good ideas that are not necessarily those of the two dominant political parties. Once in office, clean election representatives can focus on the people's business, rather than spend all their time chasing heavy-hitter and corporate money for the next campaign.

Americans across the political spectrum favor public funding rather than corporate and wealth funding of elections, and we should push to get this overdue system in place as fast as possible. Yet even as so many are working to get the Fair Elections Now Act through Congress, the corporate plutocracy is attacking even the limited public financing available now. On June 27, 2011, the Supreme Court obligingly struck down Arizona's system of allowing slightly more public funding where an extraordinarily rich or well-funded candidate spends extraordinary amounts in an election.[18] The idea behind the law had been to let people have a real choice and to hear from all sides in an election. Yet in this case, the 5–4 corporate majority on the Supreme Court that used rhetoric in *Citizens United* to suggest that under the First Amendment there never could be "too much speech" when corporations funded the "speech" struck down Arizona's law on the grounds of "too much speech" because the Arizona people had chosen public funding of that speech. So much for the purported paramount goal of fostering more information and more points of view.

Americans cannot afford to accept these results and our corporate-dominated status quo. Public funding of elections can clean the swamp of dirty, corporate-driven elections. Disclosure requirements that provide people with information about which candidates are corporate-funded will also help. As we have seen, however, much of the corruption- and greed-driven decline for America and the world results from what happens *between* elections. When corporations can spend billions of dollars on lobbying and the rest of us are more or less shut out, we have a critical problem.

Pushing for all of the reforms described in this chapter will redefine what is considered normal in Washington and in state capitals. Lobbying practices today are not "normal." Bribery is bribery. It should be a scandal, not a yawn, when politicians act like Billy Tauzin (the congressman who delivered the Medicare law for the pharmaceutical companies) and Phil Gramm (the former senator who became UBS vice chairman after stripping America of protections against financial collapse). Politicians who do that, and the corporations that pay them to do that, should not only be shamed; the individuals should be jailed and, the corporations, dechartered.

To be clear, I am not calling Tauzin and Gramm criminals. Like anyone else, they are presumably innocent until proved guilty of a crime, and they have not been accused of committing any crime. That's the problem. What they did was only shameful, low, heedless, unpatriotic, and selfish, rather than illegal. But we should change the law so that it would be a criminal act for members of Congress to go on to work as lobbyists for companies or industries that benefited from the government during their term of service. Whatever happened to the model politicians, from George Washington to Harry Truman and Dwight Eisenhower, who served their country and then returned, happily and quietly, home?

We should demand much stricter rules for disclosure but also for corporate lobbying spending itself. We should no longer allow government employees, including our representatives, to go back and forth, between government and corporate lobbying. We should have reporting and disclosure of every meeting our representatives have with lobbyists. We should ban the gift-giving, wining-and-dining, and junket-funding of our representatives by corporate lobbyists. Information in the Resources section will allow you to connect with others working to make these reforms real.

❖ ❖ ❖

Inscribed high on the walls of the Jefferson Memorial in Washington is a more moderate version of Jefferson's "water the tree of liberty with blood" recognition of the need to preserve a revolutionary spirit among the free people of America. "I am not an advocate for frequent changes in laws and constitutions," wrote Jefferson. "But laws and institutions must go hand in hand with the progress of the human mind. . . . We might as well require a man to wear still the coat which fitted him when a boy as civilized society to remain ever under the regimen of their barbarous ancestors."[19]

We now know, having seen the successful execution of the Powell-Chamber plan for a long corporate drive for power, that current interpretation of the Constitution does not simply reflect "the progress of the human mind." The creation of corporate rights and the transfer of power from the people to large corporations did not happen because we, the people, now have a more enlightened view of free speech and the Constitution. Rather, we, the people, are on the receiving end of that well-funded, well-organized, years-long corporatist campaign to twist our Constitution and subvert our government of people.

Accordingly, this is not a mere policy debate. We face a constitutional struggle, a national struggle. If that struggle is to be won, the Constitution must be returned to a charter of rights of sovereign people, a charter in which corporations have no place. With the People's Rights Amendment campaign and corporate and election law reform, we can return again to a government of the people. We will have preserved once again what the Founders' generation called the rights of man and what we, after two centuries of hard work and improbable successes by the American people, can proudly call the rights of people.

Resources

Presented here are the following resources:

The People's Rights Amendment

The People's Rights Amendment Resolution

Frequently Asked Questions About the People's Rights Amendment

Organizations and Links for Taking Action

Recommended Reading

Free Speech for People and Appalachian Voices' Request for Revocation of Massey Energy Company Charters

The People's Rights Amendment

Amendment XXVIII

SECTION I. We the people who ordain and establish this Constitution intend the rights protected by this Constitution to be the rights of natural persons.

SECTION II. The words *people, person,* or *citizen* as used in this Constitution do not include corporations, limited liability companies, or other corporate entities established by the laws of any state, the United States, or any foreign state. Such corporate entities are subject to any regulation as the people, through their elected state and federal representatives, deem reasonable and as are otherwise consistent with the powers of Congress and the States under this Constitution.

SECTION III. Nothing contained herein shall be construed to limit the people's rights of freedom of speech, freedom of the press, free exercise of religion, and all such other rights of the people, which rights are inalienable.

The People's Rights
Amendment Resolution

WHEREAS,

We the people adopted and ratified the United States Constitution to protect the free speech and other rights of people, not corporations;

Corporations are not people; they are entities created by the law of states and nations;

For the past three decades, the Supreme Court has wrongly transformed the First Amendment and Constitution into a powerful tool for corporations seeking to evade and invalidate the people's laws;

This corporate misuse of the Constitution reached an extreme conclusion in the United States Supreme Court's ruling in *Citizens United v. Federal Election Commission*;

Citizens United v. Federal Election Commission overturned long-standing precedent prohibiting corporations from spending corporate general treasury funds in our elections;

Citizens United v. Federal Election Commission unleashes a torrent of corporate money in our political process unmatched by any campaign expenditure totals in United States history;

Citizens United v. Federal Election Commission purports to invalidate state laws and even state constitutional provisions separating corporate money from elections;

Citizens United v. Federal Election Commission presents a serious and direct threat to our republican democracy;

Article V of the United States Constitution empowers and obligates the people and states of the United States of America to use the constitutional amendment process to correct those egregiously wrong decisions of the United States Supreme Court that go to the heart of our democracy and republican self-government;

and

The people and states of the United States of America have strengthened the nation and preserved liberty and equality for all by using the amendment process throughout our history, including in six of the ten decades of the twentieth century, and reversing seven erroneous Supreme Court decisions;

NOW THEREFORE BE IT RESOLVED THAT WE CALL ON THE UNITED STATES CONGRESS TO PASS AND SEND TO THE STATES FOR RATIFICATION A CONSTITUTIONAL AMENDMENT TO REVERSE CITIZENS UNITED V. FEDERAL ELECTION COMMISSION AND TO RESTORE CONSTITUTIONAL RIGHTS AND FAIR ELECTIONS TO THE PEOPLE.

By the People of _____ on _____.
                             [place]   [date]

Frequently Asked Questions About the People's Rights Amendment

The People's Rights Amendment overturns the 2010 *Citizens United* v. *FEC* ruling, a 5–4 decision of the U.S. Supreme Court that held that we, the American people, are not allowed to limit corporate spending in elections. The Court ruled that corporations—even transnationals—can spend unlimited amounts to help elect or defeat candidates for public office. The American people have overturned at least six Supreme Court cases by constitutional amendment in the past, and we need to do the same with *Citizens United*, which makes corporate money the same as "speech."

Most businesspeople, like other Americans, do not believe that corporations are people or that spending corporate capital in elections is constitutionally protected speech. Businesses are designed to provide a product or service, to employ people, and to build a strong economy. Many businesspeople exercise their rights to engage in the policymaking process, and that right never should be impeded, but allowing corporations to use their vast financial resources to buy political influence undermines the political rights of all citizens, as well as competitive markets.

The People's Rights Amendment ends the misuse and abuse of people's constitutional rights by transnational corporations to subvert democratically enacted laws and to gain advantage over competitors. The amendment makes clear that corporations are not people with constitutional rights and ensures that people, not corporations, govern in America.

What will be the impact of the People's Rights Amendment on day-to-day business operations? Don't corporations have to be "persons" in order to function in our economy?

The People's Rights Amendment will have no impact on day-to-day or other operations of corporations. No activity of a business corporation requires the fabrication of corporate constitutional rights. The rights of individual people (doing business in a corporation or otherwise) are unchanged by the People's Rights Amendment.

For two centuries, corporations were able to carry out their business purposes without the fabrication of constitutional rights, and the concept of "corporate speech rights" did not exist before 1978. Until the *Citizens United* ruling in 2010, we were free to use federal law to control corporate spending in elections and did so for more than a century.

The People's Rights Amendment restores core democratic rights to citizens without changing the productive role of corporations in our economy. State and federal laws define corporations and set the rules for the use of the corporate form. These laws are unaffected by the People's Rights Amendment.

Under state and federal law, corporations are "persons" for the purposes of contracting, suing, being sued, transacting business, and continuity of operations as employees come and go. Under state and federal law, corporations are "persons" for numerous purposes, from trademark protection to criminal prosecution. The People's Rights Amendment has no effect whatsoever on those state and federal laws.

The People's Rights Amendment stops the radical and improper application of the corporate "person" concept to the rights of real people under the Constitution and Bill of Rights.

The People's Rights Amendment would not affect the day-to-day business of corporations but would prevent misuse of our Constitution by corporations seeking to trump our laws. For example, Monsanto has used its corporate "speech rights" to strike down disclosure laws and conceal its use of genetically modified drugs in food production. This would not be allowed after the People's Rights Amendment. The People's Rights Amendment would prevent corporations from claiming the constitutional rights of persons to strike down laws enacted through our elected state and federal governments.

Following the passage of the amendment, we expect a freer, fairer, and more competitive marketplace where small and medium-size businesses will be less likely to face a competitive disadvantage due to political favoritism.

What effect will the People's Rights Amendment have on our ability to use corporate entities in our business dealings?

None. The People's Rights Amendment does not limit in any fashion the many ways in which people and the states can design and use corporate or other economic legal entities.

The People's Rights Amendment simply states a fundamental truth: whatever corporate entities the state or federal governments create do not have constitutional rights. Instead, their rights and obligations are set out in state or federal corporate laws and other laws.

The corporate form has huge advantages, and we support state policies that encourage easy incorporation. We just shouldn't confuse those policy advantages with constitutional rights.

*Does that mean people will lose their rights when they do business
in the corporate form?*

No. The People's Rights Amendment protects all rights of all people,
whether or not they own, run, work for, or buy from corporations.

Whether the rights at issue are speech, due process, or any other
human right, the people involved in a corporation—the CEO and executives, employees, shareholders, or other people in a corporation—retain all
of their rights as people.

The People's Rights Amendment simply means that we will not allow
courts to pretend that corporations are people when it comes to the Constitution and Bill of Rights.

*What about property rights? Will this change shareholder rights?
Rights to due process?*

The People's Rights Amendment protects all constitutional rights of people, be they property rights or other rights.

Take an egregious hypothetical example, just to illustrate: Say the
government decides it needs computer technology for some reason and
enacts a law requiring that Apple deliver all of its intellectual property to
the United States government. Apple sues to block the law, claiming that
the government is taking private property without due process in violation
of the Fifth Amendment (or the Fourteenth Amendment, if a state government tries this). Does Apple have constitutional rights not to have its
property taken without due process?

The due process clause says that "no person" can be deprived of life,
liberty, or property without due process. Apple is not a "person" under
the Constitution's due process clause, but there are plenty of real people
involved in this hypothetical who do have due process rights not to have the
value of their Apple shares turned over to the government without due process. Nothing about the People's Rights Amendment would prevent those
real people from protecting their rights.

The claim could be brought directly by the corporation using statutes
such as the federal Tort Claims Act. The claim could also be brought by the
corporation, if it is deemed to have standing by the Court to raise the rights
of its shareholders. The claim could be brought by the shareholders as a class.

Another possibility to litigate the question may include challenges to
the constitutional power of the federal government to take such action, an
approach taken when the Supreme Court invalidated the Truman administration's nationalization of the American steel industry in 1952. The

People's Rights Amendment does not empower the government to seize property or do anything in violation of our liberties.

The specific approach for enforcement of corporate property rights would depend on the circumstances and on the jurisprudence developed by the Court after the ratification of the People's Rights Amendment. On top of all of this, people, businesses, and legislators are extremely unlikely to sit idly by while government seizes property. It is not the unconstitutional concept of corporate rights that blocks such government overreaching but rather a healthy Constitution of checks and balances, liberties of the people, and an active, engaged citizenry. The People's Rights Amendment promotes all of this.

What will be the impact of the amendment on company political action committees (PACs) and employee contributions?

The People's Rights Amendment will have no impact on laws that apply to PAC contributions and individual contributions made by company employees or others. Instead, the People's Rights Amendment overturns *Citizens United* and restores to the people and our elected representatives the power and the duty to enact laws and regulations that ensure that elections are free and fair and serve our democracy.

The People's Rights Amendment does not say what those rules should be. Rather, it says that we, the people, and our representatives should make those rules.

Congress and the states will be free to decide on the rules for PACs, employee contributions, or even corporate spending in elections. The People's Rights Amendment clarifies that corporations don't have constitutional "rights" to trump those rules and strike down the election laws that Congress and the states enact.

Will the amendment affect my ability as a business leader to lobby on behalf of my company or with a trade group?

No. The People's Rights Amendment protects all the rights of people to associate and petition government, to speak, and to lobby.

The People's Rights Amendment does not make or change any lobbying rules. It may allow Congress or the states to make such rules, and we believe that reform of our lobbying laws is overdue.

Between 1998 and 2010, the U.S. Chamber of Commerce spent $739 million on lobbying. Pharmaceutical and health care corporations spent more than $2 billion on lobbying in the past twelve years. Three corporations seeking military contracts, Northrop Grumman, Lockheed, and Boeing, spent more than $400 million on lobbying. The list goes on.

The People's Rights Amendment will allow (but not require) Congress and the states to regulate corporate lobbying in an evenhanded way. Corporations will not have a "right" to "speak" through election cash from the corporate treasury—which is often hard to differentiate from the outright bribing of elected officials—or to corrupt our lawmaking. At the same time, the People's Rights Amendment protects the rights of human beings to say anything they want and to argue, inform, and appeal to and petition our representatives for anything at all, including laws that affect our own businesses or the industries in which we work.

The People's Rights Amendment merely distinguishes between people and corporations so that our government remains a government of, for, and by the people.

Are there aspects of the corporate rights doctrine not related to campaign finance that will be addressed by the amendment?

Yes. The recent fabrication of "corporate rights" under the Constitution goes beyond elections and money in politics. *Citizens United* is the extreme extension of a corporate rights doctrine that courts have used with increasing aggression and hostility to the judgment of people and our elected representatives since 1980.

The courts have used the fabrication of corporate rights, particularly corporate "speech," to strike down a wide range of commonsense laws in recent years, from those concerning clean and fair elections to environmental protection and energy to tobacco, alcohol, pharmaceuticals, and health care to consumer protection, lotteries, and gambling to race relations and much more.

Examples include laws to ensure an even playing field between local, regional, or national businesses that compete with global corporations, such as laws to protect consumer choice by requiring disclosure about food products derived from genetically modified drug treatments for animals or laws to protect the public interest, such as limitations on cigarette advertisements near schools or energy conservation requirements for utility corporations.

A new corporate "due process" theory has turned federal judges into overseers of state juries and courts, so that jury awards may be overturned if federal judges decide they are "too high." These "rights" have been used almost exclusively by transnational corporations to evade accountability for harmful products or actions.

Even if we think punitive damages need oversight and reform, most businesspeople do not want to twist our Constitution to prevent our government of the people from deciding on the best course. Even as shareholders, we do not need a corporate constitutional "right" to strike down decisions of a state jury because a federal judge might have reached a different conclusion. In a case where a punitive damages judgment is a real constitutional issue, it would be because of the danger that such a judgment might, in essence, confiscate shareholders' property. If it ever came to that (it never has), the human beings who are shareholders have due process rights to make any valid constitutional argument about that confiscation without the need to fabricate improper corporate constitutional rights.

In a few other instances, courts have treated corporations as people with constitutional rights, such as under the Fourth Amendment protections against unreasonable search and seizure. The People's Rights Amendment changes nothing about the rights of human beings, including the rights of employees, executives, and others against search and seizure. There is no such thing as a corporate constitutional right, but that does not relieve the courts from ensuring that government does not violate the rights of people who work in or who own corporations or anyone else.

What about freedom of the press and media—aren't they all corporations?

The People's Rights Amendment will not limit freedom of the press in any way. The First Amendment protects freedom of speech and freedom of the press, as well as freedom of religion, assembly, and petition. All of these are rights of the people. In addition, the People's Rights Amendment explicitly reaffirms these freedoms.

A ban on corporate general treasury money to run political advertisements is not the same as a ban on editorials or commentary by the press. A free press is critical to freedom and democracy. No speech, press, or other rights of the people are affected by the People's Rights Amendment.

Will an amendment affect the ability of nonprofit associations and unions to give in elections as well? Will it affect my religious institution's status as a corporation? What about nonprofit corporations? Will this silence them?

The People's Rights Amendment will have no impact on people's rights to associate freely or worship as they wish. Freedoms such as religion, speech, and assembly are not predicated on the creation by the state of corporate entities that are granted tax deductions and other state-based advantages.

The federal law (the Bipartisan Campaign Reform Act of 2002) struck down by *Citizens United* equally applied to unions, nonprofits, and for-profit corporations.

If union activity, charitable activity, or advocacy activity is done by a corporate entity, the corporation is expected to comply with laws applicable to corporations.

Whatever corporate form and rules government comes up with must be evenhanded and apply equally to all religions and all points of view. Government cannot say Protestants but not Unitarians can organize their church as a nonprofit corporation. Government cannot say that a synagogue but not a church can give tax-deductible contributions to its nonprofit corporate entity. Government cannot do that because the rights of people would be violated. That has nothing to do with whether those people use a corporation to organize the institution.

There's no reason to be afraid of a fair rule for all that says anyone who wants to organize a church using a corporate form can do so, but it must comply with corporate (and other) laws. It has always worked that way, and the People's Rights Amendment doesn't change that.

What about freedom to associate? Aren't corporations just like any other association?

A corporation is not just like any other association of people. A corporation is a specific creation of state or federal statute that may only be used for purposes defined by the statute that permitted its creation. "Those who feel that the essence of the corporation rests in the contract among its members rather than in the government decree . . . fail to distinguish, as [those in] the eighteenth century did, between the corporation and the voluntary association."[1] That distinction has always been true and is true now. A corporation is a government-created structure for doing business and is available only by statute.

We, as people, have the right to associate. We have a choice to incorporate, if we like the balance of benefits and burdens of incorporating.

Could there be unintended consequences for our economy? Corporations seem essential now. Could this amendment upend the complex workings of corporations in our economy?

The People's Rights Amendment does nothing to change the role of corporations in our economy. The responsibility for defining the economic role of corporations would remain where it had always been before the Court fabricated corporate rights: with the people and our elected representatives. The corporate entity will continue to be a very useful economic tool. Ending "corporate person" rights in the Constitution has nothing to do with federal and state laws that make corporations like "persons" who may enter into contracts, sue and be sued, and so on.

In fact, the People's Rights Amendment, while not intended as an economic reform, will probably help the economy. Corporate "rights" (which are really about global corporate power) are harming the American economy. The vast majority of businesspeople and corporations do not need or want "rights" to defy democratically enacted laws or to be pushed into buying more and more political ads. The People's Rights Amendment would not upend anything about corporations in our economy except the abuse of the Bill of Rights by transnational corporations seeking to attack our laws.

Won't this lead to big government? Government telling us how much we can spend and so on? I'm against regulation.

Then you should support the People's Rights Amendment. This amendment is not regulation. It is about liberty for us as people to debate and decide for ourselves what size government should be or what regulations make sense.

If corporations aren't "persons," how will they be prosecuted in court? Will they have due process? Equal protection?

Under the People's Rights Amendment, corporations will still be able to use the court system, of course, and they may even raise and argue constitutional claims; but they will do so as corporations, not as people. This is related to what lawyers and judges call "standing" to make arguments. Just as an environmental organization has standing to argue about a river because the organization has human beings in its membership who are personally affected by the pollution in the river, a corporation will sometimes have standing to argue the claims of its employees or shareholders.

The People's Rights Amendment will force courts to address the heart of the matter: What human rights are affected when a corporation challenges democratically enacted laws?

So when BMW claims, for example, that a $2 million punitive damage judgment violates its due process rights because the judgment is "excessive," the Court will need to be clear that due process rights belong to the human shareholders who will be affected by the judgment or the CEO, who might get a lower bonus as a result of it. Whether that violates the due process rights of the people who lose money due to such a judgment can be determined by the Court without pretending that the corporation itself has constitutional rights.

Today, the playing field is not level; the largest global corporations have far more power in the legislatures and the courts than all other businesses. After the People's Rights Amendment is added to the Constitution, all of our rights as people, as well as the checks and balances of our Constitution and our democratic process, will ensure a level playing field for all businesses.

Business and businesspeople will continue to have strong, influential weight in legislatures and agencies under the People's Rights Amendment. There are many tools to address improper rules or regulations that do not require creating constitutional rights for corporate entities.

Why do we need a constitutional amendment? Can't Congress fix this?

Congress could begin to address some of the problems of *Citizens United*. Congress could enact laws requiring disclosure of political spending by corporations, for example. It is telling, though, that even that limited measure failed to pass in a vote on the Senate floor after *Citizens United*.

Short of disregarding the Supreme Court's decision—which would undermine the Court's legitimacy—Congress cannot overrule the Supreme Court's interpretation of the Constitution without moving to amend the Constitution.

That is why constitutional amendments have always been necessary to correct egregiously wrong Supreme Court decisions, from the 1856 ruling that African Americans, "whether emancipated or not," are not citizens and "had no rights which the white man is bound to respect"[2] to the 1874 decision that even if women were citizens, they had no right to vote because the Constitution did not guarantee the right to vote as among the fundamental rights, privileges, or immunities of citizenship.[3]

Congress and the states can and should take many steps short of amendment to make elections more fair and to improve the likelihood that legislatures will reflect the will of the people, from approving public funding mechanisms to eliminating barriers to registration and voting. None of these will be sufficient, however, without the People's Rights Amendment.

I don't think we should amend the First Amendment or any other part of the Bill of Rights. That's never been done, and we shouldn't start now.

I don't think we should amend the Bill of Rights either. That's why we need the People's Rights Amendment to restore the Bill of Rights to real people. The fight to change the Bill of Rights has been going on for three decades, and the humans are losing.

With the creation of corporate "voices," "speech," and "rights," the Bill of Rights has been radically altered. The Twenty-Eighth Amendment will protect the First Amendment and the rest of the Bill of Rights for people and end the distortion of turning corporations into "people."

Eliminating corporate money in politics or eliminating the ability of corporations to strike down laws that they think will blunt their marketing campaigns will not affect the speech rights of a single person.

Organizations and Links
for Taking Action

There are a lot of ways to connect to people and organizations working to overturn *Citizens United* and restore an economy that works for everyone. Here are some useful sources of information.

About *Citizens United*

Free Speech for People has extensive resources regarding the *Citizens United* decision, its background and implications, and tools for joining the campaign for the People's Rights Amendment and other actions to balance corporate power.

http://www.freespeechforpeople.org)

The Story of Stuff Project has produced a clever explanatory video titled "The Story of *Citizens United* v. FEC."

http://storyofstuff.org/citizensunited

For a satirical take on the *Citizens United* decision, watch the Murray Hill Inc. campaign video

http://www.murrayhillincforcongress.com

On the implications of *Citizens United* for American business, visit the American Sustainable Business Council.

http://www.asbcouncil.org

Business for Democracy

http://www.businessfordemocracy.org

American Independent Business Alliance

http://www.amiba.net

The Constitutional Amendment Campaign and the People's Rights Amendment

Corporations Are Not People

http://www.corporationsarenotpeople.com

Free Speech for People

http://www.freespeechforpeople.org

Business for Democracy

http://www.businessfordemocracy.com

Move to Amend

    http://www.movetoamend.org (and member groups listed there)

People for the American Way

    http://www.pfaw.org

Public Citizen

    http://www.citizen.org
    http://www.democracyisforpeople.org

Common Cause

    http://www.commoncause.org

United for the People

    http://www.united4thepeople.org (and groups identified there)

Center for Media and Democracy

    http://www.prwatch.org
    http://www.corpwatch.org
    http://www.sourcewatch.org

We the People Campaign

    wethepeoplecampaign.org

Corporate Charter Reform and Corporate Accountability

Corporations Are Not People

    http://www.corporationsarenotpeople.com

Free Speech for People

    http://www.freespeechforpeople.org

Center for Media and Democracy

    http://www.prwatch.org
    http://www.corpwatch.org
    http://www.sourcewatch.org

Center for Corporate Policy

    http://www.corporatepolicy.org/

Green Change

    http://www.greenchange.org/

B Corporations

    http://www.bcorporation.net/

Reclaim Democracy

    http://www.reclaimdemocracy.org

Program on Corporations, Law, and Democracy
   http://www.poclad.org
Community and Environmental Legal Defense Fund
   http://www.celdf.org
Corporate Ethics International
   http://www.corpethics.org/

Corporations for the Twenty-First Century

American Sustainable Business Council
   http://www.asbcouncil.org
B Corporations
   http://www.bcorporation.net
Social Venture Network
   http://www.svn.org
CERES
   http://www.ceres.org
New Voice of Business
   http://www.newvoiceofbusiness.org
Slow Money
   http://www.slowmoney.org
Main Street Alliance
   http://www.mainstreetalliance.org
American Independent Business Alliance
   http://www.amiba.net
New Rules Project
   http://www.newrules.org
Business Alliance for Local Living Economies
   http://www.livingeconomies.org

Cleaning the Swamp: Campaign Finance and Lobbying Reform

Public Campaign
   http://www.publicampaign.org

Demos

    http://www.demos.org

Common Cause

    http://www.commoncause.org

Public Citizen

    http://www.citizen.org

Campaign Legal Center

    http://www.campaignlegalcenter.org

MoveOn/The Other 98%—Fight Washington Corruption

    http://fightwashingtoncorruption.org

Center for Responsive Politics

    http://www.opensecrets.org

National League of Women Voters

    http://www.lmv.org

Other Resources

American Constitution Society

    http://www.asclaw.org

Equal Justice Society

    http://www.equaljusticesociety.org

Brennan Center for Justice

    http://www.brennancenter.org

Constitution Accountability Center

    http://www.theusconstitution.org/

Transpartisan Center

    http://www.transpartisancenter.org

Constitution Party

    http://www.constitutionparty.com/

Alliance for Democracy

    http://www.thealliancefordemocracy.org/

I have provided a sampling of possible resources here. There are many other groups—international, national, regional, and local. If you can't find one in your area, contact me at Free Speech for People (jclements@ freespeechforpeople.org) and I'll point you in the right direction.

Recommended Reading

The following list is by no means exhaustive. Many excellent and important works are not mentioned, but these are some of my favorites.

The Constitution

Declaration of Independence

United States Constitution

Amar, Akhil Reed. *America's Constitution: A Biography.* New York: Random House, 2005.

Cogan, Neil H., ed. *The Complete Bill of Rights: The Drafts, Debates, Sources and Origins.* New York: Oxford University Press, 1997.

Frohnen, Bruce, ed. *The American Republic: Primary Sources.* Indianapolis, Ind.: Liberty Fund, 2002.

Hamilton, Alexander, James Madison, and John Jay. *The Federalist.* New York: Cambridge University Press, 2003. (Originally published 1788.)

Handlin, Oscar, and Mary Flug Handlin. *Commonwealth: A Study of the Role of Government in the American Economy, Massachusetts, 1774–1861.* Cambridge, Mass.: Belknap Press of Harvard University Press, 1947.

Horwitz, Morton J. *The Transformation of American Law, 1870–1960.* New York: Oxford University Press, 1992.

Horwitz, Morton J. *The Transformation of American Law, 1780–1860.* Cambridge. Mass.: Harvard University Press, 1997.

Kammen, Michael, ed. *The Origins of the American Constitution: A Documentary History.* New York: Viking Penguin, 1986.

Kyvig, David E. *Explicit and Authentic Acts: Amending the Constitution, 1776–1995.* Lawrence: University Press of Kansas, 1996.

Schwartz, Bernard. *The Bill of Rights: A Documentary History.* New York: Chelsea House/McGraw Hill, 1971.

Corporations and the Constitution

Hartmann, Thom. *Unequal Protection: How Corporations Became "People" and How You Can Fight Back* (2nd ed.). San Francisco: Berrett-Koehler, 2010.

Kerr, Robert L. *The Corporate Free Speech Movement: Cognitive Feudalism and the Endangered Marketplace of Ideas.* New York: LFB, 2008).

Nace, Ted. *Gangs of America: The Rise of Corporate Power and the Disabling of Democracy.* San Francisco: Berrett-Koehler, 2003.

Corporate Power and Human Life

Bakan, Joel. *The Corporation: The Pathological Pursuit of Profit and Power.* New York: Free Press, 2004.

Kelley, Marjorie. *The Divine Right of Capital: Dethroning the Corporate Aristocracy.* San Francisco: Berrett-Koehler, 2001, 2003.

Klein, Naomi. *No Logo.* New York: Picador, 2002.

Korten, David C. *When Corporations Rule the World* (2nd ed.). Bloomfield, Conn.: Kumarian Press/San Francisco: Berrett-Koehler, 2001.

Potter, Wendell. *Deadly Spin: An Insurance Company Insider Speaks Out on How Corporate PR Is Killing Health Care and Deceiving Americans.* New York: Bloomsbury Press, 2010.

Schor, J. *Born to Buy: The Commercialized Child and the New Consumer Culture.* New York: Scribner, 2004.

Schwartz, Ellen, and Suzanne Stoddard. *Taking Back Our Lives in the Age of Corporate Dominance.* San Francisco: Berrett-Koehler, 2000.

Corporate Law

Greenfield, Kent. *The Failure of Corporate Law.* Chicago: University of Chicago Press, 2006.

Henn, Harry G., and John R. Alexander. *Law of Corporations,* 3rd ed. Saint Paul, Minn.: West, 2002. (Originally published 1983.)

Cleaning the Swamp

Hacker, Jacob S., and Paul Pierson. *Winner-Take-All Politics: How Washington Made the Rich Richer—and Turned Its Back on the Middle Class.* New York: Simon & Schuster, 2010.

Kaiser, Robert G. *So Damn Much Money.* New York: Vintage Books, 2009.

Other Related Works

Chute, Carolyn. *The School on Heart's Content Road.* New York: Atlantic Monthly Press, 2008.

Diamond, Jared. *Collapse: How Societies Choose to Fail or Succeed.* New York: Viking, 2004.

Free Speech for People and Appalachian Voices' Request for Revocation of Massey Energy Company Charters

June 8, 2011

By Electronic and First Class Mail

(Attorney.General@State.DE.US)

The Honorable Beau Biden
Attorney General, State of Delaware
Carvel State Office Building
820 N. French Street
Wilmington, DE 19801

>   Re: Request to Investigate Revocation of Massey
>   Energy Company Corporate Charters

Dear Attorney General Biden:

We write today, on behalf of Free Speech For People and Appalachian Voices, to request investigation by your office into a Delaware corporation that has engaged in repeated and sustained violations of law, contributing to the deaths of people in central Appalachia and to the destruction and devastation of our environment and communities. We request that you investigate and consider bringing proceedings to revoke the charter of the Massey Energy Company corporation and its Delaware corporate subsidiaries ("Massey"). As Massey became a wholly-owned subsidiary corporation of another Delaware corporation, Alpha Natural Resources, Inc. ("Alpha"), on June 1, 2011, we request that you take appropriate steps to ensure Alpha's cooperation in your inquiry.[1]

Free Speech for People is a national campaign to combat unconstitutional doctrines of "corporate rights" that threaten our republican democracy and government of, for and by the American people. Hundreds of thousands of Americans have joined Free Speech for People's call for a constitutional amendment to restore the United States Constitution and fair elections to the people in response to the US Supreme Court's recent ruling in Citizens United v. FEC. Responsible oversight of state-created corporations is an essential obligation of citizenship and self-government, and Free Speech for People works

---

[1] U.S. Securities and Exchange Commission, Alpha Rule 424 prospectus, May 19, 2011 ("On January 28, 2011, Alpha, Mountain Merger Sub and Massey entered into an agreement and plan of merger pursuant to which Mountain Merger Sub will merge with and into Massey, which will be the surviving corporation of the Merger and a wholly owned subsidiary of Alpha.")

for accountability with respect to the privileges and conditions that apply to corporate charters granted by the people and our states.

Appalachian Voices is an award-winning, environmental organization committed to protecting the land, air and water of the central and southern Appalachian region. Since the impacts of coal threaten Appalachia more than any other single source of pollution, Appalachian Voices is committed to reducing coal's impact on the region and to advancing its vision for a cleaner energy future.

Massey Energy Company is the 4th largest coal company in the country, with revenues estimated for 2011 at more than $4 billion. The corporation keeps its headquarters in Richmond, VA and maintains substantial mine operations in central Appalachia. Although Massey avails itself of Delaware corporate charter laws, the company has virtually no business in Delaware. Following the Massey-Alpha merger, the combined company will be the second largest coal company, with estimated earnings for 2011 at more than $8 billion. Alpha also avails itself of Delaware corporate charter laws but maintains virtually no business in Delaware.

On April 5, 2010 an explosion in Massey's Upper Big Branch Mine in southern West Virginia killed 29 men working in the mine. We have attached the May 19, 2011 Report of the Governor's Independent Investigation Panel, which has determined that the explosion was preventable, and was caused by Massey's pattern of disregarding safety laws and undermining law enforcement. As discussed further herein, the Report chronicles Massey's repeated violations of law and its "normalization of deviancy."

I. The Corporate Charter in Delaware and Elsewhere Is A Privilege Subject to Revocation in Cases of Repeated Unlawful Conduct

As you know, many of the world's largest corporations, including Massey, have chosen to use corporate charters granted by the people and General Assembly of Delaware. While Delaware has welcomed the widespread use of Delaware corporate charters even for business conducted well beyond Delaware's borders, the people of Delaware and the General Assembly have always insisted that the corporate charter is a privilege, not a right. Delaware, like other states, reserves the right to revoke or forfeit state corporate charters when they are abused or misused, as in cases of repeated unlawful conduct. In Delaware and elsewhere, corporate charters are only granted "subject to dissolution or the revocation or forfeiture of the corporate charter." See 8 Del. Code § 284. See also 5 Del. Code §§ 732, 1520, 1631 (credit card and bank corporate charters subject to revocation).

The Delaware Constitution (Article IX, §1) requires that the General Assembly "shall, by general law, provide for the revocation or forfeiture of the charters or franchises." The General Assembly has followed this mandate of the people by enacting Title 8, Section 284 of the General Corporations Law entitled "Revocation or Forfeiture of Charter; Proceedings." That section provides:

(a) The Court of Chancery shall have jurisdiction to revoke or forfeit the charter of any corporation for abuse, misuse or nonuse of its corporate powers, privileges or franchises. The Attorney General shall, upon the Attorney General's own motion or upon the relation of a proper party, proceed for this purpose by complaint in the county in which the registered office of the corporation is located.

(b) The Court of Chancery shall have power, by appointment of receivers or otherwise, to administer and wind up the affairs of any corporation whose charter shall be revoked or forfeited by any court under any section of this title or otherwise, and to make such orders and decrees with respect thereto as shall be just and equitable respecting its affairs and assets and the rights of its stockholders and creditors.

In Young v. the National Association for the Advancement of White People, 35 Del.Ch. 10, 109 A.2d 29 (1954) the Chancery Court stated, "there is no question but that this Court will forfeit a corporate charter where the abuse of its privileges and franchises is clear." 109 A.2d at 31. The Court added that such revocation of a corporate charter is appropriate in cases of "a sustained course of fraud, immorality or violations of statutory law . . . ." Id. In a subsequent action brought by the Attorney General to revoke a corporate charter, the Chancery Court affirmed again that "continued serious criminal violations by corporate agents in the course of the discharge of their duties could very well constitute the misuse of a charter." Craven v. Fifth Ward Republican Club, 37 Del.Ch. 524, 528, 146 A.2d 400, 402 (1958) (granting preliminary injunction).

II. "The Normalization of Deviance"—The Report of the Governor's Independent Investigation Panel, May 19, 2011.

On April 5, 2010 an explosion in Massey's Upper Big Branch Mine in southern West Virginia killed 29 men working in the mine. The Governor of West Virginia appointed an independent investigation panel to determine the cause of the explosion, and to impartially find facts that would help prevent similar disasters in the future. Numerous Massey executives refused to cooperate with the investigation. A Massey official was indicted in March 2011, charged with lying to the Federal Bureau of Investigation.[2]

The Report of the Governor's Independent Investigation Panel (the "Report") concerning the explosion and deaths describes in more than 100 pages how Massey repeatedly placed profits ahead of worker safety and compliance with the law, and has a long history of criminal and civil violations of law. Describing a shocking corporate culture of illegality, "enemies lists", "codes of silence," and a "too big to be regulated" attitude, the Report states, "Massey exhibited a corporate mentality that placed the drive to produce above worker safety."[3]

The Report concludes that the fatal explosion at the Massey mine was caused by Massey's systemic failure to comply with basic, existing standards, such as maintaining adequate ventilation systems, complying with standards for applying rock dust and water spraying. Massey did not record many safety hazards, and when recorded, did not correct them.

The Report identifies a longstanding "culture" at Massey that is "causing incalculable damage to mountains, streams, and air in the coalfields; creating health risks for coalfield residents by polluting streams, injecting slurry into the ground and failing to control coal

---

[2] http://blogs.findlaw.com/blotter/2011/03/security-chief-from-massey-mines-explosion-charged-with-lying-to-fbi-and-obstructing-the-investigati.html

[3] Report at 99–100.

waste dams and dust emissions from processing plants; using vast amounts of money to influence the political system; and battling government regulation regarding safety in the coalmines and environmental safeguards for communities."[4]

As alarming as the corporate violations that caused the death of scores of men, the independent panel identified failures of the government agencies that should have been enforcing the law to protect the lives of the people working in Massey's mines. As the report says, "merely having laws on the books has never been enough to ensure worker safety. The ability of the government to rigorously enforce those laws is a hard-earned right paid for with the blood of coalminers."[5]

The West Virginia Independent Investigation Panel linked the failure of government's law enforcement directly to the corruption of government caused by the campaign spending and political influence of Massey and its CEO. The Report describes how, after a West Virginia Court concluded that Massey had intentionally and wrongfully acted in disregard of the rights of another business and destroyed the business, the CEO, Don Blankenship, spent $3 million to fund a vicious judicial election campaign accusing the incumbent judge of being "soft on sex offenders." That judge lost the election to "a virtually unknown lawyer" who was a "personal friend" of Blankenship and was "more sympathetic to Massey's interests."[6]

The Report provides "a graphic illustration of the intertwining of coal and government that works to the detriment of those dedicated to creating an atmosphere in which miners are assured safe working conditions."[7]

Massey "relish[ed] the opportunity to challenge inspectors' enforcement actions by disputing findings and arguing about what the law requires." The Vice-President for safety at Massey openly said, "don't worry, we'll litigate it away" about a violation found by an inspector. Still, in 2009 alone, federal inspectors wrote 515 citations and orders for safety violations and 48 "withdrawal orders" for significant and substantial violations.[8] Massey CEO's message in the Annual Report for 2009 says, "we are proud of our safety record." The CEO's message goes on to label climate change science a "misinformation scandal" and to express "concern" with "environmental extremism" and "ill-considered regulations."[9]

III. Other Violations of Law By Massey

According to the Report, in one ten-year period, Massey was cited for 62,923 federal violations including more than 25,000 considered "significant and substantial." Fifty-nine men who worked in Massey's mines were killed in accidents during that time.[10]

In January 2006, a fire at Massey's Aracoma Alma mine killed two men. Federal investigators determined that the fatal fire was caused by Massey's "reckless disregard"

---

[4] Report at 92.

[5] Report at 76.

[6] Report at 85.

[7] Report at 85.

[8] Report at 77.

[9] 2009 Annual Report at 16–17.

[10] Report at 93.

for safety rules at the Aracoma mine.[11] On December 23, 2009, Massey's subsidiary, the Aracoma Coal Company pleaded guilty to ten criminal violations of mine safety laws, including a felony conviction for a willful violation causing death, and agreed to pay a $2.5 million criminal fine. According to the Independent Investigation Report, Massey CEO Don Blankenship may have been aware of the violations before the fire occurred.

In January 2008 Massey Energy Company, Inc. paid a $20 million fine for Clean Water Act violations in West Virginia and Kentucky. The United States Department of Justice and the Environmental Protection Agency described the fine as the largest civil penalty in the history of the EPA.[12]

Under the Delaware Constitution and revocation law, the "Court will forfeit a corporate charter where the abuse of its privileges and franchises is clear." Young v. the National Association for the Advancement of White People, 35 Del.Ch. 10, 109 A.2d 29 (1954). We respectfully urge you to investigate whether, as seems clear, Massey Energy Company and its subsidiary corporations have forfeited the privilege of their corporate charters, and to initiate forfeiture proceedings using your authority under Title 8.

Thank you for your consideration. We are available to discuss this referral with you further at your convenience, and we look forward to hearing from you.

Sincerely,

Jeffrey D. Clements
General Counsel
Free Speech For People
9 Damonmill Square, Suite 4B
Concord, Massachusetts 01742

Phone: (978) 287-4901
Fax: (978) 287-4900
jclements@freespeechforpeople.org

Willa Coffey Mays
Executive Director
Appalachian Voices
191 Howard Street
Boone, North Carolina 28607

Phone: (828) 262-1500
Fax: (828) 262-1540
willa@appvoices.org

---

[11] Report at 92.

[12] January 17, 2008 announcement, Massey Energy to Pay Largest Civil Penalty Ever for Water Permit Violations, available at http://yosemite.epa.gov/opa/admpress.nsf/b1ab9f485b098972852562e7004dc 686/6944ea38b888dd03852573d3005074ba!OpenDocument

Notes

Introduction: What's at Stake

1. Bill Moyers, remarks at the fortieth anniversary of Common Cause, Oct. 6, 2010, http://www.economicpolicyresearch.org/the-financial-crisis/164-bill-moyers-jeff-madrick-and-lbj.html (accessed September 4, 2011).

Chapter One: American Democracy Works, and Corporations Fight Back

1. Bruce Frohnen, ed. *The American Republic: Primary Sources* (Indianapolis: Liberty Fund, 2002), http://oll.libertyfund.org/title/669/206314 (accessed April 6, 2011). This theory of how societies fail has been extended beyond free democratic societies. The great historian Arnold Toynbee is said to have maintained that "civilizations die by suicide, not murder," perhaps drawing on his theme in *From Civilization on Trial* (Oxford, England: Oxford University Press, 1948) concerning the decline of the Greco-Roman world. Echoing Toynbee more recently, the American scientist Jared Diamond titled his classic inquiry into the connection between unbalanced ecological and resource exploitation and the fall of societies *Collapse: How Societies Choose to Fail or Succeed* (New York: Penguin, 2005).

2. According to the 2009 *Statistical Abstract of the United States*, after-tax corporate profits in 2005 were almost $1 trillion. During the 2008 election cycle, *Fortune* 100 companies—the hundred largest corporations—alone had combined revenues of $13.1 trillion and profits of $605 billion. In contrast, during the same 2008 cycle, all political parties combined spent $1.5 billion and all of the federal political action committees spent $1.2 billion.

3. Dale Robertson, quoted in "The SCOTUS 'Corporate Cash for Candidates' Decision: Left, Right, and Tea," *Reid Report*, January 10, 2010, http://blog.reidreport.com/2010/01/supco-campaign-cash-decision-reactions/ (accessed July 21, 2011).

4. For a thorough examination of the creation and impact of the "corporate speech movement," see Robert L. Kerr, *The Corporate Free Speech Movement: Cognitive Feudalism and the Endangered Marketplace of Ideas* (New York: LFB, 2008). Kerr documents the corporate-driven transition from democracy to what he calls cognitive feudalism and, picking up on the film *It's a Wonderful Life*, "from Bedford Falls to Pottersville."

5. James Madison, "To J. K. Paulding," March 10, 1827, in Gaillard Hunt, ed., *The Writings of James Madison* (New York: Putnam, 1900), Vol. 9.

6. Thomas Jefferson, "To George Logan," November 12, 1816, in *The Works of Thomas Jefferson*, (New York: Putnam, 1904–05), Vol. 12, http://oll.libertyfund.org/title/808/88352 (accessed July 21, 2011).

7. Andrew Jackson, "Fifth Annual Message to Congress (December 3, 1833)," Miller Center, http://millercenter.org/scripps/archive/speeches/detail/3640 (accessed July 21, 2011).

8. Martin Van Buren, "First Annual Message to Congress (December 5, 1837)," Miller Center, http://millercenter.org/scripps/archive/speeches/detail/3589 (accessed July 21, 2011).

9. The background and text of the Powell memorandum, titled "Attack on American Free Enterprise System" and dated August 23, 1971, can be found at http://www.reclaimdemocracy.org/corporate_accountability/powell_memo_lewis.html (accessed June 22, 2011). The Powell memo and its contribution to the "conservative" movement have been widely described. One of the most thorough and thoughtful examinations of the memorandum and its implications is that of Jerry Landay in "The Powell Manifesto: How a Prominent Lawyer's Attack Memo Changed America," August 20, 2002, *Media Transparency*, http://old.mediatransparency.org/story.php?storyID=21 (accessed June 8, 2011). William K. Black, associate professor of law and economics at the University of Missouri–Kansas City, has examined the Powell memo and Powell's roots in the tobacco industry. See "My Class, Right or Wrong: The Powell Memorandum's 40th Anniversary," *New Economic Perspectives*, April 25, 2011, http://neweconomicperspectives.blogspot.com/2011/04/my-class-right-or-wrong-powell.html (accessed June 8, 2011).

10. See, for example, Linda Greenhouse, "The Legacy of Lewis F. Powell, Jr.," *New York Times*, December 4, 2002, http://www.nytimes.com/2002/12/04/politics/04SCOT.html (accessed June 22, 2011); Gerald Gunther, "Lewis F. Powell, Jr.: A Fine Judge, a Remarkable Human Being," *Columbia Law Review*, April 1999; and Gerald Gunther, "A Tribute to Justice Lewis F. Powell, Jr.," Harvard Law Review, December 1987.

11. Sandra Day O'Connor, *The Majesty of the Law: Reflections of a Supreme Court Justice* (New York: Random House, 2003), p. 150.

12. A possible exception came from John Conyers, Jr., and the Congressional Black Caucus, as well as from the Old Dominion Bar Association in Virginia. At Powell's confirmation hearings in November 1971, the president of the Old Dominion Bar Association asserted that Powell "for much of his life waged war on the Constitution," referring to his role as a member of the Richmond, Virginia school board during the years of the state's resistance to the *Brown v. Board of Education* decision. Conyers testified against Powell's nomination, citing Powell's professional and personal associations with racism. These included alleged discrimination at his law firm, at Philip Morris, and in Powell's private clubs, which banned African Americans (one allowed members to bring "colored servants with them to the club only if they are dressed in appropriate attire"). Presciently, Conyers expressed concern about Powell's "close association with a variety of corporate giants." U.S. Senate, Committee on the Judiciary, "Hearings on the Nominations of William H. Rehnquist, of Arizona, and Lewis F. Powell, Jr., of Virginia, to be Associate Justices of the Supreme Court of the United States," November 3–10, 1971, http://www.gpoaccess.gov/congress/senate/judiciary/sh92-69-267/browse.html (accessed June 21, 2011).

13. See notes 10 and 11.

14. Judge Gladys Kessler, the federal judge who oversaw the 2006 racketeering trial of the cigarette corporations, thoroughly documented the role of each corporate participant, including the Tobacco Institute, in the decades-long illegal cigarette corporation RICO conspiracy. Her conclusions, affirmed by the United States Court of Appeals for the District of Columbia, are set out in her final opinion of more than sixteen hundred pages in *United States v. Philip Morris USA, Inc., et. al.*, Civil Action 99-2496 (GK),

August 17, 2006, http://www.justice.gov/civil/cases/tobacco2/amended%20opinion. pdf (accessed June 22, 2011).

15. Ibid.

16. *Laurus & Brother Company* v. *Federal Communications Commission*, 447 F.2d 876 (1971).

17. The columnist Jack Anderson reported on the Powell memo in September 1972; see Landay, "Powell Manifesto." In a 1979 amicus brief filed in connection with the case of *Central Hudson Gas & Electric Corp.* v. *Public Service Commission of New York*, 447 U.S. 557 (1980), the National Chamber Litigation Center, a corporate litigation project launched in response to the Powell memo, slyly quoted a brief section of Powell's memo to suggest that corporations recognized a larger public responsibility. The brief stated:

> Indeed, one member of this Court has stated the obligation of management thusly:
> The day is long past when the chief executive officer of a major corporation discharges his responsibility by maintaining a satisfactory growth of profits, with due regard to the corporation's public and social responsibilities. If our system is to survive, top management must be equally concerned with protecting and preserving the [private enterprise] system itself. This involves far more than an increased emphasis on "public relations" or "governmental affairs"—two areas in which corporations long have invested substantial sums. [Powell, "Attack," p. 3]

18. See *First National Bank of Boston* v. *Bellotti*, 435 U.S. 765 (1978); *FEC* v. *Wisconsin Right to Life*, 551 U.S. 449 (2007) (issue advocacy advertisements of the nonprofit corporation BCRA held to violate First Amendment); *Thompson* v. *Western States Medical Center*, 535 U.S. 357 (2002) (federal restriction on advertising of compounded drugs invalidated); *Lorillard* v. *Reilly*, 533 U.S. 525 (2001) (Massachusetts regulations of tobacco advertising targeting children invalidated); *Greater New Orleans Broadcasting Association* v. *United States*, 527 U.S. 173 (1999) (federal restriction on advertising of gambling and casinos held unconstitutional); *44 LiquorMart* v. *Rhode Island*, 517 U.S. 484 (1996) (Rhode Island law restricting alcohol price advertising invalidated); *Rubin* v. *Coors Brewing Co.*, 514 U.S. 476 (1995) (federal restriction on advertising alcohol level in beer invalidated); *City of Cincinnati* v. *Discovery Network*, 507 U.S. 410 (1993) (municipal application of handbill restriction to ban news racks for advertising circulars on public property held unconstitutional); *Pacific Gas & Electric Co.* v. *Public Utilities Commission of California*, 475 U.S. 1 (1986) (invalidating California rule that utility corporations must make bill envelopes, which are property of ratepayers, available for other points of view besides that of the corporation); *Central Hudson Gas & Electric Corp.* v. *Public Service Commission of New York*, 447 U.S. 557 (1980) (New York rule restricting advertising that promotes energy consumption invalidated); *Bellsouth Telecomm.* v. *Farris*, 542 F.3d 499 (6th Cir. 2008) (Kentucky may not prohibit corporations from misleadingly including a "tax" on customer bills where consumers paid no tax because Kentucky law required that the corporation pay a fee from what would otherwise be shareholder profits); *Allstate Insurance Co.* v. *Abbott*, 495 F.3d 151 (5th Cir. 2007) (Texas law regulating advertising of auto body shops tied to auto insurers invalidated); *This That & the Other Gift & Tobacco* v. *Cobb County, Georgia*, 439 F.3d 1275 (11th Cir. 2006) (Georgia ban on advertisements of sexual devices invalidated); *Passions Video* v. *Nixon*, 458 F.3d 887 (8th Cir. 2006) (Missouri statute restricting advertisements of sexually explicit businesses invalidated); *Bad Frog Brewery* v. *New York State Liquor Authority*, 134 F.3d 87 (2d Cir. 1998) (New York regulation barring beer bottle label with gesture described by the Court as "acknowledged by Bad Frog to convey, among other things, the message 'f#*! you'" held unconstitutional); *International Dairy Foods Association* v. *Amestoy*, 92 F.3d 67 (2d Cir. 1996) (Vermont law requiring disclosure on label of dairy products containing milk from cows treated

with bovine growth hormones invalidated); *New York State Association of Realtors v. Shaffer,* 27 F.3d 834 (2d Cir. 1994) (invalidating New York law authorizing the secretary of state to declare "nonsolicitation" zones for real estate brokers); *Sambo's Restaurants v. City of Ann Arbor,* 663 F.2d 686 (6th Cir. 1981) (First Amendment allows corporation to break agreement with city and use name found to be deeply offensive and carry prejudicial meaning to African Americans); *John Donnelly & Sons v. Campbell,* 639 F.2d 6 (1st Cir. 1980) (invalidating Maine law restricting billboard pollution, even though law allowed—and paid for—commercial signs put up by state of uniform size at exits and visitor centers); *Washington Legal Foundation v. Friedman,* 13 F. Supp. 2d 51 (D.D.C. 1998) (invalidating federal law regulating drug manufacturers' use of journal reprints and drug corporation–sponsored educational seminars to promote off-label uses for prescription drugs); and *Equifax Services v. Cohen,* 420 A.2d. 189 (Me. 1980) (invalidating portions of Maine credit reporting statute as First Amendment violation). Many more such cases may be found in the state and federal reports.

19. See *First National Bank of Boston v. Bellotti,* 435 U.S. 765, 826 and n. 6 (1978) (Rehnquist, dissenting) ("The free flow of information is in no way diminished by the Commonwealth's decision to permit the operation of business corporations with limited rights of political expression. All natural persons, who owe their existence to a higher sovereign than the Commonwealth, remain as free as before to engage in political activity. . . . The Fourteenth Amendment does not require a State to endow a business corporation with the power of political speech."); *Central Hudson Gas & Electric Corp. v. Public Service Commission of New York,* 447 U.S. 557 (1980) (Rehnquist, dissenting) ("I disagree with the Court's conclusion that the speech of a state-created monopoly, which is the subject of a comprehensive regulatory scheme, is entitled to protection under the First Amendment."); and *Pacific Gas & Electric Co. v. Public Utilities Commission of California,* 475 U.S. 1, 26, 24 (1986) (Rehnquist, dissenting) ("Nor do I believe that negative free speech rights, applicable to individuals and perhaps the print media, should be extended to corporations generally. . . . PG&E is not an individual or a newspaper publisher; it is a regulated utility. The insistence on treating identically for constitutional purposes entities that are demonstrably different is as great a jurisprudential sin as treating differently those entities which are the same."). See also *Virginia Board of Pharmacy v. Virginia Citizens Consumer Council,* 425 U.S. 748, 784 (1976) (Rehnquist, dissenting) ("The Court speaks of the importance in a 'predominantly free enterprise economy' of intelligent and well-informed decisions as to allocation of resources. . . . While there is again much to be said for the Court's observation as a matter of desirable public policy, there is certainly nothing in the United States Constitution which requires the Virginia Legislature to hew to the teachings of Adam Smith in its legislative decisions regulating the pharmacy profession.").

20. Alliance for Justice, *Justice for Sale: Shortchanging the Public Interest for Private Gain* (Washington, D.C.: Alliance for Justice, 1993).

21. Amicus brief of the U.S. Chamber of Commerce, *First National Bank of Boston v. Bellotti,* U.S. Supreme Court, 1977 WL 189653 (1977).

22. *First National Bank of Boston v. Bellotti,* 435 U.S. 765 (1978).

23. *Central Hudson Gas & Electric Corp. v. Public Service Commission of New York,* 447 U.S. 557 (1980).

24. National Chamber Litigation Center, "Business Is Our ONLY Client" and "Celebrating Thirty Years of Advocacy in the Courts," *Business Advocate,* Spring 2007.

25. Center for Responsive Politics, "Lobbying: Top Spenders, 1998–2011," *OpenSecrets,* http://www.opensecrets.org/lobby/top.php?indexType=s (accessed July 21, 2011), and

"Lobbying: Top Industries, 1998–2011," *Open Secrets*, http://www.opensecrets.org/ lobby/top.php?indexType=i (accessed July 21, 2011).

26. Since 1995, Gallup has regularly polled the following question:

All in all, which of the following best describes how you feel about the environmental problems facing the earth?

(1) Life on earth will continue without major environmental disruptions only if we take additional, immediate, drastic action concerning the environment; or

(2) we should take some additional actions concerning the environment; or

(3) we should just take the same actions we have been taking on the environment.

Chapter Two: Corporations Are Not People— and They Make Lousy Parents

1. Kessler, Final Opinion, 974.

2. *Bad Frog Brewery* v. *New York State Liquor Authority*, 134 F.3d 87, 91 and n. 1 (2d Cir. 1998).

3. *Laurus & Brother Company* v. *Federal Communications Commission*, 447 F.2d 876 (1971).

4. Kessler, Final Opinion, 1207–1208.

5. Ibid., 974

6. Ibid., 1008–1115.

7. Ibid., 972.

8. Ibid., 1207.

9. Ibid., 977–978.

10. *Lorillard Corp.* v. *Reilly*, 533 U.S. 525 (2001), citing studies by the FDA that "72% of 6 year olds and 52% of children ages 3 to 6 recognized 'Joe Camel,' the cartoon anthropomorphic symbol of R. J. Reynolds' Camel brand cigarettes." After the introduction of Joe Camel, Camel cigarettes' share of the youth market rose from 4 percent to 13 percent.

11. Ibid., 534–535:

"(5) Advertising Restrictions. Except as provided in [§ 21.04(6)], it shall be an unfair or deceptive act or practice for any manufacturer, distributor or retailer to engage in any of the following practices:

"(a) Outdoor advertising, including advertising in enclosed stadiums and advertising from within a retail establishment that is directed toward or visible from the outside of the establishment, in any location that is within a 1,000 foot radius of any public playground, playground area in a public park, elementary school or secondary school;

"(b) Point-of-sale advertising of cigarettes or smokeless tobacco products any portion of which is placed lower than five feet from the floor of any retail establishment which is located within a one thousand foot radius of any public playground, playground area in a public park, elementary school or secondary school, and which is not an adult-only retail establishment." [§§21.04(5)(a)–(b)]

12. Ibid., §1.

13. *Lorillard Tobacco Co.* v. *Reilly*, 2001 WL 193609 (U.S.), 20 (U.S. amicus brief, 2001).

14. See Brief of the Washington Legal Foundation in *Lorillard Tobacco Co.* v. *Reilly*, and *Altadis U.S.A.* v. *Reilly*, 2001 WL 34135253 (U.S.):

Because it involves restrictions on wholly truthful speech— a category of speech for which extremely few restrictions are warranted, regardless whether the speech is commercial or noncommercial—this case provides a particularly appropriate occasion to provide *Central Hudson* with the overhaul it desperately requires. . . . Any First Amendment test that could even arguably be applied to uphold sweeping speech restrictions of the type at issue in this case has little to recommend itself. . . .

The importance of advertising in our free-market economy cannot easily be overstated.

15. *Lorillard Corp. v. Reilly*, 533 U.S. 525 (2001). Tom Reilly had succeed Scott Harshbarger as attorney general of Massachusetts.

16. Michael Pollan, "Playing God in the Garden," *New York Times*, October 25, 1998, http://www.nytimes.com/1998/10/25/magazine/playing-god-in-the-garden.html (accessed July 21, 2011).

17. Parliament of Canada, Standing Senate Committee on Agriculture and Forestry, "rBST and the Drug Approval Process," Interim Report, March 1999, http://www.parl.gc.ca/Content/SEN/Committee/361/agri/rep/repintermar99-e.htm#C.%20Conclusions%20Reached (accessed April 28, 2011).

18. Personal communication, March 8, 2011.

19. Vermont's proposed findings of fact no. 9, George Aff. ¶45, Ex. N (FDA letter, July 27, 1994), in *International Dairy Foods Association v. Amestoy*, 92 F.3d 67 (2nd Circ. 1996).

20. *International Dairy Foods Association v. Amestoy*, 6 V.S.A. (1996), §2754(c).

21. Affidavit of Donald George, acting commissioner and director of the Animal and Dairy Industries Division of the Vermont Department of Agriculture filed in *International Dairy Foods*.

22. Ibid.

23. Kessler, final order, 4–5, 97.

24. The industry lawyers did not bother to submit to the public process the hundreds of pages of affidavit materials that they filed in court a short time later when the industry sued to block the law after the commissioner completed the implementation of the labeling law. The commissioner viewed this as an industry attempt to "subvert the process," suspended the rule, and took all of the new material under review so that it could be considered before the final rule took effect. George affidavit, *International Dairy Foods*.

25. *International Dairy Foods*, Surreply Brief of State of Vermont, 8; Groves affidavit; Buckley affidavit.

26. *Monsanto Company v. Oakhurst Dairy*, United States District Court for the District of Massachusetts, Case 1:03-cv-11273-RCL, Answer of Oakhurst Dairy.

27. *International Dairy Foods*, Memorandum in Support of Plaintiffs' Renewed Motion for Preliminary Injunction, 2, 16.

28. *International Dairy Foods Association v. Amestoy*, 898 F.Supp. 246, 250 (D. Vt. 1995).

29. *International Dairy Foods Association v. Amestoy*, 92 F.3d 67 (2nd Cir. 1996).

30. Personal communication, March 8, 2011.

31. Powell, "Attack."

32. Thomas Jefferson, *Notes on Virginia* (1782).

33. *Wisconsin v. Yoder*, 406 U.S. 205, 213, 225 (1972).

34. Susan Linn and Courtney L. Novosat, "Calories for Sale: Food Marketing to Children in the 21st Century," *Annals of the American Academy of Political and Social Science*, 615 (2008): 133–155.

35. Campaign for a Commercial-Free Childhood, "Ronald McDonald Report Card Ads Expelled from Seminole County; CCFC Campaign Ends Controversial In-School Marketing Program," January 17, 2008, http://commercialfreechildhood.org/pressreleases/ronaldmcdonald.htm (accessed July 22, 2011).

36. Channel One, "Terms and Conditions of Network Participation," http://help. channelone.com/pdfs/12-07-07/2008-Link-LeftNav&Contact-Terms.pdf (accessed September 4, 2011), p. 4.

37. Juliet B. Schor, *Born to Buy: The Commercialized Child and the New Consumer Culture* (New York: Scribner, 2004), p. 21.

38. In 2006, 82 percent of schools had corporate advertisements. Alex Molnar, David R. Garcia, Faith Boninger, and Bruce Merrill, *A National Survey of the Types and Extent of the Marketing of Foods of Minimal Nutritional Value in Schools* (Tempe: Commercialism in Education Research Unit, Arizona State University, 2006).

39. Jennifer Medina, "Los Angeles Schools to Seek Sponsors," *New York Times*, December 15, 2010.

40. Ibid.

41. Alex Molnar, Faith Boninger, Gary Wilkinson, Joseph Fogarty, and Sean Geary, *Effectively Embedded: Schools and the Machinery of Modern Marketing: The Thirteenth Annual Report on Schoolhouse Commercializing Trends, 2009–2010* (Boulder, Colo.: National Education Policy Center, 2010), http://nepc.colorado.edu/publication/ Schoolhouse-commercialism-2010 (accessed March 15, 2011).

42. Susan Linn and Josh Golin, "Beyond Commercials: How Food Marketers Target Children," *Loyola of Los Angeles Law Review*, May 2006, p. 24, http://llr.lls.edu/ volumes/v39-issue1/docs/linn.pdf (accessed July 22, 2011).

43. Catey Hill, "10 Things Snack Food Companies Won't Say," *Smart Money*, November 15, 2010, http://www.smartmoney.com/spending/for-the-home/10-things-snack-food-companies-wont-say/?page=3 (accessed July 22, 2011).

44. California Pan-Ethnic Health Network and Consumers Union, *Out of Balance: Marketing of Soda, Candy, Snacks and Fast Foods Drowns Out Healthful Messages*, September 2005, http://nepc.colorado.edu/files/CERU-0509-140-OWI.pdf (accessed July 22, 2011).

45. "Overweight children are at risk for a number of medical problems, including hypertension, asthma, and Type 2 diabetes, a disease that previously has been found primarily in adults. Since 1980, the proportion of overweight children ages six to eleven has more than doubled to 15.3%; for adolescents, the rate has tripled to 15.5%." [Linn and Golin, "Beyond Commercials," pp. 13–14]

46. Federal Trade Commission, *Marketing Food to Children and Adolescents: A Review of Industry Expenditures, Activities, and Self-Regulation* (Washington, D.C.: Federal Trade Commission, 2008), http://www.ftc.gov/os/2008/07/P064504foodmktingreport.pdf (accessed July 22, 2011).

47. FTC Improvements Act of 1980, Pub. L. No. 96-252, Sections 11(a)(1), 11(a)(3), 94 Stat. 374 (1980), codified in part at 15 U.S.C. §57a(i).

48. Molnar et al., *Effectively Embedded*.

49. Allen D. Kanner, "Today's Class Brought to You by . . . ," *Tikkun*, January–February 2009, pp. 25–26, http://www.commercialfreechildhood.org/articles/featured/ todaysclass.pdf (accessed July 22, 2011).

50. American Petroleum Institute, "Progress Through Petroleum," http://www.classroom-energy.org/oil_natural_gas/progress_through_petroleum/index.html# (accessed August 17, 2011).

51. Ibid.

52. Ibid.

53. Center for Science in the Public Interest, "Corporate-School Partnerships Good for Profits, Not Kids," September 25, 2002, http://www.cspinet.org/new/200209252.

html (accessed July 22, 2011); Coca-Cola Company, "Mission, Vision & Values," 2010, http://www.thecoca-colacompany.com/ourcompany/mission_vision_values.html (accessed July 22, 2011).

54. U.S. Government Accountability Office, "For-Profit Colleges: Undercover Testing Finds Colleges Encouraged Fraud and Engaged in Deceptive and Questionable Marketing Practices," August 4, 2010, http://www.gao.gov/products/GAO-10-948T (accessed July 22, 2011).

55. Ibid.

56. Ibid.

57. Tom Harkin, "For-Profit College Investigation," *Tom Harkin, Iowa's Senator* (newsletter), n.d., http://harkin.senate.gov/forprofitcolleges.cfm (accessed July 22, 2011).

58. Ibid.

59. Statement of Senator Tom Harkin, chairman of the Senate Committee on Health, Education, Labor, and Pensions, March 10, 2011.

60. Tamar Lewin, "Hearing Sees Financial Success and Education Failures of For-Profit College," *New York Times*, March 10, 2011, http://www.nytimes.com/2011/03/11/education/11college.html (accessed August 17, 2011).

61. Ibid.

62. Tamar Lewin, "Flurry of Data as Rules Near for Commercial Colleges," *New York Times*, February 4, 2011, http://www.nytimes.com/2011/02/04/education/04colleges.html?pagewanted=print Page (accessed July 23, 2011).

Chapter Three: If Corporations Are Not People, What Are They?

1. Victor Hugo, *Les Miserables: A Novel*, trans. Charles Wilbour (New York: Carelton, 1862), p. 95.

2. *Citizens United*, 24.

3. *First National Bank of Boston v. Bellotti*, 435 U.S. 765, 777 (1978).

4. *Consolidated Edison Co. of New York v. Public Service Commission of New York*, 447 U.S. 530, 540 (1980). Justice Rehnquist joined Justice Blackmun in dissent: "Because of Consolidated Edison's monopoly status and its rate structure, the use of the [informational] insert [in the utility bills] amounts to an exaction from the utility's customers by way of forced aid for the utility's speech." [549]

5. *Central Hudson Gas & Electric Corp. v. Public Service Commission of New York*, 447 U.S. 557, 570 (1980). It took Justice Rehnquist in dissent to make clear that a "public utility is a state-created monopoly," and the Court failed to recognize that the state law is most accurately viewed as an economic regulation," not a "speech" restriction.

6. *Lorillard v. Reilly*, 53 U.S. 525 (2001) (Thomas, concurring). By contrast, Justice O'Connor's opinion of the Court described the cigarette manufacturers by straightforward reference to their corporate names.

7. Coors and its controlling family were active for many years in building the corporate rights offensive. In the 1970s, not long after the Powell memo to the Chamber of Commerce, Joseph Coors, the Coors Charitable Foundation, and eighty-seven corporations helped start and fund an organization called the Heritage Foundation.

8. *Rubin v. Coors Brewing Co.*, 514 U.S. 476, 479 (1995). "Respondent" refers to the party that won the case in the federal court below the Supreme Court and is "responding" to the other party's appeal.

9. "A corporation is a legal entity created through the laws of its state of incorporation." Cornell University Law School, Legal Information Institute, "Corporations: An

Overview," n.d., http://topics.law.cornell.edu/wex/Corporations (accessed July 23, 2011).

10. Harry G. Henn and John R. Alexander, *Law of Corporations*, 3rd ed. (Saint Paul, Minn.: West, 1991).

11. Kent Greenfield, *The Failure of Corporate Law* (Chicago: University of Chicago Press, 2006), pp. 30–33. Greenfield reviews and demolishes the claims of those who characterize corporations as the natural product of private contract and who discount the public interest in the corporation.

12. "Those who feel that the essence of the corporation rests in the contract among its members rather than in the government decree . . . fail to distinguish, as the eighteenth century did, between the corporation and the voluntary association." [Oscar Handlin and Mary Flug Handlin, *Commonwealth: A Study of the Role of Government in the American Economy: Massachusetts, 1774–1861* (Cambridge, Mass.: Belknap Press, 1961; originally published 1947), p. 92 and n. 18.]

13. See, for example, Virginia Statutes, §13.1-812, making it "unlawful for any person to transact business in the Commonwealth as a corporation or to offer or advertise to transact business in the Commonwealth as a corporation unless the alleged corporation is either a domestic corporation or a foreign corporation authorized to transact business in the Commonwealth. Any person who violates this section shall be guilty of a Class 1 misdemeanor."

14. "More than 50% of all publicly-traded companies in the United States including 63% of the *Fortune* 500 have chosen Delaware as their legal home," according to the state's Web site, http://www.corp.delaware.gov/aboutagency.shtml. See also Greenfield, *Failure of Corporate Law*, pp. 107–108.

15. Greenfield, *Failure of Corporate Law*, pp. 107–108. Greenfield's book offers a compelling case that in either event, the dominance by Delaware of the laws of incorporation for large companies is undemocratic and creates detrimental results for all of us.

16. Delaware Code, Annotated title 8, §102.

17. Ibid.

18. Increasing numbers of people are calling for a similar approach, whereby corporations would have to justify the corporate advantages granted by the people and come in for charter renewal based on their public benefits and compliance with the law. Links to these efforts are set out in the Resources section following Chapter Seven.

19. *Marshall v. Baltimore and Ohio Railroad Co.*, 57 U.S. 314 (1853).

20. *First National Bank of Boston v. Bellotti*, 435 U.S. 765 (1978) (Rehnquist, dissenting).

21. *Santa Clara County v. Southern Pacific Railroad Co.*, 118 U.S. 394 (1886), did not decide the corporate personhood question or any federal constitutional question. ("As the judgment can be sustained upon this [state law] ground it is not necessary to consider any other questions raised by the pleadings and the facts found by the court"; 416.)

22. Among the most thorough descriptions of the strange story of *Santa Clara* and the Supreme Court are Thom Hartmann's *Unequal Protection: How Corporations Became "People" and How You Can Fight Back*, 2nd ed. (San Francisco: Berrett-Koehler, 2010) and Ted Nace's *Gangs of America: The Rise of Corporate Power and the Disabling of Democracy* (San Francisco: Berrett-Koehler, 2003).

23. See *Pembina Consolidated Silver Mining and Milling Co. v. Commonwealth of Pennsylvania*, 125 U.S. 81, 188–189 (1888); *Missouri Pacific Railway Co. v. Mackey*, 127 U.S. 205 (1888); *Minneapolis & Saint Louis Railway Co. v. Herrick*, 127 U.S. 210 (1888); *Minneapolis & Saint Louis Railway Co. v. Beckwith*, 129 U.S. 26 (1889); *Charlotte, Columbia and Augusta Railroad Co. v. Gibbes*, 142 U.S. 386 (1892); *Covington and Lexington Turnpike Road Co. v. Sandford*, 164 U.S. 578 (1896); *Gulf, Colorado and Santa*

Fe Railway Co. v. Ellis, 165 U.S. 150 (1897); and *Kentucky Finance Corp. v. Paramount Auto Exchange Corp.*, 262 U.S. 544 (1923).

24. Henn & Alexander, *Law of Corporations*, p. 24 and n. 2, citing Edwin Merrick Dodd, *American Business Corporations Until 1860* (1954); Joseph Stancliffe Davis, *Essays in the Earlier History of American Corporations* (1917); Simeon E. Baldwin, "American Business Corporations Before 1789," in *Annual Report of the American Historical Association*, pp. 253–274 (1902). See also Handlin and Handlin, *Commonwealth*, pp. 99, 162.

25. Handlin and Handlin, *Commonwealth*, pp. 106–133; *Louis K. Liggett Co. v. Lee*, 288 U.S. 517, 548–560 (1933) (Brandeis, dissenting).

26. Restrictions on corporate purposes were the norm. See ibid. See also *Head and Amory v. Providence Insurance Co.*, 6 U.S. (2 Cranch) 127, 166–167 (1804) ("a corporation can only act in the manner prescribed by law").

27. James Wilson, "Of Corporations," in *Collected Works of James Wilson*, ed. Kermit L. Hall and Mark David Hall (Indianapolis, Ind.: Liberty Fund, 2007), vol. 2, ch. 10, http://oll.libertyfund.org/title/2074/166648/2957866 (accessed July 22, 2009).

28. *Trustees of Dartmouth College v. Woodward*, 17 U.S. 518, 636 (1819).

29. *Hope Insurance Co. v. Boardman*, 9 U.S. (5 Cranch) 57, 58 (1809).

30. *Bank of Augusta v. Earle*, 38 U.S. 519, 587 (1839).

31. *Pembina Consolidated Silver Mining and Milling Co. v. Commonwealth of Pennsylvania*, 125 U.S. 181, 188–189 (1888).

32. Grover Cleveland, "Fourth Annual Message to Congress (December 3, 1888)," Miller Center, http://millercenter.org/scripps/archive/speeches/detail/3758 (accessed July 24, 2011).

33. Theodore Roosevelt, *Theodore Roosevelt: An Autobiography* (New York: Scribner, 1929 (originally published 1913), p. 423; Theodore Roosevelt, "Sixth Annual Message to Congress (December 3, 1906)," Miller Center, http://millercenter.org/scripps/archive/speeches/detail/3778 (accessed July 24, 2011).

34. Roosevelt, *Roosevelt*, p. 425. And he went further, writing supportively of the Progressive reformers: "They realized that the Government must now interfere to protect labor, to subordinate the big corporation to the public welfare, and to shackle cunning and fraud exactly as centuries before it had interfered to shackle the physical force which does wrong by violence." [p. 425]

35. Theodore Roosevelt, speech delivered August 31, 1910, cited in Hartmann, *Unequal Protection*, p. 161.

36. *Connecticut General Life Insurance Co. v. Johnson*, 303 U.S. 77, 85–87.

37. *United States v. Morton Salt Co.*, 338 U.S. 632, 651–652 (1950).

38. Kentucky Constitution, §150 (1891):

If any corporation shall, directly or indirectly, offer, promise or give, or shall authorize, directly or indirectly, any person to offer, promise or give any money or any thing of value to influence the result of any election in this State, or the vote of any voter authorized to vote therein, or who shall afterward reimburse or compensate, in any manner whatever, any person who shall have offered, promised or given any money or other thing of value to influence the result of any election or the vote of any such voter, such corporation, if organized under the laws of this Commonwealth, shall, on conviction thereof, forfeit its charter and all rights, privileges and immunities thereunder; and if chartered by another State and doing business in this State, whether by license, or upon mere sufferance, such corporation, upon conviction of either of the offenses aforesaid, shall forfeit all right to carry on any business in this State; and it shall be the duty of the General Assembly to provide for the enforcement of the provisions of this section.

39. First National Bank of Boston v. Bellotti, 435 U.S. 765, 826 and n.6 (Rehnquist, dissenting)

40. Ibid., 822-23.

41. *Austin v. Michigan Chamber of Commerce*, 494 U.S. 652 (1990).

42. Ibid., 658–659 (1990), quoting *Federal Election Commission v. Massachusetts Citizens for Life*, 479 U.S. 238, 257 (1986).

43. *McConnell v. Federal Election Commission*, 540 U.S.93, 205 (2002).

44. Charlie Cray, "Using Charters to Redesign Corporations in the Public Interest," in William I I. Wist, ed., *The Bottom Line or Public Health* (Oxford: Oxford University Press, 2010), http://www.corporatepolicy.org/pdf/CrayCharters2010.pdf (accessed June 13, 2011).

Chapter Four: Corporations Don't Vote; They Don't Have To

1. Murray Hill Inc., "Supreme Court Ruling Spurs Corporation Run for Congress; First Test of 'Corporate Personhood' in Politics," January 25, 2010, http://www.murrayhillweb.com/pr-012510.html (accessed March 24, 2011).

2. Ibid.

3. In a comprehensive 2011 poll conducted by Hart Research Associates and Free Speech for People, only 7 percent of respondents thought that the American people were on a "fair and level" playing field with corporations in our political system, 61 percent worried "a great deal" or "quite a bit" that corporations have too much influence and control over government, and 80 percent support a constitutional amendment to overturn *Citizens United* and make clear that corporations do not have the same rights as people. Even before *Citizens United*, barely a third of Americans agreed with the statement "Most elected officials care what people like me think." Half of Americans who are eligible to vote in elections do not even bother to cast a vote, a bare-minimum effort asked of a citizen in a republic.

4. Center for Responsive Politics. "Lobbying: Top Spenders, 1998–2011"; U.S. Chamber of Commerce, "Thomas J. Donohue," http://www.uschamber.com/about/board/donohue.htm (accessed July 24, 2011); Tom Hamburger, "Chamber of Commerce Vows to Punish Anti-Business Candidates," *Los Angeles Times*, January 8, 2008, http://www.latimes.com/entertainment/la-na-chamber8jan08,0,454295.story (accessed April 14, 2011).

5. U.S. Chamber Watch inspected Chamber of Commerce tax and other filings. See its findings at U.S. Chamber Watch, "The U.S. Chamber: A Multimillion-Dollar Shell Game," 2011, http://www.fixtheuschamber.org/news/news/inside-chambers-million-dollar-shell-game (accessed April 14, 2011), and U.S. Chamber Watch, "Beyond the $86 Million Buyout: What Else We Found in the Chamber's 990s," November 17, 2010, http://www.fixtheuschamber.org/tracking-the-chamber/beyond-86-million-buyout-what-else-we-found-chambers-990s (accessed April 14, 2011).

6. Ibid.

7. Trevor Potter, quoted in Drew Armstrong, "Insurers Gave U.S. Chamber $86 Million Used to Oppose Obama's Health Law," *Bloomberg News*, November 17, 2010, http://www.bloomberg.com/news/2010-11-17/insurers-gave-u-s-chamber-86-million-used-to-oppose-obama-s-health-law.html (accessed April 4, 2011).

8. Health Care for America Now, "Breaking the Bank: CEOs from 10 Health Insurers Took Nearly $1 Billion in Compensation, Stock from 2000 to 2009," August 2010, http://hcfan.3cdn.net/684f3fa81c1e757518_01m6bxg6s.pdf (accessed March 28, 2011).

9. Wendell Potter, *Deadly Spin: An Insurance Company Insider Speaks Out on How*

Corporate PR Is Killing Health Care and Deceiving Americans (New York: Bloomsbury Press, 2010), pp. 136–141.

10. Keith Johnson, "Exodus: Apple Leaves Chamber of Commerce over Climate Spat," *Wall Street Journal*, October 5, 2009, http://blogs.wsj.com/environmentalcapital/2009/10/05/exodus-apple-leaves-chamber-of-commerce-over-climate-spat/ (accessed April 14, 2011).

11. Glenn Spencer, "*Citizens United*, Election Spending, and the DISCLOSE Act," *Chamberpost*, July 8, 2010, http://www.chamberpost.com/2010/07/citizens-united-election-spending-and-the-disclose-act/ (accessed April 14, 2011).

12. Quoted in Ryan J. Reilly, "Citizens United President Enjoys 'Bitching and Moaning' over Supreme Court Case," *TPM Muckraker*, December 1, 2010, http://tpmmuckraker.talkingpointsmemo.com/2010/12/citizens_united_president_enjoys_bitching_and_moan.php (accessed April 14, 2011).

13. Gerald Mayer, "Union Membership Trends in the United States," *Federal Publications*, paper no. 174, August 31, 2004, http://digitalcommons.ilr.cornell.edu/cgi/viewcontent.cgi?article=1176&context=key_workplace (accessed April 15, 2011).

14. Jon Youngdahl, "No Secrets Surrounding SEIU's Political Contributions" (letter), *Washington Post*, October 21, 2010, http://www.washingtonpost.com/wp-dyn/content/article/2010/10/20/AR2010102004912.html (accessed April 15, 2011).

15. Michael J. Carden, "National Debt Poses Security Threat, Mullen Says," U.S. Department of Defense, *News*, August 27, 2010, http://www.defense.gov/news/newsarticle.aspx?id=60621 (accessed April 28, 2011).

16. Congressional Budget Office, "Options for Reducing the Deficit," March 2011, http://www.cbo.gov/ftpdocs/120xx/doc12085/03-10-ReducingTheDeficit.pdf (accessed March 29, 2011).

17. Pew Charitable Trusts, "The Great Debt Shift: Drivers of Federal Debt Since 2001," April 2011, http://www.pewtrusts.org/uploadedFiles/wwwpewtrustsorg/Fact_Sheets/Economic_Policy/drivers_federal_debt_since_2001.pdf (accessed June 13, 2011).

18. Bipartisan Policy Center Debt Reduction Task Force, "Restoring America's Future: Executive Summary," November 2010, http://bipartisanpolicy.org/sites/default/files/FINAL%20DRTF%20EXECUTIVE%20SUMMARY_0.pdf (accessed March 29, 2011).

19. Chris Hellman, National Priorities Project, "$1.2 Trillion for National Security," March 1, 2011, http://nationalpriorities.org/en/pressroom/articles/2011/03/01/tomgram-chris-hellman-12-trillion-for-national-sec/ (accessed August 28, 2011).

20. Tax revenues came to 15 percent of GDP in 2009. National Commission on Fiscal Responsibility and Reform, "The Moment of Truth," December 2010, http://www.fiscalcommission.gov/sites/fiscalcommission.gov/files/documents/TheMomentofTruth12_1_2010.pdf (accessed July 25, 2011).

21. Congressional Budget Office, "Preliminary Analysis of the President's Budget for 2012," March 2011, http://www.cbo.gov/doc.cfm?index=12103 (accessed March 29, 2011).

22. Cato Institute, *Cato Handbook for Policymakers*, 7th ed. (Washington, D.C.: Cato Institute, 2010), p. 279, http://www.cato.org/pubs/handbook/hb111/hb111-26.pdf (accessed April 15, 2011); Public Citizen, "Corporate Welfare," http://www.citizen.org/congress/welfare/index.cfm (accessed April 15, 2011).

23. Chris Edwards, "Agriculture Subsidies," Cato Institute, June 2009, http://www.downsizinggovernment.org/agriculture/subsidies (accessed March 31, 2011).

24. ProPublica, "Bailout Score Card," http://projects.propublica.org/bailout/main/summary (accessed March 30, 2011).

25. SourceWatch, "Portal:Real Economy Project," February 14, 2011, http://www.sourcewatch.org/index.php?title=Portal:Real_Economy_Project (accessed September 6, 2011).

26. Theo Emery, "GE Jet Engine Program Survives House Bill," *Boston Globe*, May 27, 2011, http://www.boston.com/news/politics/articles/2011/05/27/ge_jet_engine_program_survives_house_bill/?p1=News_links (accessed May 27, 2011).

27. Organisation for Economic Cooperation and Development, "OECD Health Data, 2011: Frequently Requested Data," http://www.oecd.org/document/16/0,3343,en_2649_33929_2085200_1_1_1_1,00.html (accessed August 1, 2011).

28. CBS News and New York Times, "American Public Opinion: Today vs. 30 Years Ago," February 1, 2009, http://www.cbsnews.com/htdocs/pdf/SunMo_poll_0209.pdf (59% favor government health insurance); Henry J. Kaiser Family Foundation, "Public Opinion on Health Care Issues," July 2009, http://www.kff.org/kaiserpolls/upload/7945.pdf (single-payer government plan favored by 50%); Ricardo Alonso-Zaldivar and Janet Hook, "Times/Bloomberg Poll: Obama Healthcare Ideas Favored," October 25, 2007, http://articles.latimes.com/2007/oct/25/nation/na-poll25/2 (53% want "government-run, government-financed health insurance program that would cover all Americans"); Physicians for a National Health Program, "Where Are We on Reform?" December 31, 2007, http://www.pnhp.org/news/2007/december/where_are_we_on_refo.php (54% support a "single-payer health care system that is a national health plan financed by taxpayers in which all Americans would get their insurance from a single government plan"). All sites accessed July 25, 2011.

29. Jacob S. Hacker and Paul Pierson, *Winner-Take-All Politics: How Washington Made the Rich Richer—and Turned Its Back on the Middle Class* (New York: Simon & Schuster, 2010), p. 31: Among rich nations, "the U.S. has the highest rate of preventable death before age seventy-five" and has fewer doctors, hospital beds, and nurses per person.

30. See Olga Pierce, "Medicare Drug Planners Now Lobbyists, with Billions at Stake," ProPublica, October 20, 2009, http://www.propublica.org/article/medicare-drug-planners-now-lobbyists-with-billions-at-stake-1020 (accessed March 29, 2011).

31. Robert G. Kaiser, *So Damn Much Money* (New York: Vintage Books, 2009), p. 309.

32. Robert Pear, "House's Author of Drug Benefit Joins Lobbyists," *New York Times*, December 14, 2011, http://query.nytimes.com/gst/fullpage.html?res=9C00E2DF1430F935A25751C1A9629C8B63&pagewanted=all (accessed April 28, 2010).

33. Pierce, "Medicare Drug Planners Now Lobbyists."

34. Kaiser, *So Damn Much Money*, p. 366.

35. Robert Reich, "The White House Deal with Big Pharma Undermines Democracy, Healthcare Reform," *Salon*, August 10, 2009, http://www.salon.com/news/opinion/feature/2009/08/10/pharma (accessed March 23, 2010).

36. Potter, *Deadly Spin*, pp. 68–72.

37. Ibid., front cover.

38. Environmental Law Institute, "Estimating U.S. Government Subsidies to Energy Sources, 2002–2008," September 2009, http://www.elistore.org/Data/products/d19_07.pdf (accessed April 20, 2011).

39. George W. Bush, " President Addresses the American Society of Newspaper Editors Convention," April 14, 2005, http://georgewbush-whitehouse.archives.gov/news/releases/2005/04/20050414-4.html (accessed April 1, 2011).

40. Richard Milhouse Nixon, "State of the Union Address (January 30, 1974)," http://millercenter.org/scripps/archive/speeches/detail/3887; Gerald Rudolph Ford, "Address on Energy Policy (May 27, 1975)," http://millercenter.org/scripps/archive/speeches/

detail/3985; Jimmy Carter, "Address to the Nation on Energy (April 18, 1977)," http://millercenter.org/scripps/archive/speeches/detail/3398 (all accessed April 1, 2011).

41. "Energy Security: President Reagan's Message to the Congress, May 6, 1987," http://findarticles.com/p/articles/mi_m1079/is_v87/ai_5171542/?tag=content;col1; George H. W. Bush, "State of the Union Address (January 29, 1991)," http://millercenter.org/scripps/archive/speeches/detail/3429; Bill Clinton, "State of the Union Address (January 27, 1998)," http://millercenter.org/scripps/archive/speeches/detail/3444; George W. Bush, "State of the Union Address (January 31, 2006)" http://millercenter.org/scripps/archive/speeches/detail/4461 and "State of the Union Address (January 8, 2008), " http://georgewbush-whitehouse.archives.gov/news/releases/2008/01/20080128-13.html; Barack Obama, "Address Before a Joint Session of Congress (February 24, 2009)," http://millercenter.org/scripps/archive/speeches/detail/4612 (all accessed April 1, 2011).

42. Testimony of R. James Woolsey, U.S. House of Representatives Select Committee on Energy Independence and Global Warming, Hearings on Geopolitical Implications of Rising Oil Dependence and Global Warming, April 18, 2007, http://www.globalwarming.house.gov/tools/assets/files/0117.pdf (accessed April 20, 2011); Center for Public Integrity, "Foreign Oil Dependence Has Grown," n.d., http://www.publicintegrity.org/investigations/broken_government/articles/entry/1002/ (accessed April 2, 2011).

43. See the American Coalition for Clean Coal Electricity, "Facts & Figures: Almost Half of America's Electricity Generation," http://www.cleancoalusa.org/about-us-almost-half-america's-electricity-generation (accessed April 1, 2011).

44. Paul R. Epstein and others, "Full Cost Accounting for the Life Cycle of Coal," *Annals of the New York Academy of Sciences* 1291 (February 17, 2011): 73–98, http://onlinelibrary.wiley.com/doi/10.1111/j.1749-6632.2010.05890.x/full (accessed March 27, 2011).

45. Ibid.

46. Environmental Protection Agency, "Mercury Maps: Linking Air Deposition and Fish Contamination on a National Scale," January 2005, http://water.epa.gov/type/watersheds/datait/maps/fs.cfm (accessed April 21, 2011):

As of December 2003, 45 states had issued fish advisories for mercury covering more than 13,000,000 lake acres and over 750,000 river miles. Atmospheric deposition of mercury is a primary route of transport of mercury to water. Mercury air emissions from coal-fired power plants, waste incinerators, mercury cell chlorine manufacturing facilities, and other sources can be transported long distances before ultimately depositing on watersheds and water bodies.

47. Matthew L. Wald, "Stimulus Money Puts Clean Coal Projects on a Faster Track," *New York Times,* March 16, 2009, http://www.nytimes.com/2009/03/17/business/energy-environment/17coal.html (accessed August 30, 2011). Also see Taxpayers for Common Sense, "Clean Coal Gets Boost in House and Senate Stimulus Bills," January 30, 2009, http://www.taxpayer.net/search_by_tag.php?action=view&proj_id=1842&tag=coal%20subsidies&type=Project (accessed August 18, 2011).

48. Epstein and others, "Full Cost Accounting."

49. Pew Center on Global Climate Change, "Climate Change 101: Understanding and Responding to Global Climate Change," January 2011, http://www.pewclimate.org/docUploads/climate101-fullbook_0.pdf (accessed April 4, 2011).

50. Center for Public Integrity, "No Robust, Sustained Alternative Energy Policy," n.d., http://www.publicintegrity.org/investigations/broken_government/articles/entry/no_robust_sustained_alternative_energy_policy/ (accessed April 2, 2011).

51. Center for Responsive Politics, "Lobbying: Top Industries, 1998–2011."

52. Jim Snyder, "Oil Group Starts Political Giving as Congress Weighs Repeal of Tax Breaks," *Bloomberg*, February 24, 2011, http://www.bloomberg.com/news/2011-02-24/oil-group-starts-political-giving-as-congress-eyes-subsidies.html (accessed April 20, 2011).

53. "If you tried to fill 25 feet of the Hudson River, we would put you in jail." Quoted in Paul de Barros, "Robert Kennedy Jr. Says West Virginia Coal Industry out of Control in Documentary," *Seattle Times*, July 21, 2011, http://www.dfw.com/2011/07/21/484290/robert-kennedy-jr-says-west-virginia.html (accessed July 27, 2011).

54. Epstein and others, "Full Cost Accounting":

> More than 500 mountains have been obliterated, the adjacent valleys filled, in Kentucky, Virginia, West Virginia, and Tennessee, completely altering some 1.4 million acres, burying 2,000 miles of streams. In Kentucky alone, there are 293 MTR [mountain top removal] sites, over 1,400 miles of streams damaged or destroyed, and 2,500 miles of streams polluted. Valley fill and other surface mining practices associated with MTR bury headwater streams and contaminate surface and groundwater with carcinogens and heavy metals and are associated with reports of cancer clusters, a finding that requires further study.

55. I Love Mountains, http://www.ilovemountains.org; Appalachian Voices, http://www.appvoices.org; Kentucky Riverkeeper, http://www.appalachianstudies.eku.edu/kyriverkeeper/; Waterkeeper Alliance, http://www.waterkeeper.org.

56. Robert Kennedy Jr., "RFK Jr. on *Citizens United*" (video), June 11, 2011, http://www.freespeechforpeople.org; also available at http://www.youtube.com/watch?v=1k-DxVzq (accessed June 22, 2011).

57. "Harlan County, Kentucky: What Happened to Elmer's Fish Pond?" September 8, 2009, http://www.youtube.com/watch?v=VuPyevfufCE (accessed June 22, 2011).

58. Quoted in Mark Baller and Leor Joseph Pantilat, "Defenders of Appalachia: The Campaign to Eliminate Mountaintop Removal Coal Mining and the Role of Public Justice," 37 *Envtl. L.* 629, 640 (2007), http://legacy.lclark.edu/org/envtl/objects/37-3_Pantilat.pdf (accessed July 27, 2011).

59. *Bragg v. Robertson et al.*, Civil Action No. 2:98-0636 (U.S. D. Ct. S.D. W.Va.), Memorandum Opinion and Order Granting Preliminary Injunction, March 3, 1999.

60. *Bragg v. West Virginia Coal Association*, 248 F.3d 275, 285 (4th Cir. 2001).

61. Francis X. Clines, "Judge Takes on Bush on Mountaintop Mining," *New York Times*, May 19, 2002, http://www.nytimes.com/2002/05/19/national/19STRI.html (accessed April 21, 2011); *Kentuckians for the Commonwealth v. Rivenburgh* (KFTC I), 204 F. Supp. 2d 927, 946 (S.D. W.Va. 2002).

> When the longstanding practice was challenged, the agencies undertook to change the rule so streams could be filled as immense waste dumps if the disposal had the "effect" of filling the waters of the United States. . . . Regulators were pushing ahead rapidly to change the rules, without regard for the purposes, policy, history, or language of Act itself. [vacated, 317 F.3d 425 (4th Cir. 2003)]

62. Kennedy, "RFK Jr. on *Citizens United*."

63. John Cheves, "Coal Execs Hope to Spend Big Under New Rules to Defeat Conway and Chandler," Bluegrass Politics, July 28, 2010, http://bluegrasspolitics.bloginky.com/2010/07/27/coal-execs-hope-to-spend-big-under-new-rules-to-defeat-conway-and-chandler/ (accessed April 21, 2011).

Chapter Five: Did Corporate Power Destroy the Working American Economy?

1. Stephen Haber, "Introduction: The Political Economy of Crony Capitalism," in *Crony Capitalism and Economic Growth in Latin America: Theory and Evidence*, ed. Stephen Haber (Stanford, Calif.: Hoover Institution Press, 2002), pp. xii–xv.

2. American Sustainable Business Council, "Business for Democracy: Who's Already on Board," http://asbcouncil.org/Business_For_Democracy.html (accessed July 28, 2011). Business for Democracy was launched by the American Sustainable Business Council, which is working in partnership with Free Speech for People on the People's Rights Amendment campaign.

3. James Roberts, "Cronyism: Undermining Economic Freedom and Prosperity Around the World," Heritage Foundation, August 9, 2010, http://origin.heritage.org/Research/Reports/2010/08/Cronyism-Undermining-Economic-Freedom-and-Prosperity-Around-the-World (accessed July 28, 2011).

4. Robert Monks, quoted in Joel Bakan, *The Corporation: The Pathological Pursuit of Profit and Power* (New York: Free Press, 2004), p. 70.

5. Roosevelt, *Roosevelt*, p. 425.

6. There have been many convincing descriptions of this phenomenon in recent years. See, for example, Hacker and Pierson, *Winner-Take-All Politics*; Robert Kuttner, *The Squandering of America* (New York: Knopf, 2007); Paul Krugman, *Conscience of a Liberal* (New York, Norton, 2007); and Joseph E. Stiglitz, *Freefall* (New York: Norton, 2010).

7. U.S. Census Bureau, "State & County QuickFacts," June 3, 2011, http://quickfacts.census.gov/qfd/states/00000.html (accessed June 15, 2011).

8. Hacker and Pierson, *Winner-Take-All Politics*, p. 3.

9. Inequality.org, "By the Numbers," n.d., http://www.demos.org/inequality/numbers.cfm (accessed June 19, 2011).

10. "From 1973 to today, the top 5 percent of income earners have seen their wages rise by over 31 percent while the workers in the tenth percentile of income-earners (earning the lowest wage) have seen their wages increase by only 1 percent." Kurt Greenfield, *The Failure of Corporate Law* (Chicago: University of Chicago Press, 2006), p. 155.

11. Jared Bernstein and Karen Kornbluh, *Running Faster to Stay in Place: The Growth of Family Work Hours and Income* (Washington, D.C.: New America Foundation, June 2005, http://www.newamerica.net/files/nafmigration/archive/Doc_File_2437_1.pdf (accessed July 29, 2011): "Between 1970 and 2000, the percentage of mothers in the workforce rose from 38% to 67%."

12. Economic Policy Institute, "Wealth Flows to the Wealthiest as the Percentage of Americans Who Own Stock Falls," August 2006, http://www.epi.org/page/-/old/newsroom/releases/2006/08/SWApr-wealth-200608-final.pdf (accessed April 21, 2011).

13. Greenfield, *Failure of Corporate Law*, p. 156.

14. Gregory Leo Nagel, "The Effect of Labor Market Demand on U.S. CEO Pay Since 1980," *Financial Review*, August 19, 2009, http://papers.ssrn.com/sol3/papers.cfm?abstract_id=1095690 (accessed August 17, 2011).

15. Richard McCormack, "The Plight of American Manufacturing," *American Prospect*, December 21, 2009, http://prospect.org/cs/articles?article=the_plight_of_american_manufacturing (accessed April 3, 2011).

16. Ibid.

17. Bernstein and Kornbluh, *Running Faster*.
18. Ron Rittenmeyer, chair of Electronic Data Systems, quoted in Brian Jackson, "EDS Says Offshoring Great for Profitability, Promises to Continue," *ITBusiness.ca* (Canada), April 23, 2008, http://www.itbusiness.ca/it/client/en/home/News.asp?id=48091 (accessed July 29, 2011).
19. Bernstein and Kornbluh, *Running Faster*.
20. Robert Frank, an economics professor at Cornell University, has explored the relationship between income disparities and financial distress; links to his work are available at http://www.robert-h-frank.com/ (accessed April 12, 2011).
21. Massachusetts today remains one of only eight states with a flat income tax rate. Urban Institute and Brookings Center, *Tax Policy Center Report*, March 2007, http://www.taxpolicycenter.org/publications/url.cfm?ID=1001064 (accessed April 2, 2011).
22. John Chesto, "Procter & Gamble Unveils Plans to Cut 215 Jobs from Its Gillette Factory in South Boston over Five Years," *Patriot Ledger*, August 7, 2008, http://www.patriotledger.com/business/x1280301726/Procter-Gamble-unveils-plans-to-cut-215-jobs-from-its-Gillette-factory-in-South-Boston-over-five-years (accessed June 15, 2011).
23. "Fat Merger Payouts for CEOs," *Business Week*, December 12, 2005, http://www.businessweek.com/magazine/content/05_50/b3963106.htm (accessed June 15, 2001).
24. United for a Fair Economy, "Shareholders Press BankBoston on CEO Pay, Golden Parachutes, Layoffs After Fleet Merger," April 20, 1999, http://www.faireconomy.org/press_room/1999/shareholders_press_bankboston_on_ceo_pay_after_fleet_merger (accessed June 15, 2011); "13,000 Job Cuts Loom in Merger; FleetBoston, BofA Shareholders OK Giant Bank Deal," *San Francisco Chronicle*, March 18, 2004, http://articles.sfgate.com/2004-03-18/business/17417500_1_banking-resources-america-spokeswoman-eloise-hale-job-cuts (accessed June 15, 2011); Report of Trillium Asset Management available at http://trilliuminvest.com/resolutions/lending-4/ (accessed June 15, 2011).
25. "Digital May Fire 15,000; Major Restructuring If Buyout by Compaq Okd," *San Francisco Chronicle*, May 7, 1998, http://articles.sfgate.com/1998-05-07/business/17722530_1_chief-executive-robert-palmer-digital-compaq (accessed June 15, 2011).
26. Kerr, *Corporate Free Speech Movement*.
27. AFL-CIO, "Trends in CEO Pay," 2011, http://www.aflcio.org/corporatewatch/paywatch/pay/ (accessed March 30, 2011).
28. The rare exceptions are those affiliated with national lobbying groups such as Emily's List or the National Association of Broadcasters.
29. Thomas Edsall, "Obama Seeks to Kill Hedge Fund Tax Break," *Huffington Post*, February 26, 2009, http://www.huffingtonpost.com/2009/02/26/will-the-taxman-cometh_n_170082.html (accessed March 30, 2011).
30. Ibid.
31. Charles Ferguson's film *Inside Job* is a devastatingly accurate telling of the Citigroup story and Wall Street's takeover of the government that should have been regulating the financial markets.
32. Del Jones and Edward Iwata, "CEO Pay Takes a Hit in Bailout Plan," *USA Today*, September 9, 2008, http://www.usatoday.com/money/companies/management/2008-09-28-executive-pay-ceo_N.htm (accessed June 15, 2011).
33. Strategic Management, "As Citigroup Increases Its High-Skilled Headcount in India, Will Others Follow?" http://knowledge.wharton.upenn.edu/india/article.cfm?articleid=4187 (accessed April 11, 2011).

34. Mitchell Martin, "Citicorp and Travelers Plan to Merge in Record $70 Billion Deal: A New No. 1: Financial Giants Unite," April 7, 1998, http://www.nytimes.com/1998/04/07/news/07iht-citi.t.html (accessed April 11, 2011).

35. "The Long Demise of Glass-Steagall," *Wall Street Fix*, PBS, May 8, 2003, http://www.pbs.org/wgbh/pages/frontline/shows/wallstreet/weill/demise.html (accessed April 11, 2011).

36. Martin, "Citicorp and Travelers."

37. Eric Dash and Louise Story, "Rubin Leaving Citigroup; Smith Barney for Sale," January 9, 2009, http://www.nytimes.com/2009/01/10/business/10rubin.html?_r=1&hp=& adxnnl=1&adxnnlx=1302539819-6L7mz3lTxoRdG8bYITETvQ (accessed April 11, 2011).

38. Ibid.

39. Hacker and Pierson, *Winner-Take-All Politics*, p. 69.

40. Stiglitz, *Freefall*, p. 162.

41. Ibid.

42. Robert B. Ekelund and Mark Thornton, "More Awful Truths About Republicans," Ludwig von Mises Institute, September 4, 2008, http://mises.org/daily/3098 (accessed June 15, 2011).

43. David Corn, "Foreclosure Phil," *Mother Jones*, Spring 2008, http://motherjones.com/politics/2008/05/foreclosure-phil (accessed April 11, 2011).

44. To resolve a federal criminal investigation of its conduct in 2009, UBS admitted that "beginning in 2000 and continuing until 2007, UBS . . . participated in a scheme to defraud the United States and its agency, the IRS, by actively assisting" rich customers to conceal assets at UBS in order to avoid taxes that otherwise were due to the United States. See *United States* v. *UBS*, U.S. S.D. Fla., 09-60033-CR, Deferred Prosecution Agreement.

45. Corn, "Foreclosure Phil."

46. Patrice Hill, "McCain Adviser Talks of 'Mental Recession,'" *Washington Times*, July 9, 2008, http://www.washingtontimes.com/news/2008/jul/09/mccain-adviser-addresses-mental-recession/ (accessed April 11, 2011).

Chapter Six: Corporations Can't Love

1. James Madison, Virginia Ratifying Convention, June 20, 1788, http://press-pubs.uchicago.edu/founders/documents/v1ch13s36.html (accessed April 28, 2011).

2. *First National Bank of Boston* v. *Bellotti*, 435 U.S. 765 (1978).

3. Bank of America (admitted to illegal bid rigging in municipal bond market); *United States* v. *General Motors*, 186 F.2d 562 (1951) (convicted of conspiracy to destroy public transportation); *United States* v. *General Motors Corp.*, 121 F.2d 376 (1941), cert. denied 314 U.S. 618 (1941), rehearing denied, 314 U.S. 710 (1941) (criminal antitrust conviction upheld); *United States* v. *Credit Suisse* (2009) ("admits that it committed crimes and systematically violated both U.S. and New York State laws by moving hundreds of millions of dollars illegally through the U.S. financial system on behalf of entities subject to U.S. economic sanctions"); *United States* v. *UBS* (2009) (admitted that it conspired to "defraud the United States by impeding the Internal Revenue Service"); *United States* v. *Deutsche Bank* (2010) (admitted that it "unlawfully, willingly and knowingly participated in financial transactions execution in connection with a number of tax shelter transactions" resulting in $29 billion in bogus tax benefits); *United States* v. *WellCare Health Plans* (2009) (admitted that it "knowingly and willingly conspired, confederated and agreed with others to execute and attempted to execute a scheme and artifice to

defraud two health care benefit programs: the Florida Medicaid program and the Florida Healthy Kids Corporation program"); *United States* v. *Volvo* (2008) (admitted that "employees agents and distributors paid kickbacks to the Iraqi government in order to obtain contracts for the sale of trucks and heavy commercial equipment"). BP's crimes are too numerous to include here and are identified in the text.

4. Greenfield, *Failure of Corporate Law*, p. 76.

5. *Young* v. *National Association for the Advancement of White People*, 35 Del.Ch. 10, 109 A.2d 29 (1954).

6. More than 5,600 people have joined the "Revoke BP's Charter" Facebook page, http://www.facebook.com/pages/Revoke-BPs-Corporate-Charter/121706904534835 (accessed July 29, 2011).

7. The letter from Gary Ruskin at Green Change to Attorney General Beau Biden is available at http://www.greenchange.org/article.php?id=5947 (accessed April 23, 2011).

8. Amicus brief, *Nike* v. *Kasky*, 2003 WL 835523 (2003).

9. Ibid.

10. Charles de Secondat Montesquieu, *The Spirit of Laws: A Compendium of the First English Edition* (Los Angeles: University of California Press, 1977), p. 130.

11. See Daniel J. H. Greenwood, "Enronitis: Why Good Corporations Go Bad," *Columbia Business Law Review*, Vol. 2004, no 3 (2004), pp. 773–848.

12. Sheldon Whitehouse, speech to the U.S. Senate, "Whitehouse Slams Corporate Influence at MMS, Proposes Legislation to Defend Integrity of Government," June 17, 2010, http://whitehouse.senate.gov/newsroom/press/release/?id=90941d79-ae11-49Gc-b541-34dbb0969848 (accessed July 30, 2011).

Chapter Seven: Restoring Democracy and Republican Government

1. Jamie Raskin, quoted in "Group Calls for Constitutional Amendment to Overturn High Court's Campaign Finance Ruling," *The Public Record*, January 21, 2010, http://pubrecord.org/multimedia/6674/congresswoman-professor-movement/ (accessed July 30, 2011).

2. Theodore Roosevelt, First Annual Address, December 1, 1901.

3. See Thomas E. Baker, "Exercising the Amendment Power to Disapprove of Supreme Court Decisions: A Proposal for a 'Republican Veto,'" 22 Hastings Const. L.Q. 325, 331 (1995) ("By invoking the Article V power, 'we the people' may exercise a 'republican veto' to check the High Court's hermeneutical tendency toward judicial oligarchy.")

4. Several bills have been introduced in Congress, some of which focus more narrowly on campaign finance or corporate speech, rather than the principle that constitutional rights are for people, not corporations. These are available at the Free Speech for People Web site, http://www.freespeechforpeople.org.

5. Ibid.

6. Chuck Baldwin, "Corporate America: Freedom's Greatest Threat," *News with Views*, July 7, 2007, http://www.newswithviews.com/baldwin/baldwin385.htm (accessed July 30, 2011).

7. See Akhil Reed Amar, *America's Constitution: A Biography* (New York: Random House, 2005), and David E. Kyvig, *Explicit and Authentic Acts: Amending the Constitution, 1776–1995* (Lawrence: University Press of Kansas, 1996).

8. Greenfield, *Failure of Corporate Law*, is very helpful in this regard.

9. Ibid., p. 127.

10. Delaware Code, Title 8, Chapter 1, Section 284, http://delcode.delaware.gov/title8/c001/sc10/index.shtml#284 (accessed July 30, 2011).

11. *Young v. National Association for the Advancement of White People*, 35 Del.Ch. 10, 109 A.2d 29 (1954); *Craven v. Fifth Ward Republican Club*, 37 Del.Ch. 524, 528, 146 A.2d 400, 402 (1958).

12. *Craven v. Fifth Ward Republican Club*, ibid.

13. Kent Greenfield, "A Campaign Funding Mess," *Boston Globe*, January 23, 2010, http://www.boston.com/bostonglobe/editorial_opinion/oped/articles/2010/01/23/a_campaign_funding_mess/ (accessed April 24, 2011).

14. See B Corp, http://www.bcorporation.net/.

15. Hofstra Professor Daniel Greenwood has probed the undemocratic aspect of corporate law as we have come to accept it, the complexities of the states' race to the bottom (or top, as some would have it), and the possibilities of progress by the "repoliticizing" of corporate law. See Daniel J. H. Greenwood, "Democracy and Delaware: The Mysterious Race to the Bottom/Top," *Yale Law and Policy Review*, Spring 2005, pp. 381–454, http://people.hofstra.edu/daniel_j_greenwood/html/Mysterious04.htm (accessed June 18, 2011). See also Daniel J. H. Greenwood, "Democracy and Delaware: The Strange Puzzle of Corporate Law," 2002, http://people.hofstra.edu/Daniel_J_Greenwood/pdf/DemocAndDelGWU.pdf (accessed June 16, 2011).

16. SEC Rule 14a-11, "Facilitating Shareholder Director Nominations," August 25, 2010, http://www.sec.gov/rules/final/2010/33-9136.pdf (accessed April 24, 2011).

17. Commission on Governmental Ethics and Election Practices, *Guidebook for 2010 Gubernatorial Candidates: Running for Office in Maine*, August 20, 2009, http://www.maine.gov/ethics/pdf/publications/2010_gubernatorial_guide_mcea_final.pdf (accessed June 18, 2011).

18. *McCommish v. Bennett*, Supreme Court Case No. 10-239; *Arizona Free Enterprise Club v. Bennett*, Supreme Court Case No. 10-238.

19. Thomas Jefferson, letter to Samuel Kercheval, July 12, 1816.

Resources

1. Handlin and Handlin, *Commonwealth*, p. 92 and n. 18.

2. *Dred Scott v. Sandford*, 60 U.S. 393 (1856).

3. *Minor v. Happersett*, 88 U.S. 162 (1874).

Index

Index

About the Author

 Jeff Clements is a founder and General Counsel of Free Speech for People. Jeff is also founder of Clements Law Office, LLC, and has represented and advocated for people, businesses and the public interest since 1988. In the United States Supreme Court case of *Citizens United v. Federal Election Commission*, Jeff represented several liberty and democracy advocacy organizations in filing an Amicus Brief arguing that people, not corporations, have Constitutional rights. In 2010, he helped launch the Free Speech for People campaign to overturn the *Citizens United* ruling that corporations have a Constitutional right to spend unlimited money in American elections.

Jeff has served as Assistant Attorney General and as Chief of the Public Protection & Advocacy Bureau in the Massachusetts Attorney General's Office. As Bureau Chief, he led more than 100 attorneys and staff in law enforcement and litigation in the areas of civil rights, environmental protection, healthcare, insurance and financial services, antitrust and consumer protection. Jeff also served as an Assistant Attorney General in Massachusetts from 1996 to 2000, where he worked on litigation against the tobacco industry and handled a wide range of other investigations and litigation to enforce unfair trade practice, consumer protection and antitrust laws.

In private practice, Mr. Clements has been a partner in the Boston law firms of Clements & Clements, LLP and Mintz Levin. He has represented clients in a variety of appeals and litigation, and in investigations and prosecutions by the U.S. Attorney's Office and Maine Attorney General's Office.

Jeff was elected as a Trustee and President of the Board of Trustees of the Portland Water District, a public agency responsible for protecting and delivering safe drinking water and ensuring proper treatment of wastewater for 160,000 people in Portland and South Portland, Maine and several surrounding communities. He was a co-founder, officer, and director of Friends of Casco Bay, an environmental advocacy organization focused on protection and stewardship of Maine's Casco Bay. He also has served as a Trustee and President of the Board of The Waldorf School in Lexington, Massachusetts.

Jeff graduated with distinction in History and Government from Colby College in 1984, and magna cum laude with a concentration in Public Law from the Cornell Law School in 1988. He lives in Concord, Massachusetts with his wife and three children.

Berrett–Koehler
Publishers

Berrett-Koehler is an independent publisher dedicated to an ambitious mission: *Creating a World That Works for All.*

We believe that to truly create a better world, action is needed at all levels—individual, organizational, and societal. At the individual level, our publications help people align their lives with their values and with their aspirations for a better world. At the organizational level, our publications promote progressive leadership and management practices, socially responsible approaches to business, and humane and effective organizations. At the societal level, our publications advance social and economic justice, shared prosperity, sustainability, and new solutions to national and global issues.

A major theme of our publications is "Opening Up New Space." Berrett-Koehler titles challenge conventional thinking, introduce new ideas, and foster positive change. Their common quest is changing the underlying beliefs, mindsets, institutions, and structures that keep generating the same cycles of problems, no matter who our leaders are or what improvement programs we adopt.

We strive to practice what we preach—to operate our publishing company in line with the ideas in our books. At the core of our approach is stewardship, which we define as a deep sense of responsibility to administer the company for the benefit of all of our "stakeholder" groups: authors, customers, employees, investors, service providers, and the communities and environment around us.

We are grateful to the thousands of readers, authors, and other friends of the company who consider themselves to be part of the "BK Community." We hope that you, too, will join us in our mission.

A BK Currents Book

This book is part of our BK Currents series. BK Currents books advance social and economic justice by exploring the critical intersections between business and society. Offering a unique combination of thoughtful analysis and progressive alternatives, BK Currents books promote positive change at the national and global levels. To find out more, visit **www.bkconnection.com**.

Berrett–Koehler
Publishers

A community dedicated to creating
a world that works for all

Visit Our Website: www.bkconnection.com

Read book excerpts, see author videos and Internet movies, read
our authors' blogs, join discussion groups, download book apps, find
out about the BK Affiliate Network, browse subject-area libraries of
books, get special discounts, and more!

Subscribe to Our Free E-Newsletter, the *BK Communiqué*

Be the first to hear about new publications, special discount offers,
exclusive articles, news about bestsellers, and more! Get on the list
for our free e-newsletter by going to **www.bkconnection.com**.

Get Quantity Discounts

Berrett-Koehler books are available at quantity discounts for orders
of ten or more copies. Please call us toll-free at (800) 929-2929 or
email us at **bkp.orders@aidcvt.com**.

Join the BK Community

BKcommunity.com is a virtual meeting place where people from
around the world can engage with kindred spirits to create a world
that works for all. BKcommunity.com members may create their own
profiles, blog, start and participate in forums and discussion groups,
post photos and videos, answer surveys, announce and register for
upcoming events, and chat with others online in real time. Please join
the conversation!

MIX
Paper from
responsible sources
FSC www.fsc.org **FSC® C012752**